Apache Tomcat Security
Handbook

John Turner
Ben Galbraith
Brian P. Rickabaugh
Vivek Chopra
Gotham Polisetty

Wrox Press Ltd. ®

Apache Tomcat Security

Handbook

© 2003 Wrox Press

First published January 2003

Published by Wrox Press Ltd,
Arden House, 1102 Warwick Road, Acocks Green,
Birmingham, B27 6BH
United Kingdom
Printed in the United States
ISBN 1-86100-830-9

Trademark Acknowledgments

Wrox has endeavored to provide trademark information about all the companies and products mentioned in this book by the appropriate use of capitals. However, Wrox cannot guarantee the accuracy of this information.

Credits

Authors
John Turner
Ben Galbraith
Brian P. Rickabaugh
Vivek Chopra
Gotham Polisetty

Technical Reviewers
Benson Kerberos
Deepak Thomas
Ben Galbraith
Ramesh Mani
Chris Curtis
Chad Fowler

Technical Editor
Kedar Kamat

Project Manager
Abbas Saifuddin Rangwala

Author Agent
Safiulla Shakir

Managing Editor
Paul Cooper

Commissioning Editor
Nilesh Parmar

Production Coordinator
Rachel Taylor

Index
Vinod Shenoy

Cover
Santosh Haware

Proof Readers
Jennifer Williams
Victoria Blackburn

Editorial Thanks
Dilip Thomas

About the Authors

John Turner

John Turner is a senior application developer and UNIX systems administrator with Advertising Audit Service, Inc. in Farmington Hills, Michigan. A technology professional for over 10 years, John has experience in the automotive, health care, advertising, and finance industries. His industry interests include vintage technology, open source, mobile computing, and wireless networking. Outside interests and hobbies include cottage farming, dogs, recycling, history, tattoos, travel, multimedia, and electronica.

Ultimate thanks and gratitude go to my parents William and Susan, my sister Becki, and my extended family for their love and support. I'd like to thank Rodrigo, Peter, Linda, Rich, Jessica, Debbie, Jerry, Clarissa, my devoted friend Meg, and the ninjas at computerninja.com for their friendship, advice, and encouragement. My participation on this project would not have been successful without them. Thanks also to Nilesh, Safi, and the rest of the team at Wrox for this opportunity. When in doubt, focus on the positive and have fun.

Ben Galbraith

Before graduating from high school, Ben Galbraith was hired by a major Silicon Valley computer manufacturer to develop Windows-based client-server applications with international deployments and hundreds of users. In 1995, Ben began developing for the Web and fell in love with Unix, vi, and Perl. After building countless web applications with Perl, Ben discovered server-side Java in 1999 and his relationship with Perl has since become somewhat estranged.

Ben is presently a consultant in Provo, Utah. He regularly lectures, evangelizes, and gives classes on Java technology. Ben has no college degree but if he had the time he would study both ancient and modern history.

Brian P. Rickabaugh

Brian is a senior systems architect for a large global conglomerate in the financial, manufacturing, and media industries. He is also president of StrayCat Incorporated, a small business focused primarily on software consulting services. He has been developing web-centric, object-oriented software in C/C++ and Java for six years. He is also a huge proponent of open source software and the positive impact it can have on small, medium, and large organizations. His current focus is on XML and implementing web services technologies for internal and external systems integration.

When he isn't developing software, he enjoys spending time with his girlfriend Renee and cat Chloe. Brian holds a Bachelor of Science degree in Computer Information Systems from Roanoke College in Salem, Virginia. Brian currently lives in Louisville, Kentucky and would like to thank Renee for her guidance and support.

Vivek Chopra

Vivek Chopra has extensive experience in software design and development. He has worked on a range of technologies, including compilers, programming tools, middleware, and XML/web services. He has authored a number of books on web services technologies and on Apache Software. He is actively involved with Open Source software, and is a committer for the UDDI4J API.

Vivek holds a Bachelor's degree in Electronics and a Master's degree in Computer Science. He lives and works in the San Francisco Bay Area, and can be contacted at vivek@soaprpc.com.

Gotham Polisetty

Gotham Polisetty is the founder and principal architect of Global Software Solutions, Inc. in Charlotte, North Carolina. Gotham currently consults for large Fortune 500 companies and helps them architect complex distributed systems and solve problems related to the distribution of data and processing within these systems. Gotham has been involved in the IT industry since 1982 and consults extensively on the design and architectural issues involved in implementing large web-based corporate ERP systems. Gotham Polisetty can be reached at **gotham@glosoft.com**

Apache Tomcat Security

Handbook

Table of Contents

Table of Contents

Introduction   **1**

  Who Is This Book For?   **1**

  What This Book Covers   **2**

  What You Need to Use This Book   **3**

Chapter 1: Understanding Tomcat Security   **5**

  Vulnerability Overview   **6**
    Ten Most Common Security Problems   6
    Known Tomcat Vulnerabilities   8

  Installation   **9**
    Running Tomcat as a Service   10
    Using an Unprivileged User Account   11
    Using a Firewall   12
    Connector Management   14

  Default Tomcat Applications   **15**
    The Manager Application   16
    The Admin Application   18
    The examples Application   19
    The WebDAV Application   19

  Summary   **21**

Chapter 2: Tightening File System Screws   **23**

  Permissions   **23**
    The Heterogeneity of Permissions   24
      Windows Permissions   24
      NTFS Permissions   26
      Unix Permissions   27

  Users, Groups, and Owners   **27**
    Creating Users and Groups in Windows   28
    Creating Users and Groups in Unix   29

Assigning Permissions   **31**

Permissions in Windows   31

   Inherited Permissions   32
   Group Permissions   33
   Verifying Permissions   35
   Command-line Permissions   35

Permissions in Unix   36

   Unix versus Windows   37
   Changing Permissions   38
   Changing Ownership   39
   SUID/SGID Bits   39

Planning Security Permissions   **40**

Use the Latest Version   40
Separate Tomcat Account   40

   Suggested Account Settings for Unix   40
   Suggested Account Settings for Windows   41

Starting Tomcat as a Service   42
Configuring File Permissions   45
Issues Related to tomcat-users.xml   47
Disable the UserDatabaseRealm   48
Read-only Webapps Directory   48
Secure Your Files   48
Knowing If You've Been Violated   49
Read-Only File Systems   49

Summary   **49**

Chapter 3: Java Security Manager   **51**

Security Manager Features   **52**

Configuring the Security Policy File   **55**

Policy File Format   55

   keystore Entry   55
   grant Entry   56

Property Expansion in Policy Files   59

Java Security Permissions   **61**

Why Tomcat Needs the Security Manager?   **62**

Configuring Tomcat with the Java Security Manager   **63**

Tomcat's Policy File   64

   System Code Permissions   64
   Catalina Code Permissions   65
   Web Application Permissions   66

java.util.PropertyPermission   68
java.lang.RuntimePermission   69
java.io.FilePermission   73
java.net.SocketPermission   75
java.net.NetPermission   76
java.lang.reflect.ReflectPermission   77
java.security.SecurityPermission   78
java.security.AllPermission   80
Debugging Java Security Manager Installation   81
Installation Check   82

Summary   **84**

Chapter 4: Security Realms   87

Realms   87
Security and Web Applications   88
Authentication Mechanisms   89
    HTTP BASIC Authentication   89
    HTTP DIGEST Authentication   90
    FORM-Based Authentication   90
    HTTPS CLIENT Authentication   92
    Using HTTP BASIC and FORM-based Authentication over SSL   94
    Choosing an Authentication Mechanism   94
Authorization: Security Models for Web Applications   95
    Container-Managed Security   95
    Programmatic Security   96
    Pros and Cons of Container-Managed Security (Realms)   97

Tomcat's Realms   97
Adding Security Constraints to Web Applications   99
Single Sign On (SSO) for Web Applications   101
    Security Considerations for Single Sign On   101

Memory Realm   102
Configuration   102
Adding a User   103
Using Encrypted Passwords   105
    Choosing between MD5 and SHA   106
Deleting a User   107
Pros and Cons of Memory Realms   107

UserDatabase Realm   107
Configuration   107
Adding a Role   109
    Adding a User   111
    Using Encrypted Passwords   *112*
    More on UserDatabases: Using the UserDatabase API   115
Pros and Cons of UserDatabase Realms   116

JDBC Realm   117
Configuration   117
Adding a User   123
Adding a Role   124
Deleting a User   124
Deleting a Rrole   125
Pros and Cons of JDBC Realms   125

JNDI Realm   126
Configuration   127
Attributes of the JNDI Realm   130
Adding Roles and Users   133
Remove a Role or a User   133
Pros and Cons of JNDI Realms   133

JAAS Realm   134
Configuration   135
Adding or Deleting Users and Roles   138
Developing Custom Realms   138

Choosing a Realm Implementation — 139
Performance — 139
Security — 139
Add/Change Users, Roles Without Restarts — 139
Managability — 139
Custom Management Applications — 140

Summary — 140

Chapter 5: Secure Sockets and Tomcat — 143

PKI — 144
What is PKI? — 144
Encryption — 144
Symmetric — 144
Asymmetric — 145
Digital Certificates — 145
Certificate Authorities — 146
Certificate Chains — 148
Digital Signatures — 149

SSL — 149
What is SSL? — 149
Why is SSL Needed? — 150
How it Works — 150

Why Tomcat and SSL? — 151

Configuring Tomcat and SSL — 152
JSSE Install — 153
JDK keytool Utility — 155
Creating a New Keystore from Scratch — 155
The Cacerts Keystore — 157
Generating a Certificate Signing Request — 158
Trusting a Certificate Authority — 159
Importing a Certificate into a Keystore — 160
Configuring an HTTPS Connector — 161
Installation Caveats — 163
Known Issues — 164

SSL Web Resource Protection — 164
WidgetWorld — 165
Looking at web.xml — 165
Looking at server.xml — 166

SSL and Apache — 168
Installing mod_ssl — 170

SSL and AJP — 173
Overview Of AJP — 173
Overview of mod_jk — 173
Installing mod_jk — 173
SSH Tunneling — 175
Establishing the Tunnel — 175
Configuring mod_jk — 176
Caveats — 177

Ongoing SSL Management — 177

Summary — 178

Chapter 6: Application Security   181

What is Application Security?   181

Validation   183
Using Regular Expressions   183
Obscure Form Data Values   185
SSL Protocol Validation   188

Cookies and Session IDs   189
Minimize Cookie Usage   189
Cookie Validation   190
Using Sessions with JSESSIONID   191

SQL Security   193
Securing Connection Parameters   193
Prepared Statements   196
Stored Procedures   198

Securing Your Java Package   199
Java.security   199
Protecting Packages   199

Known Issues   202
The Default Invoker Servlet   202
Symbolic Links   204
JK Synchronization   205
Protecting WEB-INF   205

Summary   206

Appendix : Support, Errata, and Code Download   209

How to Download the Sample Code for the Book   209

Errata   210

E-Mail Support   210

p2p.wrox.com   211

Index   213

Apache Tomcat Security

Handbook

Introduction

Introduction

Security is among the most important concerns of the computer industry today and most of the information on the Internet is exchanged using browsers and web servers. As a large proportion of the dynamic content is served using JSPs and servlets, the use of the Tomcat servlet container is ever increasing. However, the increase in usage is also attracting many hackers.

The belief in the often quoted axiom that "just because you can't think of a way to break into your system, it doesn't mean that someone else won't find a way" is not just a paranoia but also an awareness of risk. In fact, your servers, or applications that run on your servers, are as secure as the weakest link. Hackers often find the weakest link to undermine your well-laid plans.

Tomcat has come a long way now, and being open source software, it is evolving and gaining acceptance. Just upgrading Tomcat is not enough, as many of these vulnerabilities are due to the bugs in your code or system configuration. This places some responsibility on system administrators and programmers to find ways around these security breaches. If you are exchanging sensitive information using Tomcat and you cannot afford to compromise your system, then this is the book for you.

Who Is This Book For?

This book is targeted at Tomcat developers who are contemplating Tomcat for production-level deployment, and for developers that have already embraced this option. We will assume a working knowledge of Java web applications and competence with JSPs and servlets. Very precisely, the core target reader will be the experienced Tomcat developer, who wants to know the potential problem spaces that exist within the Tomcat security domain, and the options that are available to solve these problems.

What This Book Covers

This book covers every area where Tomcat, or the applications running within Tomcat, needs to be secure. Here is what you will find in each chapter:

❑ **Chapter 1: Understanding Tomcat Security**

This chapter is about understanding what Tomcat security is all about. It shows vulnerabilities that exist in Tomcat at various levels, explains why one needs to know security, talks about the things to remember prior to installation and deployment, and discusses tools and methods for securing the entire system.

❑ **Chapter 2: Tightening File System Screws**

This chapter, as the name says, is about setting the permissions on files and directories on the server. It discusses the security policies and configuration of Windows and Unix-based file systems. It then explains what permissions should be set for files on the server, and shows how to run Tomcat as a service with an unprivileged user account.

❑ **Chapter 3: Java Security Manager**

This chapter starts by explaining the Java Security Manager and its role in Tomcat. It shows the range of permissions that can be set on various classes and their components using the Tomcat security policy file. It also discusses the Tomcat security policy file in depth, with its structure and syntax.

❑ **Chapter 4: Security Realms**

This chapter looks at how Realms are used to add security to your Java web applications. It starts with an introduction to what Realms are and where they fit in the general area of web application security. It then goes on to cover Tomcat's Realms in detail and the different implementations they provide – Memory, UserDatabase, JDBC, JNDI, and JAAS. This chapter also covers the set up and configuration for each Realm, and also how (and why) a custom implementation can (or should) be developed.

❑ **Chapter 5: Secure Sockets and Tomcat**

This chapter starts with a background discussion of PKI and SSL and then describes in detail how we can configure our Tomcat server to fully utilize SSL. It then looks at how to configure the Apache web server to act as an SSL front-end to Tomcat.

❑ **Chapter 6: Application Security**

This chapter is about the dos and don'ts of developing a web application. It is a guide for building a secure web application in an event of a code injection attack, SQL injection attack, source exposure, or similar known attacks.

What You Need to Use This Book

To make use of this book, you need to have Tomcat 4.1 installed. Wherever applicable, we have also discussed security issues relating to earlier versions of Tomcat. Since Java is platform-independent, the examples in this book should work on UNIX-based and Windows platforms without any modifications.

Apache Tomcat Security

Handbook

1

1

Understanding Tomcat Security

In the rush to bring products and services online, security is typically the one area that gets the least attention, even though it is arguably the most important. The reasons for neglecting security vary. In some cases, implementing good security is seen as too much work in a compressed timeline. In other cases, an organization chooses to rely on the security features built into another product, such as an operating system or application server, rather than enhance that security with additional steps.

Even if your system doesn't deal with financial transactions, security should still be a high priority. Security isn't just about protecting money anymore. In the Internet age, many other issues require strong security, from personal privacy to medical information. Organizations that have well-established privacy policies and have a track record of taking security seriously, often attract more customers and clients than those who don't.

The Apache Project's web servers are the most popular web servers in the world with over 63% of web sites, according to the ongoing survey from Netcraft: http://www.netcraft.com/Survey. That doesn't even include the number of private web servers in use, such as corporate intranets and personal desktops. While the Apache numbers are obviously due to the popularity of the Apache HTTP server, Apache Tomcat is popular in its own right, with millions of downloads since its release. In addition, many web servers use Tomcat as the servlet container of choice, so while a survey such as Netcraft's can only determine the actual server serving the request, there could be any number of Apache Tomcat installations supplying the actual content. Thus, devoting resources and effort to securing your Apache Tomcat installation is just as important as securing your applications, your operating systems, and your networks.

Vulnerability Overview

Web applications are complex systems by definition. Several different components are needed to make a complete system, including:

- ❑ The operating system and its file systems
- ❑ The web server itself, serving HTTP requests
- ❑ A dynamic content engine, such as Tomcat, executing the application and assembling responses
- ❑ A database
- ❑ A network or networks
- ❑ The Java Virtual Machine (JVM) in the case of applications designed with servlets and JSPs
- ❑ Any-third party packages or libraries

A vulnerability can be found in any one of these components. Even more frustrating, a specific combination of components can have a vulnerability not found in another combination. For example, a vulnerability found when using Tomcat with a certain relational database may not be an issue if a different database was used. Likewise, a problem with one version of a component might not be a problem with an older or newer version.

Ten Most Common Security Problems

The Open Web Application Security Project (OWASP) is an Open Source community project staffed entirely by volunteers. The group has highlighted the ten most common vulnerabilities in web applications and services, noting that these problems are as serious as network security problems and deserve just as much attention.

Vulnerability	Description
Unvalidated Parameters	Information from web requests is not validated before being used by a web application. Attackers can use these flaws to attack backend components through a web application.
Broken Access Control	Restrictions on what authenticated users are allowed to do are not properly enforced. Attackers can exploit these flaws to access other users' accounts, view sensitive files, or use unauthorized functions.

Vulnerability	Description
Broken Account and Session Management	Account credentials and session tokens are not properly protected. Attackers that can compromise passwords, keys, session cookies, or other tokens can defeat authentication restrictions and assume other users' identities.
Cross-Site Scripting (XSS) Flaws	The web application can be used as a mechanism to transport an attack to an end user's browser. A successful attack can disclose the end user's session token, attack the local machine, or spoof content to fool the user.
Buffer Overflows	Web application components in some languages that do not properly validate input can be crashed and, in some cases, used to take control of a process. These components can include CGI, libraries, drivers, and web application server components.
Command Injection Flaws	Web applications pass parameters when they access external systems or the local operating system. If an attacker can embed malicious commands in these parameters, the external system may execute those commands on behalf of the web application.
Error Handling Problems	Error conditions that occur during normal operation are not handled properly. If an attacker can cause errors to occur that the web application does not handle, they can gain detailed system information, deny service, cause security mechanisms to fail, or crash the server.
Insecure Use of Cryptography	Web applications frequently use cryptographic functions to protect information and credentials. These functions and the code to integrate them have proven difficult to code properly, frequently resulting in weak protection.
Remote Administration Flaws	Many web applications allow administrators to access the site using a web interface. If these administrative functions are not very carefully protected, an attacker can gain full access to all aspects of a site.
Web and Application Server Misconfiguration	Having a strong server configuration standard is critical to a secure web application. These servers have many configuration options that affect security and are not secure out of the box.

The OWASP Top Ten list is a "living" document. It can and will change over time. To get the latest version, and to participate in the project itself, visit the OWASP web site at http://www.owasp.org/.

It's important to remember that the list is not specific, nor can it be. Each web application is different, so instead of thinking in terms of specific problems, it is more effective to think in terms of the types of problems, as shown in the list. All web applications suffer from these types of vulnerabilities, and it is up to the development team, the systems administration team, and the organization supporting them, to make correcting these problems a priority. Above all, remember that your web application is a critical part of your security model. Web application security techniques are discussed in Chapter 6. For now, let's address the last item in the list: "Web and Application Server Misconfiguration."

Known Tomcat Vulnerabilities

Tomcat, like any other application, is not bug free. A fundamental part of any security policy is not only staying abreast of known vulnerabilities, usually through a mailing list like the **BUGTRAQ** list or one of many others, but also staying current with recent patch levels and versions of the software. Since Tomcat's version 4 was released, several vulnerabilities have been found and resolved. As of this writing (January 2003), the recommended versions of the Tomcat 4 branch are 4.0.6 and 4.1.18. The 4.0 branch is no longer actively developed, and work on Tomcat 5 has already started. If you are unable to use Tomcat 4 for some reason, the recommended version is 3.3.1.

Servlet/JSP Spec	Tomcat version
2.4/2.0	5.0.0 Alpha
2.3/1.2	4.1.18
2.2/1.1	3.3.1

Even if you have the latest version of Tomcat installed, you still need to worry about potential vulnerabilities. In a web server environment, Tomcat is only one piece of the entire system, so while you may have the latest security patches for Tomcat itself, your system can still fall prey to attacks and exploits that target web applications or other external system components.

Recently discovered Tomcat vulnerabilities have focused on problems with Tomcat installation defaults, such as the Invoker servlet being enabled by default, allowing an attacker to craft a URL that will display the source code of a JavaServer Page instead of the content that the page generates. More on web application vulnerabilities can be found in Chapter 6, Web Application Security.

Here's a list of the known vulnerabilities in Tomcat 4 through January 2003:

Date Announced	Vulnerability
2003-01-09	Invoker servlet file disclosure vulnerability
2002-12-10	Default Servlet file disclosure vulnerability
2002-12-09	Mod_jk chunked encoding denial of service vulnerability
2002-08-21	JSP request cross site scripting vulnerability
2002-06-12	JSP engine denial of service vulnerability
2002-04-23	Servlet path disclosure vulnerability
2002-04-19	System path information disclosure vulnerability

As you can see, the majority of the problems found are application or configuration oriented, not necessarily problems with Tomcat itself, such as a buffer overflow. All vulnerabilities found so far have known workarounds and solutions; it is up to the administrator to implement them in a timely manner. Any solutions to these vulnerabilities not covered by upgrading to the latest version of Tomcat are discussed in upcoming chapters.

For future reference, you can subscribe to various mailing lists to stay abreast of vulnerabilities as they are found. Two popular mailing lists are the *BUGTRAQ* mailing list, and the *Web Application Security* mailing list, known as **webappsec**. Information on both, including charters, archives, and subscription information, can be found at http://online.securityfocus.com/archive. In addition, vulnerability databases can be found at http://online.securityfocus.com/bid and http://www.kb.cert.org/vuls. The CERT® Coordination Center at Carnegie Mellon University is also an excellent source of Internet-related security information, including up-to-date alerts and status reports on the newest vulnerabilities. The CERT® Coordination Center web site can be found at http://www.cert.org.

Installation

Right from the start, the decisions you make when installing Tomcat can have a significant impact on the security of your installation. From a pre-installation planning perspective, you will
want to consider:

- ❑ How will starting and stopping Tomcat be controlled?
- ❑ Which user account is used to run Tomcat?

❑   Which ports will Tomcat use, and how will access to those ports be controlled?

❑   What are Tomcat installation defaults, and do they fit our security model?

Running Tomcat as a Service

Like most applications designed to provide services for many users and accept requests from other applications, Tomcat can be used in one of two ways. First, Tomcat can run as a standard user-level application. In other words, users log into their account, start up Tomcat, do their work, shut Tomcat down, and log out. In a single-developer/single-desktop scenario, this may be ideal and all that is needed. The second way is to run Tomcat as a service. By running it as a service, you are making it available to serve requests to more than just the person logged in, and you are making sure that Tomcat is available for those requests whether anyone is logged in or not. For a web server, this is the standard setup.

If you're using Linux or another type of UNIX-like operating system, you'll want to set up a script that starts and stops Tomcat as needed. Typically, this script would be called in the system's boot routine, and called again when the system shuts down. This allows Tomcat to be available to serve requests as much as possible. By including this script in your system's `init` configuration, Tomcat will be available to accept requests whenever the server is up.

If you're installing Tomcat on Microsoft's Windows operating system, you'll want to install Tomcat as a Windows service so that it stays running without requiring that a user stay logged in while it's running. Depending on the install method that you use for Tomcat, there are two different ways to set up Tomcat as a service on Windows. The first is the easiest: if you download the Tomcat self-installer package, there will be an option to install Tomcat as a service when you run it. This can be seen in the screenshot below:

By selecting the box labeled NT Service (NT/2k/XP only), the installer will take care of setting up Tomcat as a Windows service instead of as a stand-alone application controlled by a typical user. If, on the other hand, you installed Tomcat from a ZIP archive or even built it yourself from source, you can still install it as a service after the fact.

Note that installing and uninstalling Tomcat as service is not the same as starting and stopping Tomcat. You only need to do the service installation once. After that, you can use the Services control applet or the command line to start and stop your Tomcat service as needed. Running Tomcat as a service on Windows and UNIX-like platforms is discussed in Chapter 2. For more detailed information on installing Tomcat, consult *Professional Apache Tomcat (ISBN 1-861007-73-6)* from *Wrox Press*.

Using an Unprivileged User Account

One of the problems encountered when running web servers and other publicly accessible applications is the concept of permissions. While your application might use access controls to limit what certain users can do, that only applies to the application. What about Tomcat itself? Buffer overflows, probably the most common exploit, highlight the problems with running server applications under user accounts that have total access to the system. For example, if a web server is running as root, administrator, or superuser, and an attacker is able to send a request such that the web server fails and allows arbitrary commands to run within its environment, those commands will run with a superuser access.

The solution is to avoid using a privileged account to run Tomcat whenever possible. By using an unprivileged user account, you can take the first step to protecting against a future exploit that involves causing Tomcat to allow the execution of arbitrary commands issued by an attacker. If Tomcat, running as an *unprivileged* user, were to fail or for some reason allow an attacker access to the operating system, the only permission level the attacker would typically have would be the permission level of the Tomcat user, instead of administrator or superuser access.

Different operating systems have different ways of denoting the superuser account, or administrator account. On UNIX variants, the administrator account is known as root. On Windows systems, the administrator account is known as SYSTEM. UNIX-like operating systems further complicate matters by requiring that all services listening on ports less than 1024 run as root. This poses a problem, since popular Internet services like e-mail, web browsing, and file transfers all occur on ports less than 1024 by default. If one of those services was attacked and failed to handle the attack appropriately, an attacker might gain access to that service's environment, in this case an administrator environment. The *less than 1024* rule doesn't apply to Windows servers, since services run as SYSTEM by default, regardless of the port being used.

So, how do we use Tomcat as a stand-alone web server on port 80? By default, Tomcat listens on port 8080 for HTTP requests. To get Tomcat to listen on port 80, the default HTTP port, you have to do two things:

1. Change the org.apache.coyote.tomcat4.CoyoteConnector on port 8080 in server.xml to port 80

2. Start, stop, and run Tomcat as root if you're using a UNIX-like operating system.

As discussed earlier, running publicly available web services as `root` or superuser is typically a bad idea, so the solution is to avoid using Tomcat as a stand-alone web server on port 80 by integrating it with a standard HTTP web server such as Apache, Microsoft's Internet Information Server, or Sun Microsystem's iPlanet. In the case of Apache, the *less than 1024* port restriction is handled nicely by Apache starting up as `root`, binding to port 80, and then forking child processes to handle actual HTTP requests. These child processes do not run as `root`, but as some other unprivileged user, typically a user account known as `nobody`, set up specifically for Apache's use. Creating and running Tomcat with unprivileged user accounts on Windows and UNIX-like platforms is discussed in Chapter 2. For more detailed information on integrating Tomcat with a HTTP server, consult *Professional Apache Tomcat (ISBN 1-861007-73-6)* from *Wrox Press.*

Using a Firewall

While a detailed discussion of firewalls is beyond the scope of this book, they can play a key role in protecting your Tomcat installation, so we'll take a quick look at the basics: what they do, why they're important, and some simple examples of how you can use them.

Simply put, a firewall protects a computer or computer network from unauthorized access. A firewall can be software, hardware, or a combination of both. There are different types: proxy servers, packet filters, and stateful inspection firewalls. Firewalls use rules to determine which network traffic should be allowed to pass, and which shouldn't. These rules can be very simple, such as "deny all traffic to port 23," or complex, such as "deny all traffic to port 3389, unless it comes from a certain list of IP addresses, and arrives during a certain part of the day but only Monday through Friday." The rules can also determine whether certain traffic is logged or not.

Most environments include a firewall that is a distinct component from the server hosting Tomcat. Typically, the firewall is located between the public, untrusted Internet, and the trusted application network. This location allows the firewall to analyze all traffic as it passes in and out. The problem with relying on this firewall for protection of your Tomcat installation is that by default, this firewall has to include rules that apply to all nodes in the network that it is protecting. If the only node it is protecting is the machine hosting Tomcat, all is good. If the firewall is protecting a number of different networks, and dozens or even hundreds of nodes, it is possible that the firewall rule set may not be restrictive enough to provide the protection you desire for your Tomcat installation. In this scenario, you have additional tools you can use to add layers of protection.

Linux kernels since version 2.0 have included support for firewall rules. The 2.0 kernels used a tool called `ipfwadm`, while the 2.2 kernels used `ipchains`. The 2.4 kernels have yet another framework for setting up firewalls, and that is through `netfilter` and `iptables`.

Let's take a look at a simple firewall rule. Assume that the environment is Tomcat integrated with the Apache HTTP server using a web server connector such as JK or JK2. By default, Tomcat will use `org.apache.coyote.tomcat4.CoyoteConnector` to listen on port 8009 for communications from Apache. In a single server scenario, that means that traffic for port 8009 should never be received from any other machine at any other address besides localhost, or 127.0.0.1. Leaving a connector port, such as 8009, open to any traffic from anywhere is inviting trouble. So, on a Linux system, a rule for rejecting traffic on port 8009 from any address but 127.0.0.1 might look like this:

```
ipchains -A input -s ! 127.0.0.1 -d 0/0 8009 -p all -y -j REJECT
```

Going from left to right, this particular rule says, "add an input rule for all traffic from any host except localhost, destined for port 8009 on any address, any protocol, and reject it." By implementing a rule like this on the server itself, you can add one or more layers of protection to your installation beyond the protection provided by an external firewall.

The rule shown above is just an example. Your environment and requirements might need different rules, or you might not want to use a firewall on your server at all. In a load-balancing environment, your Tomcat installation might receive requests on port 8009 from any number of IP addresses on your local network. In that case, you would change the rule to use a different source parameter, like this:

```
ipchains -A input -s ! 192.168.1.0/24 -d 0/0 8009 -p all -y -j REJECT
```

As shown, the rule would reject traffic destined for port 8009 unless it came from the 192.168.1.0 Class C network, which might be the addresses used by your Apache servers. A rule for `iptables` would be similar. Either way, the point is that using a local firewall or packet filter can add protection to your Tomcat installation without requiring Tomcat to handle the network traffic.

Firewalls and packet filters are worthy of a book themselves and can't be covered thoroughly here. For more information on `ipchains` and `iptables`, consult the manual pages and documentation, or check the HOWTOs and FAQs at http://www.netfilter.org/. If you're using a UNIX variant besides Linux, consult your vendor's product pages or investigate open source options. Many different solutions exist, especially for open source operating systems like FreeBSD and OpenBSD.

If you're using a Windows server, you will need to install and configure Microsoft's Internet and Security Acceleration (ISA) server or investigate a third-party firewall package for your server, as there is no firewall or packet filter built into the Windows server kernel. For more information on using Microsoft's ISA server, consult the Microsoft MSDN HOWTO articles for ISA Server:
http://msdn.microsoft.com/howto/security.asp or the ISA Server homepage at http://www.microsoft.com/isaserver/.

Connector Management

In Tomcat parlance, a *connector* is an implementation of a particular Java class that is configured to listen on a specific port with varying parameters, such as timeout or the maximum number of connections. There are two different types of connectors: those that allow browsers to connect directly to Tomcat; and those that listen for and handle traffic from web servers like Apache or Microsoft's IIS. For example, a connector of the first type would be the default HTTP connector on port 8080. A connector of the second type would be the default JK/JK2 connector on port 8009. From the start, Tomcat comes with some connectors enabled in `server.xml`, and several disabled.

For Tomcat 4.1.18, the default connectors and their initial statuses are:

Port Number	Connector Type	Default Status
8080	HTTP/1.1	Enabled
	`org.apache.coyote.tomcat4.CoyoteConnector`	
8443	SSL HTTP/1.1	Disabled
	`org.apache.coyote.tomcat4.CoyoteConnector`	
8009	JK/JK2 AJP 1.3	Enabled
	`org.apache.coyote.tomcat4.CoyoteConnector`	
8009	Legacy JK AJP 1.3	Disabled
	`org.apache.ajp.tomcat4.Ajp13Connector`	
8082	Proxied HTTP/1.1	Disabled
	`org.apache.coyote.tomcat4.CoyoteConnector`	
8083	Legacy HTTP/1.1	Disabled
	`org.apache.catalina.connector.http.HttpConnector`	
8084	Legacy SSL HTTP/1.1	Disabled
	`org.apache.catalina.connector.http.HttpConnector`	
8008	WARP	Disabled
	`org.apache.catalina.connector.warp.WarpConnector`	

Once you have Tomcat installed, you will want to review `server.xml` and decide which connectors you need, and which you don't. Disable the connectors you don't need by commenting them out in `server.xml` and restarting Tomcat. The `server.xml` excerpt below shows the connector on port 8080 enabled:

```
<!-- Define a non-SSL Coyote HTTP/1.1 Connector on port 8080 -->
<Connector className="org.apache.coyote.tomcat4.CoyoteConnector"
           port="8080" minProcessors="5" maxProcessors="75"
           enableLookups="true" redirectPort="8443"
           acceptCount="100" debug="0" connectionTimeout="20000"
           useURIValidationHack="false" disableUploadTimeout="true" />
```

And the one below shows a disabled connector:

```
<!-- Define a non-SSL Coyote HTTP/1.1 Connector on port 8080 -->
<!--
<Connector className="org.apache.coyote.tomcat4.CoyoteConnector"
           port="8080" minProcessors="5" maxProcessors="75"
           enableLookups="true" redirectPort="8443"
           acceptCount="100" debug="0" connectionTimeout="20000"
           useURIValidationHack="false" disableUploadTimeout="true" />
-->
```

At a minimum, you will need at least one connector. If you disable all connectors, Tomcat will be unable to listen for requests. If you're using Tomcat in stand-alone mode as its own HTTP server, then you'll need the HTTP/1.1 connector on port 8080 or 80, and you won't need the JK/JK2 connector on port 8009. Likewise, if you are using Tomcat with a HTTP server and not stand-alone, you won't need the HTTP/1.1 connector on port 8080. Instead, you would use the JK/JK2 connector on port 8009 or some other port of your choosing, or even the WARP connector on port 8008. For more on configuring and using the JK/JK2 and other connectors in `server.xml`, consult *Professional Apache Tomcat (ISBN 1-861007-73-6)* from *Wrox Press*.

If you don't disable the connectors you aren't using, you allow Tomcat to receive traffic on that port. An attacker could send all kinds of different packet types to that port, looking for a vulnerability, and you would never know it was happening since it wouldn't be interfering with connectors listening on other ports. In short, make sure Tomcat is only listening on the ports you want it to use.

Default Tomcat Applications

Just as Tomcat has various connectors enabled by default, it also has several web applications included and enabled by default. These applications consist of the following:

- ❏   The Manager application
- ❏   The Admin application
- ❏   The WebDAV application
- ❏   The examples application

The applications are there for a reason, but that doesn't mean you have to sit back and accept the way they are installed or the way they are configured by default. Analyzing the default applications, determining which ones you need and which ones you don't, and taking appropriate action might make the difference between being susceptible to a vulnerability down the road, and being protected.

The Manager Application

The Manager application included with Tomcat is designed for ease of deployment and management of web applications without having to affect the entire servlet container.

With the Manager application, you can:

❑ Deploy a new web application, on a specified context path, from the uploaded contents of a WAR file

❑ Install a new web application

❑ List the currently deployed web applications, as well as the sessions that are currently active for those web apps

❑ Reload an existing web application, to reflect changes in the contents of /WEB-INF/classes or /WEB-INF/lib

❑ List the available global JNDI resources

❑ List the available security roles defined in the user database

❑ Remove an installed web application, start and stop an application, and undeploy an application

At first glance, it might seem like the Manager application is not included with your Tomcat installation. That's because the Context element for /manager is not included in server.xml. The Manager application uses the Automatic Deployment feature of Tomcat, and is deployed as a valid Context at startup because of the manager.xml file in the webapps directory of your Tomcat installation. Manager.xml looks like the following:

```
<Context path="/manager" docBase="../server/webapps/manager"
        debug="0" privileged="true">

    <!-- Link to the user database we will get roles from -->
    <ResourceLink name="users" global="UserDatabase"
                type="org.apache.catalina.UserDatabase"/>

</Context>
```

If you'd rather have the Context for the Manager application in your server.xml, you can do this simply by copying the contents of manager.xml into server.xml and restarting Tomcat. However, this will make management for many applications and virtual hosts in Tomcat harder. By taking advantage of the Automatic Deployment feature of Tomcat, you can install the Manager application for many virtual hosts simply by copying manager.xml to each host's webapps folder.

While the Manager application is available by default, access to it is disabled by default. The Manager application requires a user account with a role of **manager** in `tomcat-users.xml`, which is located in Tomcat's `conf` directory. The `tomcat-users.xml` file does not include a user with Manager access permissions out of the box. To enable Manager application access for a specific user, edit `tomcat-users.xml` so that is looks like the following:

```
<?xml version='1.0' encoding='utf-8'?>
<tomcat-users>
  <role rolename="tomcat"/>
  <role rolename="role1"/>
  <role rolename="manager"/>
  <role rolename="admin"/>
  <user username="tomcat" password="tomcat" roles="tomcat"/>
  <user username="role1" password="tomcat" roles="role1"/>
  <user username="both" password="tomcat" roles="tomcat,role1"/>
  <user username="admin" password="tomcat" roles="admin,manager"/>
</tomcat-users>
```

Note the role of `manager` added to the user account `admin`. Obviously, in your own installation, you will want to change the password from `tomcat` to something else. You can also use JDBC Realms and JNDI Realms to hold your user account and permission information if you want to integrate with existing authentication systems and avoid having to edit `tomcat-users.xml`.

If you wanted to further restrict access to the Manager application, you could do so by restricting access to a certain IP address or host name by using a `Valve`. For example, by adding a `RemoteAddrValve` or `RemoteHostValve` to manager.xml, you could restrict access to only those computers on a local network or even to the Tomcat server itself. In the example below, access to the `/manager` Context is restricted to requests from IP address `127.0.0.1`:

```
<Context path="/manager" debug="0" privileged="true"
         docBase="/usr/local/kinetic/tomcat4/server/webapps/manager">
         <Valve className="org.apache.catalina.valves.RemoteAddrValve"
                allow="127.0.0.1"/>
</Context>
```

Once you have a user account with the appropriate permissions set up in `tomcat-users.xml`, and any desired address or hostname restrictions in place using a `Valve`, you can access the manager application in one of three ways:

❑   Via a web browser using a URL like:
    `http://localhost/manager/html/`

❑   Via HTTP requests, suitable for use in scripts set up by system administrators

❑   As a set of task definitions for the Ant (version 1.4 or later) build tool

For more information on the Manager application, consult the Manager HOWTO at: http://jakarta.apache.org/tomcat/tomcat-4.1-doc/manager-howto.html. For more on creating users and roles, and using alternate methods to `tomcat-users.xml`, consult Chapter 4.

The Admin Application

Similar to the Manager application, Tomcat 4 and 5 include an administration application by default. Just as is the case with the Manager application, the Admin application uses a file called `admin.xml` in Tomcat's webapps directory to auto-deploy the `/admin` Context instead of including the Context in `server.xml`.

The contents of `admin.xml` look like this:

```
<Context path="/admin" docBase="../server/webapps/admin"
         debug="0" privileged="true">

<!--
<Valve className="org.apache.catalina.valves.RemoteAddrValve"
  allow="127.0.0.1"/>
-->

<Logger className="org.apache.catalina.logger.FileLogger"
        prefix="localhost_admin_log." suffix=".txt"
        timestamp="true"/>

</Context>
```

As you can see, it looks very similar to `manager.xml`, including the use of a `Valve` to restrict access to a specific IP address or range of addresses. The value of `allow` in the `Valve` can be a comma-delimited list of IP addresses, or even a regular expression such as `192.168.1.*`.

What's the difference between Admin and Manager? The Manager application is for managing web application deployment. The Admin application is for managing the server itself. With the Admin application, you can do the following:

❏   Add and delete `Connectors`, as well as change their parameters

❏   Add, delete, and manage `Hosts`

❏   Add, delete, and manage `Contexts` within `Hosts`

❏   Manage `Resources`, such as `DataSources` and other `Environment` parameters

❏   Manage `Users` and `Roles`

In short, rather than editing `server.xml` directly, you can accomplish the same tasks by using the Admin application. It goes without saying, then, that access to the Admin application should be monitored carefully and granted judiciously. Having access to the Admin application is essentially the same as being able to edit `server.xml`.

Just like the Manager application, you can grant access to the Admin application using `tomcat-users.xml`. While the Manager application requires a user account with a role of `manager`, the Admin application requires a user account with the role of **admin**. In the `tomcat-users.xml` file for our Manager example, for instance, the user admin has both *admin* and *manager* privileges.

By default, the Admin application can be reached at the following URL for your Tomcat installation: `http://localhost:8080/admin/`. Once you've considered the ramifications of changing the defaults, you can modify `admin.xml` and `tomcat-users.xml` to grant access to the Admin application to other users and hosts. For more on creating users and roles, and using alternate methods to `tomcat-users.xml`, consult Chapter 4.

The examples Application

By default, Tomcat includes a set of JavaServer Pages and servlets as examples of how to use Tomcat to serve web applications. In a production situation, the `/examples` Context is unnecessary, and should be disabled. If left enabled, an attacker can use some of the examples as a means of discerning information about the Tomcat installation, such as pathnames and other information, all of which is better left hidden.

Disabling the `/examples` Context is easy. Simply comment out that `Context` in `server.xml`, or delete it entirely. In fact, Tomcat 4.1.18 comes with a second `server.xml` file called `server-noexamples.xml.config`. This file is identical to `server.xml`, but without the `/examples` Context. Simply rename the default `server.xml` to `server-examples.xml.config`, and then copy `server-noexamples.xml.config` to `server.xml` and restart Tomcat. You now have a default Tomcat installation without the `/examples` Context.

Because of the Automatic Deployment feature, performing the operation above won't have any effect on the Manager or Admin applications. Both will still be available to the hostnames where they're installed.

The WebDAV Application

The fourth and final application included with Tomcat 4 is the WebDAV application. WebDAV is a method of allowing **remote authoring** of a web site using a compatible WebDAV client. Tomcat 4.1.18 supports WebDAV 2, and compatible clients include:

❑ Adobe GoLive 5.0 (and other WebDAV-enabled Adobe products like Photoshop)

❑ Internet Explorer 5 and 5.5 (Windows 2000)

❑ Jakarta Slide 1.0 WebDAV client library

❑ Office 2000 (Windows 2000)

By default, the /webdav Context is distributed with **read-only** access enabled. In order to use WebDAV for a particular Context, you'll need to make it **read-write** instead. For example, to make the /webdav Context included with Tomcat 4.1.18 read-write instead of read-only, you would edit the web.xml file found in webapps/webdav/WEB-INF/ and change the following:

```
<!--
    <init-param>
      <param-name>readonly</param-name>
      <param-value>false</param-value>
    </init-param>
-->
```

to this:

```
    <init-param>
      <param-name>readonly</param-name>
      <param-value>false</param-value>
    </init-param>
```

Also in web.xml, you can configure particular roles as listed in tomcat-users.xml, granting them particular access to the /webdav Context. For example, to enable access to /webdav for the user tomcat as defined in tomcat-users.xml, you would set up the following in web.xml:

```
<security-constraint>
  <web-resource-collection>
    <web-resource-name>The Entire Web Application</web-resource-name>
    <url-pattern>/*</url-pattern>
  </web-resource-collection>
  <auth-constraint>
    <role-name>tomcat</role-name>
  </auth-constraint>
</security-constraint>

<login-config>
  <auth-method>BASIC</auth-method>
  <realm-name>Tomcat Supported Realm</realm-name>
</login-config>

<security-role>
  <description>
    An example role defined in "conf/tomcat-users.xml"
  </description>
  <role-name>tomcat</role-name>
</security-role>
```

Once you have granted and enabled read-write access, you can reach the `/webdav` `Context` by pointing to the `/webdav` path of your Tomcat installation using your WebDAV client.

Tomcat 4 uses the Jakarta Slide WebDAV module, implemented as a servlet, to provide WebDAV services. For more info on Jakarta Slide, visit http://jakarta.apache.org/slide/index.html and for more info on WebDAV itself, visit http://www.webdav.org/. For other links and more information on Tomcat's implementation of WebDAV, consult the http://localhost:8080/webdav/index.html URL of your Tomcat installation.

Summary

As pointed out by the Open Web Application Security Project, misconfiguration and improper installation of web and application servers can be a serious problem and adversely affect the integrity of your web application and its components. In addition, neglecting to analyze things like remote administration applications that may be included can be another cause for problems. In this chapter we discussed:

❑ The top ten web application vulnerabilities as listed by the Open Web Application Security Project

❑ Proper installation of Tomcat as a service running under an unprivileged user account

❑ Using a local firewall to add additional layers of security to network traffic

❑ Managing `Connectors` in `server.xml` so only those needed are enabled

❑ Proper management of default applications and `Contexts` included with Tomcat to minimize possible entry points for attacks

In short, it is up to the server administrator to be proactive and manage the default installation of any web or application server under their control. By merely accepting the defaults, an administrator leaves themselves open to more potential attack points and may even compromise their installation, since they are simply trusting someone else to ship the product with secure defaults.

Apache Tomcat Security

Handbook

2

Tightening File System Screws

There are multiple ways for any hacker to break into your system. Any service that accepts socket connections can potentially be exploited in some unimagined and unintended way; new such *exploits* are found all the time.

It is possible that Tomcat can be exploited by a hacker in some way. While as of this writing there are no known exploits in the latest version of Tomcat (4.1.18), with the passing of time and new versions, the chances are quite good that some will be found.

The focus of this chapter is essentially *damage control*: minimizing what hackers can do if they discover some malicious way of using Tomcat. Since most common exploits of manipulating Tomcat are retrieve and execute sensitive files, this chapter's focus is on securing your server's file system against such exploits.

We will begin our discussion by reviewing how file system security works on both *Unix-derived* and *Windows* operating systems. If you are an experienced system administrator, you can probably skip or skim the first section, entitled *Permissions*. Following that section, we will discuss our recommendations on configuring your file system's security options.

Permissions

Both Windows and Unix share the same security paradigm for their file system: **permissions**. File system permissions are a fine-grained way for controlling which files users are allowed to view, execute, manipulate, and so forth. In other words, in either of these operating systems, users cannot access the file system in any way without being given explicit permission to do so.

The scope of this chapter therefore is to use these file system permissions to our advantage and to create a secure environment for our Tomcat installation.

The Heterogeneity of Permissions

While both the Windows and Unix file systems are based on the notion of permissions, they have implemented this concept in slightly different ways. We will therefore discuss the permissions available to these operating systems separately.

Windows Permissions

First of all, Windows has several different file system types. We will consider them in the order of oldest to newest.

FAT

All early versions of Windows are based on the classic **FAT (File Allocation Table)** file system, which traces its proud heritage back to the classic MS-DOS operating system and its immediate ancestor, QDOS. FAT is capable of abstracting bytes into files and directories, but not much more. It is because of FAT that legions of PC users had to create filenames no longer than eight characters.

NTFS

Realizing that FAT was all about limitations and was quite short on features, Microsoft developed the much improved **NTFS (NT file system)** for use with its next generation Windows NT operating system. NTFS is better than FAT in every way. The latest incarnation of NTFS (available in Windows 2000/XP) supports security through permissions and encryption, long file names, networking, journaling, disk quotas, and so forth. To top it off, NTFS stores files in a much more efficient way than FAT, and is much more reliable.

FAT32

In the era of Windows 95, Microsoft had to deal with a problem: consumer-grade hard drives were beginning to bump against the limitations of FAT, which could only handle up to two gigabytes of information. While Microsoft did have NTFS, the file system had been designed for the Windows NT family and was inappropriate for Windows 9x. As a result, Microsoft created an enhanced version of FAT, dubbed FAT32.

FAT32 betters its predecessor by supporting two terabytes of space (that's 2,000 gigabytes) as well as storing data in a more efficient way. FAT32 is available on Windows 95, Windows 98, Windows ME, and Windows XP.

NTFS Required

Of these three file systems, only NTFS supports any semblance of file system security. As a result, your server will need to use the NTFS file system. Thus, you'll need to use Windows NT 4/2000/XP Professional to get anything out of this chapter. Note, however, that our instructions were written with Windows 2000 and Windows XP in mind; users of Windows NT 4.0 may need to refer to their documentation.

Even if you're using Windows 2000/XP, it's possible that you're using the FAT32 file system. Take the time now to check which file system you are using. You can accomplish this by going to My Computer and viewing the properties for your partition(s) – check all of them if you have more than one. The property window for your partition will look something like this:

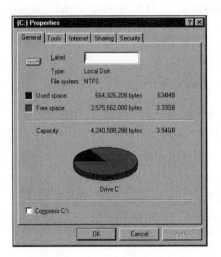

If you see FAT32 and not NTFS, don't panic. Windows 2000/XP comes with a command-line conversion utility, convert, which will upgrade your file system to NTFS. To upgrade your hard drive to NTFS, you can issue the following command:

```
convert c: /fs:ntfs
```

Here c: would be replaced by your hard drive's letter(s) as appropriate.

> **While this command should not be a destructive exercise, you should consider backing up data in case something goes wrong. This conversion is one-way; you cannot convert an NTFS volume back into a FAT/FAT32 volume.**

You must have quite a bit of free space for the conversion to occur. The formula for computing the space that you'll need is not easy to explain. If you're interested in learning more go to: http://support.microsoft.com/default.aspx?scid=KB;en-us;q156560.

> **Note: If you receive an error message "Insufficient disk space for conversion" when attempting to convert your hard drive, and you do have several gigabytes of free space, you may need to obtain service packs for your operating system. See the following Microsoft articles for details:**
> http://support.microsoft.com/default.aspx?scid=KB;en-us;q271644.

NTFS Permissions

Now that we've explained the file systems on Windows, let's discuss all the individual permissions that NTFS makes available. The permissions are divided into two categories: **folder permissions** and **file permissions**. These permissions are shown in the tables below.

Folder Permissions

Permission	Actions Permitted
Read	View files and subfolders; view folder ownership, permissions, and file system attributes (read-only, hidden, etc).
Write	Create files and subfolders; view folder ownership and permissions, change folder attributes.
List Folder Contents	View names of files and subfolders in folder.
Read and Execute	Allows user to move through folder to get to subfolders and files; includes permissions from "Read" and "List Folder Contents" as well.
Modify	Delete the folder; rename the folder; includes permissions from "Read and Execute" and "Write."
Full Control	Includes all other folder permissions; delete files and subfolders; take ownership; change permissions.

File Permissions

Permission	Actions Permitted
Read	View the file contents; view file ownership, permissions, and file system attributes.
Write	Overwrite the file; view file ownership and permissions; change file attributes.

Permission	Actions Permitted
Read and Execute	Execute the file; includes permissions from "Read."
Modify	Modify file; delete file; includes permissions from "Read and Execute" and "Write."
Full Control	Includes all other file permissions; take ownership; change permissions.

We will discuss how these permissions can be assigned to users in a moment.

Unix Permissions

The Unix-derived file systems, which include those used in Linux, FreeBSD, and Mac OS X, are somewhat simpler to explain. Security has always been an inherent aspect of the Unix file system design, and as such (like Windows) there are no histories to relate or utilities to introduce. The Unix permissions are the same for directories and files. These permissions are:

File and Directory Permissions

Permission	Actions Permitted
Read	View the contents of the file or directory.
Write	Modify or delete if a file; create files if a directory.
Execute	Execution if a file; access for directories.

Users, Groups, and Owners

We've now seen what permissions are available in both Windows and Unix-derived operating systems. To make use of these permissions, we need to consider how to assign these permissions to the various users who will be using our operating system.

❑ **Users**

Both Windows and Unix include the concept of user accounts. Anyone who wishes to log into these operating systems must know an account name and its associated password. Each user can be assigned one or more of the permissions we've discussed above and thus be granted authority to manipulate objects (files or directories) in the file system.

❑ **Groups**

In addition, both Windows and Unix support adding users to a group. Groups can then receive permissions, and all users that belong to a group share those permissions.

❏ **Owners**
And finally, both operating systems share the concept of a file/directory owner. An owner is a user who ultimately has complete control over what permissions other users or groups have for a given resource, regardless of what permissions the user has been granted.

❏ **Superusers**
Our discussion would not be complete without including one additional detail. Windows and Unix both have so-called *superuser* accounts. These accounts have complete and unrestricted access to your system, regardless of any other permission that has been set. On Windows, the default superuser account is called *Administrator*, and on Unix the default superuser account is called *root*.

The password for these accounts should be extremely well chosen and extremely well guarded. You are advised not to use these accounts for your day-to-day operations, as any virus or other malicious program may inadvertently execute when running, as this account has complete control of your system.

Creating Users and Groups in Windows

Now that we've discussed what users and groups are in relation to permissions, let's see how to create new users and groups. In Windows, a special application called *Computer Management* is used for this purpose. To reach it, open the Control Panel, double-click on the Administrative Tools icon, and then double-click on the Computer Management icon. You should see a screen like this:

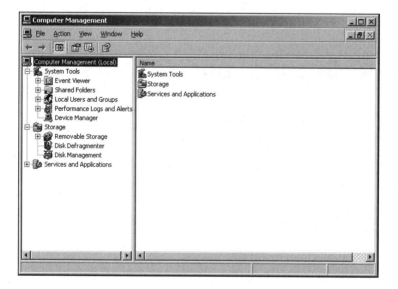

Now, click on the Local Users and Groups icon. It will expand as shown below:

You can add, modify, and delete users and groups by selecting either of these two folders, and right clicking on the list of users or groups shown on the right. All of these tasks are rather intuitive in this application, and we will not go further in the details here.

Creating Users and Groups in Unix

It will not surprise you to learn that Unix uses a series of command-line utilities to control the creation and manipulation of users and groups. Let us consider all of them in their context.

Note that the utilities we review here are from Linux operating systems; other Unix operating systems may use different utilities, although their functionality will be quite similar. If you are using a different operating system, your documentation will tell you what commands to use if they differ from those shown here.

Viewing All Users

Most Unix-derived operating systems maintain a list of all user accounts in the /etc/passwd file. The exact contents of this file can vary from operating system, but at the very least you will see a list of users with various attributes to the right of the username. Below is a typical example:

```
mel:*:25619:100:Braveheart:/home/mel:/bin/tcsh
tom:*:65191:65191:M. Report:/home/tom:/bin/tcsh
bruce:*:25622:100:Signs:/home/bruce:/bin/tcsh
kenneth:*:65523:65523:Much A. About N.:/home/kenneth:/bin/tcsh
matt:*:25624:100:Good W. H.:/home/matt:/bin/tcsh
```

In the example above, everything from the left of each line to the first colon is the username. The rest of the information determines various information about the users, and as stated varies depending on your exact operating system.

Determining a User's Group(s)

Once you know a username, you can determine which groups a user belongs to with the groups command, as shown below:

```
$ groups mel
mel : actors aussies smokers millionaires
```

In the example above, we've used groups to determine that user mel belongs to four very diverse groups.

Adding a New User

New users are added using the useradd command. The simplest way to add a new user is:

```
$ useradd [user]
```

The above syntax will also create a new group with the same name of the user and will add the user to that group. Using the -g parameter, you can specify a different group for a new user, such as:

```
$ useradd [user] -g [group]
```

If you wish to add a user to multiple groups, you can use the -G parameter, which takes as many groups as you want to throw at it, separated by commas. Note: the groups to which you wish to assign the user must already exist. The following are some valid examples:

```
$ useradd tom
$ useradd tom -g actors
$ useradd tom -g actors -G oscar_winners,californians
```

Modifying a User's Group(s)

You can modify the groups to which an existing user belongs with the usermod command. It takes the same -g and -G parameters as the useradd command. The following example of the usermod command will make user tom only belong to the actors group:

```
$ usermod -g actors -G "" tom
```

Deleting a User

Users can be deleted at any time using the following command:

```
$ userdel [user]
```

Adding a Group

Groups can be added with the following command:

```
$ groupadd [name]
```

Deleting a Group

The command to delete groups is:

```
$ groupdel [group]
```

Assigning Permissions

While Windows and Unix both make use of users, groups, and owners, you will shortly see that they differ quite significantly in how permissions are assigned to users and groups. Windows actually gives system administrators much more flexibility in the assignment of permissions than does Unix. However, this flexibility comes with a steep price: your security configuration can rapidly deteriorate into an unmaintainable mess if you are not careful. The Unix model, on the other hand, trades the complexity of Windows for a simplicity that is easy to understand and easy to administer. We will review how to assign permissions in both operating systems.

Permissions in Windows

There are two ways to manipulate a file's permissions in Windows: a GUI interface, and a command-line interface. The majority of this section will use the GUI method. We will briefly cover the command-line utility at the end of this section.

To view permissions in Windows, open the Windows Explorer, pick the file or directory whose permissions you wish to view, and right-click on it. In the context menu, choose Properties. A window will appear, entitled [filename] Properties. Click on the Security tab, and you will see something similar to the following screen:

In the Security tab, you can see two sections: Group or user names, and Permissions for [user/group]. The Group or user names section has all the users and groups who have received explicit permissions for this object. By clicking on the users and groups shown here, you can see the permissions they have been assigned in the Permissions for [user/group] section.

No Security Tab?

If you're using Windows XP Professional and you don't see a security tab, don't panic. Default configurations of Windows XP Professional often hide this security tab. To enable it, go to the Control Panel and select Folder Options. Click on the View tab, and scroll all the way to the bottom of the Advanced settings list. You will find at the bottom of the list an item entitled Use simple file sharing (Recommended). Make sure this is unchecked, as shown below:

Inherited Permissions

You may notice that some of the checkboxes that accompany permissions have been grayed out and cannot be changed. These grayed-out checkboxes indicate that the permissions in question have been inherited from a parent folder. By default, all files and directories inherit the permissions that have been assigned to their parent object. This permission inheritance is recursive; that is, each folder inherits permissions from its parent, all the way to the root directory of the file system.

This inheritance explains why there are two separate checkboxes for allowing and denying a permission, as shown below:

When a permission is inherited you cannot clear the Allow checkbox. The Deny checkbox exists to allow you to explicitly deny a permission that would otherwise be inherited. Deny settings always override Allow settings, for this reason.

Revoking Inherited Permissions

Rather than denying permissions that have been inherited, you also have the option of turning off permission inheritance for an object. To do so, click on the Advanced button on the Security tab. You will be presented a window entitled Advanced Security Settings for [object]. At the bottom of this screen, you'll see a checkbox labeled Inherit from parent the permission entries that apply to child objects. Uncheck the box, and you will no longer inherit permissions and can explicitly define them all for your object.

Group Permissions

The situation with group permissions is very similar to the situation with inherited permissions. Often, a user may receive inherited permissions through membership in a group. In these cases, you may want to assign additional explicit permissions to a user.

For example, let's say you have a group named Users, and in that group you have three users: Jim, Frank, and Mary. Frank and Mary are both very well-behaved users. You suspect, however, that Jim is not as trustworthy as the other two. Let us also suppose that you have a file, sensitive.txt, that is especially sensitive. Here are the permissions for the Users group on that file:

You decide therefore that you want to continue to allow the Users group to have access to this file, but you want to revoke Jim's access to this file. You could remove Jim from the Users group, but this would be a pain, as you do want him to have access to all of the resources that Users has access to. Instead, you decide to deny Jim access to just the sensitive.txt file. To do this, first you must add Jim to the Group or user names section of the Security tab. To do this, click on the Add... button. You'll see the following screen:

You can either type the name Jim into the textbox labeled Enter the object names to select, or you can click on the Advanced... button, which will take you to a directory of all users and groups. After adding Jim, we will now deny Jim every kind of access we can to the file, as shown below:

Now even though the Users group has access to sensitive.txt, Jim will be denied access.

Denial Precedence

In the event that a user has been assigned conflicting permissions through membership in multiple groups, permission denials always take precedence over permission allowances.

Verifying Permissions

As you begin assigning permissions to groups and users, you may occasionally become rather confused about who has access to what. Windows provides a feature to verify the permissions that a user has. This can be done by clicking on the Advanced button and selecting the Effective Permissions tab from the Advanced Security Settings window that appears. You can then select a group or user to verify, as is shown in the example below:

We can now verify which permissions we have, even if they were obtained via inheritance or group membership. You will note that the permissions here are more numerous and have different names than in other screens. Windows 2000 added some additional, finer-grained permissions to the NTFS security model introduced in Windows NT 4. If you find yourself wanting finer-grained control over your permissions, you can find more about these special permissions on Microsoft's web site. As of this writing, the following URLs will take you to a few such articles:

http://support.microsoft.com/default.aspx?scid=kb;en-us;Q308419&sd=tech
http://www.microsoft.com/mspress/books/sampchap/6103c.asp?#130

Command-line Permissions

In addition to all of the GUI windows, tabs, and so forth that we've just seen, Windows also has a command line utility, `cacls`, with which you can modify permissions. We'll not cover it in detail here, since most Windows users will prefer the GUI interface. We will, however, provide some brief examples.

Our examples will repeat the process we used to restrict Jim's access to `sensitive.txt`. First, let's view the permissions for `sensitive.txt` by issuing the following command:

```
C:\> cacls sensitive.txt
```

The output will be the following:

```
C:\sensitive.txt BUILTIN\Administrators:F
                 NT AUTHORITY\SYSTEM:F
                 FRANKLIN\bgals:F
                 BUILTIN\Users:R
                 Everyone:R
```

If we were to deny permissions for sensitive.txt to Jim via the command-line as we did in our previous example, the command we would issue is:

```
C:\> cacls sensitive.txt /E /D Jim
```

The result of this operation can be seen below:

```
C:\sensitive.txt FRANKLIN\Jim:N
                 BUILTIN\Administrators:F
                 NT AUTHORITY\SYSTEM:F
                 FRANKLIN\bgals:F
                 BUILTIN\Users:R
                 Everyone:R
```

The cacls utility is an interesting attempt by Microsoft to expose NTFS permissions to the command-line, but falls far short of the functionality (not to mention ease of use) of the permissions GUI. For more information on cacls, you can execute it with no options and see all of the parameters it supports.

Permissions in Unix

The permissions system in Unix is quite a bit easier to understand and interact with. To view permissions, all one needs is the ls utility. The following command will display the contents of a directory complete with permissions information:

```
$ ls -l
```

The -l parameter tells the ls command to display the so-called *long* file directory format, which includes the permissions. The output of this command looks like the following:

```
$ ls -l
drwxr-xr-x   2 tomcat    tomcat      4096 Aug 13 01:28 bin
drwxr-xr-x   2 tomcat    tomcat      4096 Jun 10 23:09 classes
drwxr-xr-x   4 tomcat    tomcat      4096 Jun 10 23:09 common
drwxr-xr-x   2 tomcat    tomcat      4096 Aug 13 01:28 conf
drwxr-xr-x   2 tomcat    tomcat      4096 Aug 13 01:28 lib
-rw-r--r--   1 tomcat    tomcat      4568 Jun 10 23:09 LICENSE
...
```

In this output, we see a series of columns that correspond to each file or directory in the current directory. We're only concerned with the first, third, fourth, and last columns. Let's define each of those, and drop out the other columns that are irrelevant to our discussion:

```
Permissions   Owner    Group    Filename
========================================
drwxr-xr-x    tomcat   tomcat   bin
drwxr-xr-x    tomcat   tomcat   classes
drwxr-xr-x    tomcat   tomcat   common
drwxr-xr-x    tomcat   tomcat   conf
drwxr-xr-x    tomcat   tomcat   lib
-rw-r--r--    tomcat   tomcat   LICENSE
```

Now, let's break down the values of each entry in the permission column. At first glance, they may seem somewhat cryptic, but it's actually quite simple. The permissions column can itself be viewed as four separate columns: file type, owner permissions, group permissions, and permissions for other users. Let's take the first and last files from our list above and break down the permissions column for each:

```
File Type   Owner P.   Group P.   Other P.   Filename
=====================================================
d           rwx        r-x        r-x        bin
-           rw-        r--        r--        LICENSE
```

The first subcolumn of the permissions column dictates the file type, such as "d" for directory, "l" for link, or "-" for a normal file. All of the remaining columns display whether or not the owner, group, or other users have read ("r"), write ("w"), or executable ("x") access to that file (remember that for directories, the executable property indicates whether the user has access to the directory). In the case of the bin directory, the first listing, all three of these groups have read and execute rights, but only the owner of the bin directory can write to the directory. For the second file, LICENSE, the owner, group, and public can read the file, but only the owner can modify the file.

Unix versus Windows

The discussion above brings up an interesting point about how assignment of permissions is different in Windows and Unix. In Windows, as we saw above, you can assign different permissions to each and every user on your system, as well as each and every group on your system. This can add up to an unlimited number of different permission scenarios. It can also be quite a weighty responsibility to maintain permission information in Windows.

Unix, on the other hand, is dramatically more limited in how you can assign permissions. The file's owner can receive one permission configuration, a group can receive another, and then all other users receive a third separate permission configuration. This simplicity can be an advantage, however, as it is quite easy to maintain Unix permissions.

One other important point: permissions are *not* inherited in Unix. New files or directories are assigned the permissions of their parent directory upon their creation, but these permissions will not change if the parent's permissions are changed in the future.

However, it is possible to use a more sophisticated permissions system in Unix. Replacement file systems are available that introduce the same concepts we've reviewed in Windows to virtually any Unix-like operating system. Should you be using one of these file systems, please review the documentation to determine how permissions work.

Changing Permissions

To change the permissions of a file, the chmod utility is used. For example, we can change the permissions of the LICENSE file so that every user can read and write to the file by executing chmod with the following parameters:

```
$ chmod u=rw,g=rw,o=rw LICENSE
```

The "u" parameter is used to set the permissions for the owner of the file, the "g" parameter is used to set the permissions for the group associated with the file, and "o" is used to set the permissions for everyone else. You can use one, two, or all three of these parameters. Let's see the results of our operation:

```
$ chmod u=rw,g=rw,o=rw LICENSE
$ ls -l | grep LICENSE
-rw-rw-rw- ... LICENSE
```

Let's look at the chmod command in some additional detail:

chmod Parameter	Description
[u,g,o,a]=[r,w,x]	This is the parameter we saw in the example above. On the left side of the equals sign, we choose one of the following to which we can assign permissions: the owner (u), group, others, or all three of these (a). On the right side, we choose from: read permission, write permission, or executable permission. We can combine the permissions on the right as also shown. We can issue this parameter multiple times if it is separated by a comma. Here are some examples: a=rw u=rwx,g=rx,o=rx

chmod Parameter	Description
[u,g,o,a][+,-][r,w,x]	This parameter is the same as the above, except it either adds or removes a permission from existing permissions. For example, to remove the group's write permission without altering its other permissions, we would use the following parameter: `g-w`
-R	This is the recursive parameter, meaning that the permission assignments will be made to the directory and any of its subdirectories and files, and any of their subdirectories, and so forth.

Changing Ownership

To change the owner of a file, and the group with which the file is associated, the chown command is used. The syntax of chown is:

```
$ chown user[:group] filename
```

So, if we want to change the owner of the LICENSE file from tomcat to bobcat, we would issue this command:

```
$ chown bobcat LICENSE
```

SUID/SGID Bits

Unix actually stores two more pieces of metadata with every file that relate to our security discussion. These are called the **SUID** and **SGUI bits**. If a file has the SUID bit set, it indicates that any user who executes the file will execute it as though they were the owner of the file. For example, if a file named program was owned by root and it had the SUID bit set, and if another user executed program, the operating system would execute program as though the user were root.

The SGID bit is similar. Any file with the SGID bit will make the user who executes that file a member of the group associated with the file for that file's execution.

The SUID and SGID bits can be set with the chmod utility. The syntax is as follows:

```
chmod u+s [filename]    (sets the SUID bit)
chmod g+s [filename]    (sets the SGID bit)
```

The SUID and SGID bits show up in the executable column of the permissions of each file as an "s," as shown below:

```
-rwsr-sr-x   2 tomcat   tomcat      4096 Aug 13 01:28 someprogram
```

Of course, you should use the SUID/SGID bits with great caution. We will not use them in this chapter.

Planning Security Permissions

Now that we've discussed how file system permissions work in Windows and Unix and how to can configure them, let's talk about how to secure your system through the use of wise permissions configurations.

Use the Latest Version

Before we discuss anything specific, let us reiterate the importance of using the absolute latest version of Tomcat. Using the latest version helps ensure that there are not any known exploits in your version of Tomcat. Not using the latest version makes you a target for hackers eager to try out all of the exploits they've read about.

Separate Tomcat Account

Some users run Tomcat with their normal user account or with the superuser account. Both of these are bad ideas. If Tomcat ever becomes compromised, it could use the permissions granted to the account that started it (such as your own account or the all-powerful superuser account) to wreak havoc.

Thus, you can do much to secure your file system by creating a special user account just for the purpose for running Tomcat. This distinct account should be assigned only those permissions necessary to run Tomcat, and nothing more. Let's review exactly what those permissions are. Because Unix and Windows differ significantly in their permissions models, we will cover them separately below.

Suggested Account Settings for Unix

We recommend that your unique account for running Tomcat be named `tomcat`. You should only include `tomcat` in one group, also named `tomcat`.

Disabling Login

Because you'll want to run Tomcat as a service, you should disable the account from being used for console logins (We discuss running Tomcat as a service in the next section). Disabling login ability is often achieved by *starring* the account's password.

We'll demonstrate two examples of this technique. The first example is from a BSD-like system that does not use a shadow password file:

`/etc/passwd:`

```
tomcat:*:23102:100:Tomcat:/:/bin/csh
```

The second example is from a Linux system that does use a shadow password file:

/etc/passwd:

```
tomcat:x:502:502:Tomcat:/:/bin/bash
```

/etc/shadow:

```
tomcat:*:12040:0:99999:7:::
```

Suggested Account Settings for Windows

Under Windows, you should create a new user named tomcat. Make sure that the tomcat account doesn't belong to any groups, including the default Users group. *Also, make sure that you give the account a password.* Windows cannot use the tomcat account to launch services without giving it a password. For maximum security, the password should be at least six characters in length and consist of letters of mixed cased, numbers, and special characters.

Disabling Login

You should run Tomcat as a **service**; we'll discuss more about that in the next section. Because of that, you'll need to disable the tomcat account from logging from the console, and instead only give it permissions to run services. While we discussed configuring file system permissions earlier in this chapter, we have not discussed how Windows treats other types of permissions.

Windows exposes many additional permissions mostly unrelated to the file system. These permissions are defined in a *Security Policy*. Windows security policies may be defined on the machine itself (a *Local Security Policy*) or may be defined in a central network location (a *Domain Security Policy*). We will discuss configuring your local security policy to disallow logging in but allow running services.

You can modify your machine's local security policy by going to the Control Panel, opening Administrative Tools, and double-clicking on Local Security Policy. You will see a screen similar to the following:

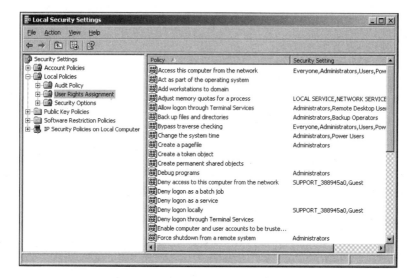

You'll need to expand the Local Policies node on the left, and then select User Rights Assignment, as shown in the screenshot above. On Windows XP, your screen will display exactly as shown. Windows 2000 is similar, but has slightly different columns. These minor differences will not impact your ability to carry out these instructions on either operating system.

You'll need to make two changes to your local security policy:

1. First, we need to disable the `tomcat` account's ability to log in. While `tomcat`'s lack of membership in any group implicitly denies `tomcat` this ability, we should explicitly deny this privilege for completeness. Double-click on the entry in the Policy column entitled Deny logon locally. In the screen that appears, add the `tomcat` account to this policy. Do the same for the following policies: Deny access to this computer from the network, Deny logon as a batch job, and Deny logon through Terminal Services.

2. Next, we need to grant permission to `tomcat` to run services. Double-click on Log on as a service and add `tomcat` to this policy.

Starting Tomcat as a Service

As we've alluded to earlier, in most server environments you'll want to configure Tomcat as a *service*. In the context of Windows and Unix, a service is a program whose life-cycle is managed automatically by the operating system. This means that the operating system will automatically start Tomcat when the system boots up and shuts Tomcat down when the system is halted. This is quite a bit more desirable than manually running $CATALINA_HOME/bin/startup.sh every time the system is started.

Configuring Tomcat as a Service in Unix

The various Unix operating systems have several mechanisms for creating and configuring services. Perhaps the most popular mechanism is the so-called SysV-style mechanism, which is almost universally supported amongst Unix-like operating systems. We'll discuss configuring Tomcat as a SysV service, but you may choose any mechanism that is more appropriate for your own operating system.

Creating a SysV-style Service

Various SysV mechanisms may vary; our explanation was tested on RedHat Linux 7.3. Check your operating system documentation to see how it may vary.

The first step in creating a SysV service is to create a script in the /etc/rc.d/init.d directory. We've included an example script below, which we've saved as /etc/rc.d/init.d/tomcat:

```bash
#!/bin/bash
#
# chkconfig:
# description: SysV script for Tomcat

# Source function lib
. /etc/init.d/functions

RETVAL=$?
export JAVA_HOME=/usr/java/jdk
export CATALINA_HOME=/usr/local/java/jakarta-tomcat

case "$1" in
  start)
          if [ -f $CATALINA_HOME/bin/startup.sh ];
             then
               echo $"Starting Tomcat"
               /bin/su tomcat $CATALINA_HOME/bin/startup.sh
          fi
          ;;
  stop)
          if [ -f $CATALINA_HOME/bin/shutdown.sh ];
             then
               echo $"Stopping Tomcat"
               /bin/su tomcat $CATALINA_HOME/bin/shutdown.sh
          fi
          ;;
  *)
          echo $"Usage: $0 {start|stop}"
          exit 1
          ;;
esac

exit $RETVAL
```

Now that we've created the basic startup script, we need to create symbolic links in the various rc directories. This can be accomplished by executing the following commands:

```
cd /etc/rc.d/rc0.d
ln -s ../init.d/tomcat K15tomcat
cd /etc/rc.d/rc1.d
ln -s ../init.d/tomcat K15tomcat
cd /etc/rc.d/rc2.d
ln -s ../init.d/tomcat K15tomcat
cd /etc/rc.d/rc6.d
ln -s ../init.d/tomcat K15tomcat
cd /etc/rc.d/rc3.d
ln -s ../init.d/tomcat S70tomcat
cd /etc/rc.d/rc4.d
ln -s ../init.d/tomcat S70tomcat
cd /etc/rc.d/rc5.d
ln -s ../init.d/tomcat S70tomcat
```

Configuring Tomcat as a Service in Windows

The easiest way to create a service for Tomcat is to use the .EXE installer available from the Jakarta Tomcat web site. The installation program will give you the option of installing a Windows service.

If, for whatever reason, you do not use the installer, you can create a Windows service from the command line. Here's an example of that:

```
%CATALINA_HOME%\bin\tomcat.exe -install "Apache Tomcat 4.1.18" \
%JAVA_HOME%\jre\bin\server\jvm.dll \
-Djava.class.path=%CATALINA_HOME%\bin\bootstrap.jar; \
%JAVA_HOME%\lib\tools.jar -Dcatalina.home=%CATALINA_HOME% -server \
-Xms64m -Xmx256m -Xrs \
-start org.apache.catalina.startup.BootstrapService \
-params start -stop org.apache.catalina.startup.BootstrapService \
-params stop -out %CATALINA_HOME%\logs\stdout.log \
-err %CATALINA_HOME%\logs\stderr.log
```

The above command should be entered on the same line. Of course, the continuation character \ simply indicates that the lines should be concatenated and should itself be omitted. Once you've executed the above command, you should see the following output:

```
The service was successfully installed.
```

Incidentally, you can remove the service in the future by executing this command:

```
%CATALINA_HOME%\bin\tomcat.exe -uninstall "Apache Tomcat 4.1.18"
```

We now need to configure our service to be started automatically, and make sure that our tomcat account is used to start the service. Go to the Control Panel, double-click on Administrative Tools, and then double-click on Services. You should see your new Tomcat service, which is labeled Apache Tomcat 4.1 if you used the EXE installer, or Apache Tomcat 4.1.18 if you installed the service manually with the instructions above. Double-click on the Tomcat service from the list of services. Ensure that the Startup type value is set to Automatic. Next, click on the Log On tab. From here you can click on This account and set tomcat as the account to use to launch the service, as shown below:

```
Apache Tomcat 4.1 Properties (Local Computer)          [?] [X]

 General   Log On   Recovery   Dependencies

    Log on as:

    ○  Local System account
          □ Allow service to interact with desktop

    ●  This account:        .\tomcat            Browse...

        Password:          ●●●●●●●●●●●●●●●

        Confirm password:  ●●●●●●●●●●●●●●●


    You can enable or disable this service for the hardware profiles listed below:

    ┌─────────────────────────────────┬──────────────┐
    │ Hardware Profile                │ Service      │
    ├─────────────────────────────────┼──────────────┤
    │ Profile 1                       │ Enabled      │
    │                                 │              │
    │                                 │              │
    │                                 │              │
    └─────────────────────────────────┴──────────────┘

                                    Enable      Disable


                    OK          Cancel          Apply
```

> Note: you will not be able to launch this service until we
> assign some additional file permissions to the tomcat
> account later in this chapter.

Configuring File Permissions

Up to now we've created a special tomcat account, and created a service for it and
instructed our operating system to launch the service with our tomcat account. We
now consider how to configure our file system's permissions. We will consider
Windows and Unix separately.

Windows File Permissions

Our tomcat user account will by default be given read access to many locations on
the file system. Let's start by revoking all file system permissions for the root directory
of all of your partitions. You can accomplish this by going to My Computer and viewing
the properties for each hard disk partition. In the Security tab, add the tomcat account,
and disable all of its permissions, as shown here:

Now we need to grant read access to the JDK directory so that Java can execute Tomcat. Locate the directory where you have installed JDK which will be used to run Tomcat (identified by the JAVA_HOME variable) and give the tomcat account Read & Execute, List Folder Contents, and Read permissions. Depending on where you have installed your JDK, you may first need to set the folder not to inherit security permissions from its parent. The best way to do this is to instruct Windows to copy (not remove) the formerly inherited permissions, and then remove any conflicting entry for the tomcat account.

Finally, we need to grant various permissions to the Tomcat directory hierarchy:

Tomcat Directories	Permissions for Tomcat Account
CATALINA_HOME CATALINA_HOME/bin CATALINA_HOME/common CATALINA_HOME/conf CATALINA_HOME/server CATALINA_HOME/shared CATALINA_HOME/webapps	Allow: Read & Execute, List Folder Contents, and Read Deny: Write
CATALINA_HOME/temp CATALINA_HOME/work CATALINA_HOME/logs	Allow: Modify, Read & Execute, List Folder Contents, Read, Write

We've essentially made everything read-only except those locations that Tomcat will need to modify: the `temp` directory for JVM temporary files, the `logs` directory, and the `work` directory for Tomcat's own temporary working files.

Unix File Permissions

The following table defines the directory and owner/group and file permission combinations that we recommend:

Directory/File	Owner/Group	Permissions
CATALINA_HOME	root/tomcat	rwxr-x---
CATALINA_HOME/bin	root/tomcat	rwxr-x---
CATALINA_HOME/bin/*.sh	root/tomcat	rwxr-x---
CATALINA_HOME/common	root/tomcat	rwxr-x---
CATALINA_HOME/conf	root/tomcat	rwxr-x---
CATALINA_HOME/logs	root/tomcat	rwxrwx---
CATALINA_HOME/logs/*.*	root/tomcat	rw-rw----
CATALINA_HOME/server	root/tomcat	rwxr-x---
CATALINA_HOME/shared	root/tomcat	rwxr-x---
CATALINA_HOME/temp	root/tomcat	rwxrwx---
CATALINA_HOME/webapps	root/tomcat	rwxr-x---
CATALINA_HOME/work	root/tomcat	rwxrwx---

If not otherwise indicated, all files in the listed directories above should have the same ownership as its containing directory and have `rw-r-----` permissions.

Issues Related to tomcat-users.xml

Because `tomcat-users.xml` stores your username and password for Tomcat's management applications, you may wish to switch to a different realm, as discussed in Chapter 4. Otherwise, a hacker may view this file and gain access to your Tomcat management applications. Because the `tomcat` account only has read access to the `webapps` directory, the hacker could not modify your web applications, but he could stop or reload your web applications on demand.

Thus, if you stick with the Tomcat realms that use `tomcat-users.xml`, you should consider removing the *admin* and *manager* web applications. You may remove these applications by deleting the $CATALINA_HOME/webapps/admin.xml and $CATALINA_HOME/webapps/manager.xml files.

Disable the UserDatabaseRealm

The most recent versions of Tomcat use the UserDatabaseRealm for their default realm. This realm is handy in that it lets you make changes to its database, the $CATALINA_HOME/conf/tomcat-users.xml file, and have those changes take effect without a restart. However, the realm requires write access to the tomcat-users.xml file, and under Unix it requires write access to the $CATALINA_HOME/conf directory. This is not wise from a security standpoint.

We therefore strongly recommend that you edit the $CATALINA_HOME/conf/server.xml file and switch the security realm to either a database realm or the older MemoryRealm, which does not require such permissions.

To change to the MemoryRealm, comment out the following lines in server.xml, as shown:

```
<!--
    <Realm className="org.apache.catalina.realm.UserDatabaseRealm"
            debug="0" resourceName="UserDatabase"/>
-->
```

Next, uncomment the following line:

```
<Realm className="org.apache.catalina.realm.MemoryRealm" />
```

Read-only Webapps Directory

You will note that we have recommended that you set read-only permissions on the webapps directory. This is to prevent hackers from modifying your web applications. This also means, however, that you will not be able to use WAR files when running Tomcat with the tomcat account, since Tomcat will not be able to expand the WAR into the file system.

Thus, you will need to either unzip the WAR file yourself when you deploy it, or run Tomcat as root from the console when you deploy new WAR files for the first time. This also means that your web applications must not write to their directories. This is a recommendation from the Servlet specification, however, because it is assumed that some servlet containers will run WAR files without exploding them into the file system and would thus not write changes to the WAR's ZIP stream.

Secure Your Files

You should review your operating system for any additional files stored on the server that should be secured. You should consider either moving these files to another server, or ensuring that the tomcat account does not have any permissions for them. On Windows, this is achieved by adding the tomcat user to the Security tab for the file or directory and explicitly clicking on the disabled checkboxes. In Unix, this is achieved by setting the permissions for *Others* to nothing (-rwx).

Once you have created the `tomcat` account, you should prevent it from accessing any sensitive files on the system. These files can include both system files and files that you may have created.

Knowing If You've Been Violated

Despite your best efforts, it is possible that a hacker may exploit Tomcat (or another service) and modify your file system in some unimagined way. A category of software, Intrusion Detection Systems, exists to help you detect when your file system has been tampered with. **Tripwire** is one of these programs, and Red Hat includes instructions for installing and configuring Tripwire in their *Official Red Hat Linux Reference Guide*. If you're not using Red Hat Linux, see http://www.tripwire.com/ for more information.

Read-Only File Systems

Some operating systems support the concept of a **read-only** file system. In this concept, available only to Unix-like operating systems, you would configure two separate file systems. The first file system, a `root` file system, would contain your operating system configured just the way you need it, such as creating a Tomcat service. You then set this file system as read-only (or for ultimate security, transfer this root file system to a read-only medium, such as a CD-ROM or a hard drive that can configure in a read-only mode). The second file system would be contained on a read-write medium, and it would contain your Tomcat installation and other files that must be modified.

Should you wish to take this (highly secure) step, you will need to find documentation for your specific operating system. There is no standard Unix way to achieve this functionality. You must exercise caution if you attempt this route; once you mark your root file system as read-only, you'll need a boot disk to make any changes.

Summary

Unix-derived operating systems and Windows 2000/XP both include file systems with security features. The features are built around the core concepts of users, groups, owners, and permissions. Windows primarily uses a GUI interface to control file system security, whereas Unix uses a variety of command-line utilities.

We recommend that you configure your file system to run Tomcat under its own account, and to restrict the access that the Tomcat account has to your system.

In this way, Tomcat is isolated from the remainder of your server, and should a hacker successfully exploit Tomcat, the damage the hacker can do will be severely limited.

Apache Tomcat Security

Handbook

3

Java Security Manager

You must be familiar with the fact that Java applies certain restrictions on applets. The Java security architecture uses the security manager to implement security and to apply rules that restrict applets from accessing files on the local file system, connecting to a host other than the one the applet was loaded from, and so on. The security manager is also used to provide a secure and controlled environment for stand-alone Java applications such as *Tomcat*.

One of the reasons that Java is a superior programming environment for applications that run on the web is due to the security features that Java provides. It provides both:

❑ **Language-level security** – such as automatic garbage collection, final modifier for methods, and so forth.

❑ **Virtual machine-level security** – that performs runtime checks, including those for access control.

The Java Virtual Machine (JVM) provides virtual machine-level security at runtime by presenting a controlled and secure environment for Java programs. The *Java class loader* verifies the byte codes that it loads from class files before creating the actual classes. The class loader is also responsible for other security functions, such as ensuring that any core class libraries are not loaded from the network. This is done to make sure that the JVM is not tricked using fake core class libraries that attempt to break the Java security model. Once the classes are loaded, the JVM performs its runtime checks. These checks include runtime **type checking** and **array bounds checking**. The security manager is responsible for a key element of Java platform security architecture – it manages security by implementing the security policy to restrict code from accessing protected resources and performing prohibited operations.

The JVM uses its security manager to implement the system's security policies by controlling access to the system resources of the computer in which it runs. By default, an application running in the JVM gets very minimal access to the local system resources. The security manager assigns access to additional resources to applications based on the permissions that are explicitly granted in a **policy file**. We will discuss how the Java security manager design allows fine-grained access control to local system resources by using this policy file.

Security Manager Features

The security manager implements the security policy by checking whether a particular permission is granted to a requesting object. The security system in Java 2 SDK transitioned to a primarily *declarative system* from a purely procedural system in its earlier versions; in other words, it is a system where application developers and system administrators describe what security settings they want instead of how to implement them. In addition to the JDK 1.1 way of implementing security procedurally, the new security architecture allows the security policies to be set by the system administrators at deployment time instead of the developers implementing the policies procedurally in code.

The security manager provides:

- ❑ Fine-grained access control

- ❑ Easily configurable security policy

- ❑ Easily extensible access control structure

- ❑ Extension of security checks to all Java programs, including applications as well as applets

Some important concepts and building blocks of Java platform security are:

- ❑ **Permission**, which is the explicit approval to perform tasks or access system resources in a specific mode (like read or write).

- ❑ **Principal**, which is an entity (person or system) in the computer system to which permissions are granted.

- ❑ **Protection domain** (referred to as domain for short), that conceptually encloses the set of objects whose instances are currently granted the same set of permissions when being executed on behalf of a given set of Principals.

The combination of permissions and their domains determine the security policy in effect. The relation between the Permission, Principal, and Protection domain is shown in the diagram below:

Figure 1

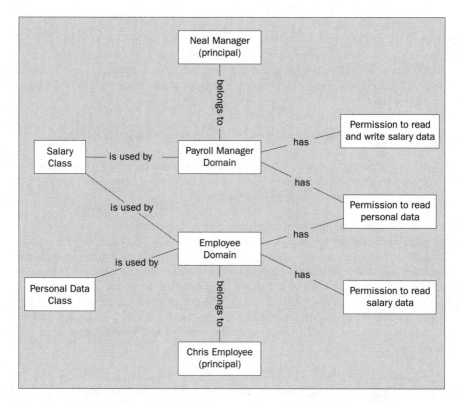

Java 2 SDK system code invokes security manager methods to check the policy currently in effect and performs access control checks. Each JVM can have at the most one security manager installed at any given time. Once a security manager is installed it cannot be replaced. This is to prevent a program from maliciously changing the security policy by replacing the security manager using the System.setSecurityManager() method.

Most browsers, including those from Netscape and Microsoft, install a default security manager. The security manager of these browsers provides a secure *sandbox* for executing applets loaded over the network. It is important to note that a security manager is not automatically installed when a stand-alone application is invoked.

An application installs the *default* security manager to apply security policies by doing one of the following:

❑   Invoking the JVM with the command-line argument:

```
$ java -Djava.security.manager MyApp
```

❑ Calling the System.setSecurityManager() method in the application code itself to install a security manager.

One way of implementing context-based security is to derive a *custom* security manager from the SecurityManager class. This custom security manager can then be installed by an application by calling the System.setSecurityManager() method. It is also possible to install the custom security manager while invoking the JVM from the command line, as in:

```
$ java -Djava.security.manager=COM.abc.MySecurityManager MyApp
```

In JDK 1.1, sub-classing of the SecurityManager was the only way to implement context-based security. This method is both difficult and error prone and is not the preferred way, expect for very unusual situations.

The preferred method of implementing context-based security is by using the configurable **security policy file** mechanisms introduced in Java 2 SDK. The policy file (system or user) consists of a series of statements, referred to as *grant entries*. Each grant entry identifies the permissions granted to certain code. It is based on three factors: the location from which it is loaded, signers of the code, and the principal executing the code. The policy file format and the structure of grant entries will be explained further as the chapter progresses. This new Java security policy mechanism is one the main reasons for the power, flexibility, and ease of configuration of the security system.

The default Java security policy file is configured such that when the Security Policy is initialized, the *system* policy file will be loaded in first, and then the *user* policy file is added to it. If neither policy files exist, a built-in policy similar to the original JDK 1.1 *sandbox* policy is applied.

> *Please refer to http://java.sun.com/products/archive/jdk/1.1/index.html for more information on JDK 1.1 security.*

It is also possible to specify an additional or a different policy file to be used when invoking execution of an application. This can be done via the –Djava.security.policy command-line argument, which sets the value of the java.security.policy property. In the example below, the policy file pfURL is loaded in addition to those specified in the security properties file:

```
$ java -Djava.security.manager -Djava.security.policy=pfURL MyApp
```

This next example below with the == syntax would result in the JVM using only the specified policy file pfURL and ignoring all other default policy files:

```
$ java -Djava.security.manager -Djava.security.policy==pfURL MyApp
```

> **Tomcat's startup script, when run with the -security switch, uses the method described above to make sure that the JVM uses *only* those permissions granted in Tomcat's policy file while ignoring all the default policy files.**

We will explain Tomcat's startup script and its policy file under the *Configuring Tomcat with the Java Security Manager* section.

Configuring the Security Policy File

A security policy for a Java environment represents the permissions that are available for the application code from various sources. In the `Policy` reference implementation, the policy can be specified within one or more policy configuration files. The policy files indicate what permissions are allowed for code from specified code sources. Let us look at the structure of the policy file.

Policy File Format

The policy file is made up of permissions that are granted to an application code at a specified code source. A policy configuration file is a simple text file containing a list of entries. This list is made up of at most one `keystore` entry and zero or more `grant` entries.

The snippet below shows a sample policy file:

```
// Keystore on Gorham's computer is called gotham.keystore
keystore "gotham.keystore";

// grant code signed by our trusted friend "Neal" all permissions
grant SignedBy "neal" {
    permission java.security.AllPermission;
};
```

> **The keywords in the policy file are not case sensitive.**

keystore Entry

A **keystore** is a database of private keys and their associated digital certificates such as X.509 certificate chains authenticating the corresponding public keys. All code, whether it is an applet that is loaded from a remote host or an application from the local file system, is associated with a *code source*. A code source is the URL from which the code loaded may be associated with a list of *signers* of the code. A signer is identified by a name associated with the signer's public key. This name is referred to as an *alias*. Aliases and keys are stored in the keystore.

There can be only one `keystore` entry in the policy file, and it can be anywhere in the file. It has the following syntax:

```
keystore "my_keystore_url", "keystore_type";
```

The following rules apply to the `keystore` entry:

1. `keystore_type` specifies the keystore type. This parameter is optional and it defines the properties of keystore data such as its storage and data format, the algorithms used to protect private keys in the keystore file, and so forth. If the keystore type is not specified, the type is assumed to be Sun's proprietary `JKS`. This default keystore type is specified by the `keystore.type` property in the delivered java.security file.

2. `my_keystore_url` specifies the URL location of the keystore.

3. The URL can be specified either in a *relative* manner or in an *absolute* manner. If a relative URL is specified, then its file location is relative to the policy file's location.

Some examples of the keystore declarations are:

Absolute:

```
keystore "http://abc.glosoft.com/conf/keystore";
```

Relative:

```
keystore "keystore";
```

In the case of the relative `keystore` URL declaration above, if the policy file is loaded from `$CATALINA_HOME/conf/catalina.policy`, then the keystore will be loaded from `$CATALINA_HOME/conf/keystore`.

grant Entry

Each `grant` entry in a policy file essentially consists of a code source (a URL and a list of signers) and its permissions. The system creates the corresponding `CodeSource` object after consulting the keystore to determine the certificate(s) of the specified signer(s). The `grant` entry grants a specified code source a set of permissions. The format of a `grant` entry in the policy file is as follows:

```
grant [SignedBy "signer_names"] [, codeBase "URL"]
      [, Principal [principal_class_name] "principal_name"]
      [, Principal [principal_class_name] "principal_name"]... {
    permission permission_class_name [ "target_name" ]
               [, "action"] [, SignedBy "signer_names"];
    permission ...
};
```

An example of the grant entry in a policy file is shown below:

```
// grant all objects the ability to read the user.home system property
grant {
    permission java.util.PropertyPermission "java.home", "read";
};

// grant any code signed by "sysadmin" permission to manipulate the
security providers
grant signedBy "sysadmin" {
    permission java.security.SecurityPermission
                              "Security.insertProvider.*";
    permission java.security.SecurityPermission
                              "Security.removeProvider.*";
};
```

The following rules apply to grants:

1. The leading grant is a reserved word that signifies the beginning of a new entry.

2. Optional items are allowed in square brackets in the grant entries.

3. Within each grant entry, a leading permission is a reserved word that marks the beginning of a new permission in the entry.

4. White spaces are allowed immediately before or after any comma.

5. The name of the permission class must be a fully qualified class name; therefore a class name such as java.io.FilePermission cannot be abbreviated to FilePermission.

6. The action field is optional in that it can be omitted if the permission class does not require it. If it is present, then it must come immediately after the target field.

7. The codeBase (URL) field is optional. Lack of this field signifies "any code base."

8. In addition to specifying an actual file name, the code base URL can end with a wildcard. The different kinds of wildcards for the code base URLs are given below:

    •   A URL trailing with a "/" matches all class files but not JAR files in the specified directory. For example, codeBase "file:${catalina.home}/webapps/finance/WEB-INF/classes/" matches all the class files in the /WEB-INF/classes directory.

    •   A URL trailing with a "/*" matches all class files and JAR files in the specified directory. For example, codeBase "file:${catalina.home}/webapps/finance/WEB-INF/classes/*" matches all the class and JAR files in the /WEB-INF/classes directory.

- A URL trailing with a "/-" matches all class files and JAR files not only in the specified directory but also in all subdirectories under the specified directory, recursively. For example, codeBase "file:${catalina.home}/webapps/finance/WEB-INF/classes /-" matches all the class and JAR files in the /WEB-INF/classes directory and those in all subdirectories under the /WEB-INF/classes directory, recursively.

9. The first SignedBy field is optional. This field is a string alias that is mapped, using a separate mechanism, to a set of public keys that are associated with the signers. These keys, within certificates in the keystore, are used to verify that certain signed classes are really signed by these signers.

10. The second SignedBy field, inside a permission entry, represents the alias to the keystore entry containing the public key corresponding to the private key used to sign the byte codes that implemented the said permission class. This permission entry is effective (access control permission will be granted based on this entry) only if the byte code implementation is verified to be correctly signed by the stated alias.

11. This signer_names field can be a comma-separated string containing names of multiple signers. For example the string "Adam,Eve,Charles" means signed by *Adam and Eve and Charles* (the relationship is AND, not OR).

12. If the SignedBy field is omitted, it signifies *any signer*, in which case it doesn't matter whether the code is signed or not.

13. A keystore entry must appear in a policy configuration file if any grant entry specifies signer aliases.

14. A Principal field in the grant entry specifies a class_name/ principal_name pair. The class_name in the principal value field is the name of the class that implements the java.security.Principal interface and encapsulates a principal entity. The principal_name would be a text string such as the user's login-id.

   A principal is one of the many identities that are associated with a subject, where a subject is defined as the entity in the system that is granted permissions. A subject could be an employee of the organization, say *Neal Polis*. This subject may have one principal associated with its login-id on the organization's accounting system and another principal associated with its login-id on the payroll system, and so on.

   An authenticated principal can be associated with the executing thread's access control context and perform a privileged action by calling the either the doAs or doAsPrivileged method. Refer to Sun Microsystem's JDK 1.4 documentation for more details on using subject-based authorization. The Principal field is optional. If the Principal field is omitted, then it signifies *any principal*. An example of a principal-based grant entry that uses Kerberos authentication mechanism is shown below:

```
grant principal javax.security.auth.kerberos.KerberosPrincipal
     "neal@KRB.GLOSOFT.COM"   {

   permission java.util.PropertyPermission "java.home", "read";
   permission java.io.FilePermission "foo.txt", "read";
};
```

If the class_name of the principal is not given while specifying the principal value as shown in the example below, then the class name is assumed to be javax.security.auth.x500.X500Principal. Therefore, the next two grant specifications shown below are equivalent:

```
grant principal "alice" {
   permission java.io.FilePermission "/tmp/games", "read, write";
};

grant principal javax.security.auth.x500.X500Principal
"cn=alice"{
   permission java.io.FilePermission "/tmp/games", "read, write";
};
```

15. The order of codeBase, SignedBy, and Principal fields in the policy file does not matter.

The *keytool* utility is used to create and administer keystores. The keystore specified in a policy configuration file is used to look up the public keys of the signers specified in the grant entries of the file.

Property Expansion in Policy Files

Property expansion is similar to expanding variables in a shell. That is, when a string like "${some.property}" appears in a policy file, or in the security properties file, it will be expanded to the value of the specified system property. Using property expansion makes Java Security policy files more portable. The "policy.expandProperties" property in the security properties file controls whether property expansion is allowed. If the value of this property is true (the default), expansion is allowed.

Property expansion takes place anywhere a double quoted string is allowed in the policy file and the security properties file. The signedBy, codeBase, target_names, and actions fields in the policy file can be made more portable by property expansion. Since the property $(java.home) is used in the permission shown below, this permission grant would work as-is regardless of where the Java runtime system is installed. On our computer, we have the following permission entry:

```
permission java.io.FilePermission "${java.home}", "read";
```

This will expand to:

```
permission java.io.FilePermission "/java/1.2", "read";
```

Since file paths in the policy file must be specified in a platform-dependent format, in some cases, using property expansion may help keep the policy file platform-independent. The special notation of "${/}" is a shortcut for "${file.separator}". This notation is particularly useful in maintaining platform-independent policy files. Examples of property expansion, assuming the user.home system property is set to /home/gotham on Unix and c:\users\gotham on Windows, are shown below. The permission entry:

```
permission java.io.FilePermission "${user.home}${/}*", "read";
```

This will expand to either of the two lines:

```
permission java.io.FilePermission "/home/gotham/*", "read";   (Unix)
permission java.io.FilePermission "c:\home\gotham\*", "read"; (Windows)
```

Since a codeBase is always a URL, any file separator characters will be automatically converted to a "/". This conversion of the file separator character would take even if the system were Windows based. Thus ${/} is not necessary in codeBase strings. For example, in Windows:

```
grant codeBase "file:/${java.home}/lib/ext/"
```

This will be converted to:

```
grant codeBase "file:/C:/j2sdk1.2/lib/ext/"
```

Notes:

1. Nested properties cannot be used. For example, "${user.${foo}}" does not work.

2. If a property can't be expanded in a grant entry, permission entry, or keystore entry, that entry is ignored. For example, if there is no system property foo then all the permissions in the grant shown below are ignored:

```
grant codeBase "${foo}" {
  permission ...;
  permission ...;
};
```

Java Security Permissions

For a web application (or an applet) running under a security manager to be allowed to perform secured actions, such as reading or writing a file, it must be granted permission for that particular action. The only exception is that code always automatically has permission to read files from its same CodeSource and subdirectories of that CodeSource; it does not need explicit permission to do so.

In Java, permissions are represented by the abstract class java.security.Permission. The java.security.Permission class is sub-classed, as appropriate, to represent actual permissions. Additionally, one can also sub-class an existing sub-class of java.security.Permission class to implement a new permission. In this chapter, we will refer to these sub-classes that implement actual system permissions as the **Permission Classes**.

Permissions commonly have two parameters; the first parameter usually specifies the target of the permission, and the second parameter usually specifies the action(s) on the target. Generally, a set of actions can be specified together as a comma-separated composite string. For example, a code can be granted permission to java.io.FilePermission with the target "/tmp/*" and actions of "read,write" as shown below:

```
grant  "/tmp/*" {
permission "java.io.FilePermission " , "read,write"
}
```

This grants the code base permission to read any file in the /tmp/ directory but not in any of its sub-directories.

There are a number of permission classes that are a standard part of the JDK, and web application developers can also create their own custom permission classes. New custom permissions are created either by sub-classing the java.security.Permission class or one of its sub-classes, such as the java.security.BasicPermission. A sub-classed custom permission (other than BasicPermission) is usually defined in the package providing the resource being protected. Thus, FilePermission is found in the java.io package.

The use of Java security policies and permissions that are relevant to Tomcat to control access to system resources will be explained in the *Configuring Tomcat with the Java Security Manager* section.

Why Tomcat Needs the Security Manager?

Tomcat's access controls are implemented using Java platform security architecture's security manager and its associated security policy declaration mechanisms. For Tomcat's system administrators to effectively configure Java's security manager, it is important for them to understand its role in Java platform's security architecture. The `SecurityManager` and its associated `AccessController` and `ClassLoader` are key components of Java platform security.

The Java security architecture is conceptually simple. Throughout the JDK, the Java security team had to:

- ❑ Identify operations in the code that might pose a security risk.

- ❑ Find places in the code where checks could be placed to guard these operations (but do so without creating any bottlenecks).

- ❑ Throw an exception if the caller is not allowed to proceed.

The security manager is used to protect the Tomcat server from potentially harmful servlets, JSPs, beans, and tag libraries in the same way it is used by web browsers to protect the client from untrustworthy applets. Code can be harmful not only because of malicious developers but also because of inadvertent programming mistakes. Some of the security manager's duties include:

- ❑ Managing access to socket operations

- ❑ Guarding access to protected resources including files, confidential data, and so on

- ❑ Controlling the creation of, and all access to, operating system programs and processes

- ❑ Preventing the installation of new Class Loaders

- ❑ Maintaining thread integrity

- ❑ Controlling access to Java packages·

A Tomcat installation that is not secured by the Java security manager will give a JSP or class file unfettered access to system resources and privileged actions. For example, a JSP with `<% System.exit(1); %>` can terminate Tomcat each time it executes the JSP.

The Java security manager is the *primary* security tool for the system administrator to control resource access by the web applications running inside the Tomcat server.

Configuring Tomcat with the Java Security Manager

This section explains the mechanics of starting Tomcat with the security manager. The intent here is to deliver enough information to a systems administrator to configure and run Tomcat with the security manager installed.

Tomcat can be started with the security manager installed by using the -security option as shown below:

Tomcat 4.1:

```
$CATALINA_HOME/bin/startup.sh    -security    (Unix)
%CATALINA_HOME%\bin\startup.bat -security    (Windows)
```

Tomcat 3.2:

```
$TOMCAT_HOME/bin/startup.sh -security      (Unix)
%TOMCAT_HOME%\bin\startup    -security      (Windows)
```

When Tomcat 4.1 or Tomcat 3.2 is started with the -security switch, the batch (or shell) script installs the default Java security manager and specifies that Tomcat's policy file should only be used and to ignore all others policy files. The -security switch causes the script to invoke the JVM with the command line arguments shown below:

Tomcat 4.1:

```
-Djava.security.manager
-Djava.security.policy==$CATALINA_BASE/conf/catalina.policy    (Unix)
-Djava.security.policy==%CATALINA_BASE%\conf\catalina.policy (Windows)
```

Tomcat 3.2:

```
-Djava.security.manager
-Djava.security.policy==${TOMCAT_HOME}/conf/tomcat.policy    (Unix)
-Djava.security.policy==%TOMCAT_HOME%\conf\tomcat.policy    (Windows)
```

When Tomcat is started as shown above the default Java security manager gets installed in place and this security manager enforces the security policies that are configured in catalina.policy for Tomcat 4.1 or tomcat.policy in the case of Tomcat 3.2. Please note that this policy file installed with Tomcat will completely override all other policy files, including the user's default policy file, if it is present in his home directory and the system default policy file (java.policy) is present in the JDK or JRE system directories.

Tomcat's policy file follows the standard java.policy file format. Hence, the catalina.policy file can be edited by any text file editor, or by a **policytool** application that comes with Java 1.2 or later. The Tomcat systems administrator should modify the security policies in Tomcat's policy file based on the site security requirements and the permissions required by the web applications installed on the system. The location of the policy file is:

Tomcat 4.1:

```
$CATALINA_HOME/conf/catalina.policy          (Unix)
%CATALINA_HOME%\conf\catalina.policy         (Windows)
```

Tomcat 3.2:

```
${TOMCAT_HOME}/conf/tomcat.policy            (Unix)
%TOMCAT_HOME %\conf\tomcat.policy            (Windows)
```

Tomcat's Policy File

The security policy files used by both Tomcat 4.1 and Tomcat 3.2 are similar in structure and organization. This section will use the $CATALINA_HOME/conf/catalina.policy file that is installed with Tomcat 4.1 to explore the structure of Tomcat's policy file and the permissions granted by this file to itself and those web application that run in its JVM. Tomcat's system administrators should become familiar with this policy file, as they will have to tailor the permissions in this file based on the web applications installed and run on the server.

Tomcat 4.1's policy file is divided into system code permissions, Catalina code permissions, and web application code permissions. Each of these sections of the policy file will be listed in the order below. The comments in the policy file are very instructive and at most times give the reason for the entry. The meaning of individual grants is explained later in this chapter:

```
============================================================================
// catalina.corepolicy - Security Policy Permissions for Tomcat 4.0
// This file contains a default set of security policies to be
//  enforced (by the JVM) when Catalina is executed with the
// "-security" option.  In addition to the permissions granted here,
// the following additional permissions are granted to the codeBase
// specific to each web application:
//
// * Read access to the document root directory
//
// $Id: catalina.policy,v 1.27 2002/09/08 18:04:02 glenn Exp $
//
============================================================================
```

System Code Permissions

Tomcat's policy file grants all permissions to javac and Java standard system extensions. The javac tool is used by Tomcat to compile JSP pages into servlets. The grants in this section ensure that the system code permissions will work when the JVM is run either from JDK or the JRE. Additional grants may be necessary in this section if the JVM uses different paths for the JARs and classes of its standard extensions (Mac OS X needs additional grants, for example):

```
// ========== SYSTEM CODE PERMISSIONS =============================

// These permissions apply to javac
```

```
grant codeBase "file:${java.home}/lib/-" {
  permission java.security.AllPermission;
};

// These permissions apply to all shared system extensions
grant codeBase "file:${java.home}/jre/lib/ext/-" {
  permission java.security.AllPermission;
};

// These permissions apply to javac when ${java.home] points at
// $JAVA_HOME/jre
grant codeBase "file:${java.home}/../lib/-" {
  permission java.security.AllPermission;
};

// These permissions apply to all shared system extensions when
// ${java.home} points at $JAVA_HOME/jre
grant codeBase "file:${java.home}/lib/ext/-" {
  permission java.security.AllPermission;
};
```

Catalina Code Permissions

This section grants all permissions for its own code. This code is needed to start up and run the Tomcat server and JSP container. Note that the "manger" and "admin" web applications are granted all permissions in this section:

```
// ========== CATALINA CODE PERMISSIONS ============================

// These permissions apply to the server startup code
grant codeBase "file:${catalina.home}/bin/bootstrap.jar" {
  permission java.security.AllPermission;
};

// These permissions apply to the servlet API classes and those shared
// across all class loaders located in the "common" directory
grant codeBase "file:${catalina.home}/common/-" {
  permission java.security.AllPermission;
};

// These permissions apply to the container's core code, plus any
// additional libraries installed in the "server" directory
grant codeBase "file:${catalina.home}/server/-" {
  permission java.security.AllPermission;
};

// These permissions apply to the jasper page compiler.
grant codeBase "file:${catalina.home}/shared/lib/jasper-compiler.jar"
{
  permission java.security.AllPermission;
};

// These permissions apply to the jasper JSP runtime
grant codeBase "file:${catalina.home}/shared/lib/jasper-runtime.jar" {
```

```
  permission java.security.AllPermission;
};

// These permissions apply to the privileged admin and manager web
// applications
grant codeBase "file:${catalina.home}/server/webapps/admin/WEB-
INF/classes/-" {
  permission java.security.AllPermission;
};

grant codeBase "file:${catalina.home}/server/webapps/admin/WEB-
INF/lib/struts.jar" {
  permission java.security.AllPermission;
};
```

Web Application Permissions

Tomcat allows read access to various system properties:

```
// ========== WEB APPLICATION PERMISSIONS ===========================

// These permissions are granted by default to all web applications
// In addition, a web application will be given a read FilePermission
// and JndiPermission for all files and directories in its doc root.
grant {
  // Required for JNDI lookup of named JDBC DataSource's and
  // javamail named MimePart DataSource used to send mail
  permission java.util.PropertyPermission "java.home", "read";
  permission java.util.PropertyPermission "java.naming.*", "read";
  permission java.util.PropertyPermission "javax.sql.*", "read";

  // OS Specific properties to allow read access
  permission java.util.PropertyPermission "os.name", "read";
  permission java.util.PropertyPermission "os.version", "read";
  permission java.util.PropertyPermission "os.arch", "read";
  permission java.util.PropertyPermission "file.separator", "read";
  permission java.util.PropertyPermission "path.separator", "read";
  permission java.util.PropertyPermission "line.separator", "read";

  // JVM properties to allow read access
  permission java.util.PropertyPermission "java.version", "read";
  permission java.util.PropertyPermission "java.vendor", "read";
  permission java.util.PropertyPermission "java.vendor.url", "read";
  permission java.util.PropertyPermission "java.class.version",
                                            "read";
  permission java.util.PropertyPermission
                     "java.specification.version", "read";
  permission java.util.PropertyPermission "java.specification.vendor",
                                            "read";
  permission java.util.PropertyPermission "java.specification.name",
                                            "read";
```

```
  permission java.util.PropertyPermission
                      "java.vm.specification.version", "read";
  permission java.util.PropertyPermission
                      "java.vm.specification.vendor", "read";
  permission java.util.PropertyPermission
                      "java.vm.specification.name", "read";
  permission java.util.PropertyPermission "java.vm.version", "read";
  permission java.util.PropertyPermission "java.vm.vendor", "read";
  permission java.util.PropertyPermission "java.vm.name", "read";

  // Required for getting BeanInfo
  permission java.lang.RuntimePermission
                      "accessClassInPackage.sun.beans";
  permission java.lang.RuntimePermission
                      "accessClassInPackage.sun.beans.*";

  // Required for sevlets and JSP's
  permission java.lang.RuntimePermission
                  "accessClassInPackage.org.apache.catalina.util";
  permission java.lang.RuntimePermission
                  "accessClassInPackage.org.apache.catalina.util.*";

  // Required for running servlets generated by JSPC
  permission java.lang.RuntimePermission
                  "accessClassInPackage.org.apache.jasper.runtime";
  permission java.lang.RuntimePermission
                  "accessClassInPackage.org.apache.jasper.runtime.*";

  // Required for OpenJMX
  permission java.lang.RuntimePermission "getAttribute";

  // Allow read of JAXP compliant XML parser debug
  permission java.util.PropertyPermission "jaxp.debug", "read";
};
...
```

Tomcat utilizes a custom permission class called `org.apache.naming.JndiPermission`. This permission controls read access to JNDI-named file-based resources. The permission name is the JNDI name and there are no actions. A trailing `"*"` can be used to do wild card matching for a JNDI-named file resource when granting permission. For example, the permission below will match any JNDI resource in the web application deployment descriptor (`/WEB-INF/web.xml`) of the web application `examples`:

```
  permission org.apache.naming.JndiPermission "jndi://myhost/examples/*"
```

In addition to the custom `JndiPermission` class, Tomcat uses the sub-set of the standard system security manager Permission classes shown below:

- ❏ `java.util.PropertyPermission`
- ❏ `java.lang.RuntimePermission`
- ❏ `java.io.FilePermission`
- ❏ `java.net.SocketPermission`

❑   `java.net.NetPermission`

❑   `java.lang.reflect.ReflectPermission`

❑   `java.security.SecurityPermission`

❑   `java.security.AllPermission`

There is a magic list of permissions that can or cannot be granted to applications. All of these permission have legitimate uses in applications. However, granting of any permission will have some risks associated with the permission and these risks vary with the target of the permission and the actions allowed. The system administrator is strongly encouraged to understand the permission being granted and assess the risks involved before it grants the permission to an application. Assessing the risks may include understanding the application by looking at the source code, discussing the application's security requirements with the application developers, verifying the trustworthiness of the source of the application, the sensitivity and the criticality of the resource at risk, and so forth. The details of these permissions are specified below.

java.util.PropertyPermission

This class controls read/write access to JVM properties such as `java.home`, `tomcat.home`, and `os.name`. Code can be granted permission to *set* or *get* these properties using the `setProperty()` and the `getProperty()` methods of `java.lang.System`.

Since most of these system properties are application-specific, Tomcat administrators should take care in examining the risks before granting read and/or write permission to any given property. While getting information about system properties (using the `getProperty()` method) does not by itself compromise the system, this information can be used later to mount attacks against the system. For example, granting of *read* permission to the `"java.home"` system property gives malevolent code-sensitive information about the system environment – the location of the runtime environment's directory.

Target(s)

The names of various Java properties as set in various property files. Targets can be specified as `"*"` (any property), `"a.*"` (any property whose name has a prefix `"a."`), `"a.b.*"`, and so on. Note that the wildcard can occur only once and can only be at the rightmost position.

Action(s)

These include `read` and `write`:

❑   The `read` permission allows the `getProperty()` method in `java.lang.System` to be called to get the property value.

❑   The `write` permission allows the `setProperty()` method to be called to set the property value.

Example

This segment of Tomcat's policy file shown below grants various `java.util.PropertyPermissions` necessary for JNDI lookup to all web applications. Note the absence of the `CodeSource` attribute for this `grant`. This lack of `CodeSource` grants these permissions to *all* code running under this security manager:

```
grant {
    // Required for JNDI lookup of named JDBC DataSource's and
    // javamail named MimePart DataSource used to send mail
    permission java.util.PropertyPermission "java.home", "read";
    permission java.util.PropertyPermission "java.naming.*", "read";
    permission java.util.PropertyPermission "javax.sql.*", "read";
};
```

java.lang.RuntimePermission

This class controls the use of some System/Runtime functions like `exit()` and `exec()`, and so on. Tomcat administrators should make sure that the code being granted runtime permissions is trusted, since a lot of these runtime permissions can be used to mount attacks on the Tomcat system. For example, malicious code with the `createClassLoader` permission can instantiate its own class loaders, which could then load its own rogue classes into the system. These newly loaded classes could be placed into any protection domain by the class loader, thereby automatically granting the classes permissions for that domain.

Target(s)

The target for this class is a string that specifies a runtime permission being granted. For example, `RuntimePermission("createClassLoader")` denotes the permission to instantiate a new class loader. The target names with their details are given in the table below:

Permission Target Name	What the Permission Allows	Risks of Allowing this Permission
createClassLoader	Creation of a class loader	A malicious application can instantiate a class loader and then use it to load rogue classes into trusted protection domains. These classes will be granted permissions for that domain.

Table continued on following page

Permission Target Name	What the Permission Allows	Risks of Allowing this Permission
getClassLoader	Getting a reference to the class loader for the caller's class.	Once code has access to a class loader, it can load any class that is available to the class loader using the ClassLoader.loadClass( ) method. The classes loaded using this method can include those classes that are not normally available to the code.
setContextClassLoader	Setting of the context class loader used by a thread using Thread.setContextClassLoader	setContextClassLoader permission would allow code to change which context class loader is used for a particular thread, including system threads.
setSecurityManager	Setting of the security manager of new security manager or replacing an existing security manager using System.setSecurityManager(SecurityManager)	A malicious application can replace Tomcat's security manager with a rouge security manger that it created. This rouge security manager can be used to bypass all the security checks.
createSecurityManager	Create (Instantiate) a new security manager.	A malicious application can create a rouge security manager and replace Tomcat's security manager with the setSecurityManager() method as explained above.
exitVM	Halting of the Java Virtual Machine.	A System.exit call in a servlet of JSP will bring down the Tomcat server.

Permission Target Name	What the Permission Allows	Risks of Allowing this Permission
shutdownHooks	Registration and cancellation of virtual-machine shutdown hooks using the `Runtime.addShutdownHook(Thread)` and `Runtime.removeShutdownHook(Thread)` methods.	Malicious code can register a rogue shutdown hook that interferes with the clean shutdown of the virtual machine.
setFactory	Setting of the socket factory used by `ServerSocket` or `Socket`, or of the stream handler factory used by the URL.	Malicious code can set the implementation of these factories to a rogue implementation.
setIO	Setting of standard system streams: `System.out`, `System.in`, and `System.err`.	`System.in` can be changed to monitor and steal user input. Further, `System.err` can be set to a "null" `OutputSteam`, effectively hiding any error messages sent to `System.err`.
modifyThread	Modification of threads, for example, via calls to Thread `stop`, `suspend`, `resume`, `setPriority`, and `setName` methods.	Malicious code can try to destabilize the system by starting and suspending threads in the system.
stopThread	Stopping of threads via calls to the Thread `stop` method.	Malicious code may corrupt the system by killing threads.
modifyThreadGroup	Modification of thread groups, for example, via calls to `ThreadGroup` `destroy`, `getParent`, `resume`, `setDaemon`, `setMaxPriority`, `stop`, and `suspend` methods.	Malicious code can create thread groups and set their run priorities.

Table continued on following page

Permission Target Name	What the Permission Allows	Risks of Allowing this Permission
getProtectionDomain	Retrieval of the reference to the ProtectionDomain for a class.	The ProtectionDomain of a class can be used to retrieve sensitive information such as the code source and the permissions for the domain. This information can be used for future attacks.
readFileDescriptor	Reading of file descriptors.	Malicious code can confidential read data from the file associated with the file descriptor.
writeFileDescriptor	Writing to file descriptors.	Malicious code can write to the file associated with the file descriptor. This allows an attacker to corrupt the file or even fill up the entire file system.
loadLibrary.{library name}	Dynamic linking of the specified native system library.	Native system libraries bypass the Java security architecture; hence there is no protection from malicious behavior native library code.
accessClassInPackage. {package name}	Access to the specified package via a class loader's loadClass method.	Malicious code may load classes that it normally does not access by using the loadClass method and thereby compromise the security in the system.
defineClassInPackage. {package name}	Definition of classes in the specified package, via a class loader's defineClass method.	Malicious code can define rogue classes in trusted packages like java.security or java.lang.

Permission Target Name	What the Permission Allows	Risks of Allowing this Permission
accessDeclaredMembers	Access to the declared members of a class. This grants code permission to call the Class. GetDeclaredMethods() method to query a class for its public, protected, default (package) access, and private fields and/or methods.	Malicious code may use this information to better aim an attack.
queuePrintJob	Initiation of a print job request.	Attacker can print out sensitive information or simply waste paper.

Action(s): none.

Example

The segment of Tomcat's policy file shown below grants the java.lang.RuntimePermission with the targets of accessClassInPackage.sun.beans and accessClassInPackage.sun.beans.*. This allows all applications running under the security manager to access classes in the packages mentioned:

```
grant {
    // Required for getting BeanInfo
    permission java.lang.RuntimePermission
                        "accessClassInPackage.sun.beans";
    permission java.lang.RuntimePermission
                        "accessClassInPackage.sun.beans.*";
    };
```

java.io.FilePermission

This class controls read/write/execute access to files and directories. Tomcat administrators should not grant web application more access to files and directories than they absolutely need. Malicious code with read permissions can be used to steal sensitive data. Even worse, code with write or delete permissions can be used to overwrite crucial system or data files.

> **Code does not need explicit permission to read a file from the same directory it is in or a subdirectory of that directory.**

In a Windows system, a grant entry specifying a file path would look like:

```
grant {
  permission java.io.FilePermission "C:\\users\\gotham\\*", "read";
};
```

Target(s)

The targets are the directory and file names. These name strings cannot contain white spaces. File paths must be specified in a *platform-dependent* format.

The following syntax is used to specify the target directories and files:

❑   `file`
This specifies the named file.

❑   `directory/*`
This specifies all files the named directory.

❑   `Directory`
This is same as directory/ (all files in the named directory).

❑   `directory/file`
This specifies the named file in the named directory.

❑   `*`
This specifies all files in the current directory.

❑   `directory/-`
This specifies all files in the file system under this named directory and files under its sub-directories recursively.

❑   `-`
This specifies all files in the file system under the current directory.

❑   `"<<ALL FILES>>"`
This is a special string that specifies all files in the file system. In the case of Unix this includes all files under the root directory and in the case of Windows it includes all files on all drives.

Action(s): `read, write, delete, and execute.`

Example

The example shown below grants the code in
`${catalina.home}/webapps/hr/WEB-INF/classes` (and code in its subdirectories recursively) read and write access to all files under `${catalina.home}/data/hr/` directory and those under its sub-directories recursively:

```
grant codeBase "file:${catalina.home}/webapps/hr/WEB-INF/classes/-"
{
    permission java.io.FilePermission "${catalina.home}/data/hr/-",
                                        "read, write";
};
```

java.net.SocketPermission

This class controls the use of *network sockets*. Tomcat administrators should note that granting web applications permission to accept or make connections to remote hosts might be dangerous because malevolent code can then easily transfer any confidential data to parties who may not otherwise have access.

Target(s)

The target for this class can be given as host_id_value:port_range. The host_id_value can either be a numerical IP address or a standard DNS name of the form hostname, hostname.domain, or hostname.subdomain.domain. The host_id_value for the local machine can be specified as "localhost" or " ". The wildcard "*" may be included once in the DNS host name specification. If a wildcard is included, it must be in the leftmost position, as in "*.sun.com". Wildcards allowed in host name specifications are:

- ❑ *.domain (all hosts in the domain)
- ❑ *.subdomain.domain
- ❑ * (all hosts)

The port_range is in the format PORT1-PORT2, where the PORT1 and PORT2 are integers between 0 and 65535. The port range value will be interpreted as below:

- ❑ PORT1 (a single port)
- ❑ PORT1- (all ports numbered PORT1 and above)
- ❑ -PORT2 (all ports numbered PORT2 and below)
- ❑ PORT1-PORT2 (all ports between PORT1 and PORT2, inclusive)

Action(s)

Actions include – accept, connect, listen, and resolve. The action resolve is implied by accept, connect, and listen – those who can listen or accept incoming connections from or initiate outgoing connections to a host should be able to look up the name of the
remote host.

Examples

The segment of the Tomcat's policy file shown below grants the code in
${catalina.home}/webapps/examples/WEB-INF/lib/driver.jar permission to connect to the computer dbhost.glosoft.com on port 5432. Note, this permission is commented out in the delivered Tomcat file and is intended to only serve as an example:

```
// The permission granted to your JDBC driver
 grant codeBase "jar:file:${catalina.home}/webapps/examples/WEB-
INF/lib/driver.jar" {
     permission java.net.SocketPermission "dbhost.glosoft.com:5432",
"connect";
 };
```

Let's consider another example. The segment of the Tomcat's policy file shown below grants the code in ${catalina.home}/webapps/myWebApp/WEB-INF/classes/mailApp.jar the permission to connect to port 25 on an SMTP server. This permission is required by the web application to send e-mails:

```
 grant codeBase "file:${catalina.home}/webapps/myWebApp/WEB-
INF/classes/mailApp.jar" {
   permission java.net.SocketPermission "mail.glosoft.com:25",
                                                      "connect";
 };
```

java.net.NetPermission

This class controls use of *network connections*. The Tomcat systems administrator should assess risks before granting the web application NetPermssions.

Target(s)

The targets include the following:

❑ RequestPasswordAuthentication
This permission allows the code to ask the authenticator registered with the system for a password. Malicious code can steal this password.

❑ setDefaultAuthenticator
This permission allows the code to set the default authenticator that will be used by the networking code when a proxy or HTTP server asks for authentication. A malicious authenticator can monitor and steal authentication that is entered by the user.

❑ SpecifyStreamHandler
This permission allows the code to specify a stream handler to construct a URL. Malicious code may create a bogus URL that gets the actual bytes from someplace it does have access to. Thus it might be able to trick the system into putting rogue classes in trusted protection domain or code source.

Action(s): none.

Example

The segment of the policy file shown below grants all code access to
java.net.Authenticator. GetPasswordAuthentication() method. This method
will return an object containing the userid and password from the authenticator:

```
grant {
permission java.net.NetPermission "requestPasswordAuthentication";
};
```

java.lang.reflect.ReflectPermission

This class controls the use of reflection to do class introspection. A
ReflectPermission is a named permission (like RuntimePermission).
suppressAccessChecks is the only target name currently defined. This target for
ReflectPermission allows the accessible flag of a reflected object to be set by
calling AccessibleObject.setAccessible(..). Setting the accessible flag in a
reflected object permits sophisticated applications with sufficient privileges, such as
Java Object Serialization or other persistence mechanisms, to manipulate objects in a
manner that would normally be prohibited.

> *Extreme caution should be taken before granting this
> permission to code*, **for it provides the ability to access or
> invoke even private fields and methods of a class.**

Target(s)

suppressAccessChecks allows suppressing the standard Java programming language
access checks – for public, default (package) access, protected, and private members –
performed by reflected objects at their point of use.

Action(s): none.

Example

The segment of the policy file shown below permits code to change the accessible flag
of reflected objects. Setting the accessible flag of a reflected object to true will
suppress Java language access checks for public, default (package) access, protected,
and private members for both Fields and Methods:

```
grant {
    permission java.lang.reflect.ReflectPermission
                                    "suppressAccessChecks";
};
```

java.security.SecurityPermission

This class controls access to `Security` methods that are used to access security-related objects, such as `Security`, `Policy`, `Provider`, and `Signer` objects. The Tomcat system administrator has to be aware that there are major risks involved in granting code any security permissions. For example, granting code the `securityPermission` with the `setPolicy` target is extremely dangerous, as malicious code may grant itself all the necessary permissions it needs to successfully mount an attack on the system. Another example of a security risk to watch out for is that the permission to `getSignerPrivateKey` will allow code to retrieve a signer's secret private key. The intruder can use this private key to sign various files and claim the signature came from the Signer.

Target(s)

The targets for this permission class are:

❏ `getPolicy`
This permits code to retrieve permissions granted to a given `CodeSource` by using the `getPermissions` method. Malicious code can use the vulnerabilities exposed by this information to aim an attack.

❏ `setPolicy`
This permits code to set the system-wide security policy. Granting this permission is extremely risky. Malicious code can grant itself all the necessary permissions it needs to successfully attack the system.

❏ `getProperty.{key}`
This permits code to retrieve the security property with the specified key. Malicious code can use the vulnerabilities exposed by this information to aim an attack.

❏ `setProperty.{key}`
This permits code to set the security property with the specified key. These properties include the security provider, location of the system-wide security policy, and so on. Malicious code that has permission to set a new security provider can set a rogue provider that steals confidential information such as cryptographic private keys. Code that has permission to set the location of the system-wide security policy can point it to a security policy that grants the attacker all the necessary permissions it requires to successfully mount an attack on the system.

❏ `insertProvider.{provider name}`
This permits code to add a provider with the specified name. An attacker can insert a rogue provider at the highest level and have it steal the private keys passed to it.

❏ `removeProvider.{provider name}`
This permits code to add a provider with the specified name. Malicious code can remove a provider and cause instability in the cryptography system.

❑ SetSystemScope

This permits code to configure the system identity scope. Malicious code can configure the system identity scope with bogus certificates. The attacker can then use malicious application code signed with those certificates to disrupt the system. Note that the IdentityScope class is deprecated.

❑ SetIdentityPublicKey

This permits code to set the public key of an Identity. An attacker can change the public key of a "trusted" identity to a bogus public, thereby granting "trusted" privileges to rogue application code signed with that public key. Note that the Identity class is deprecated.

❑ setIdentityInfo

This permits code to set the general information string for an Identity. Malicious code with this permission can trick applications into using a different identity than intended.

❑ printIdentity

This permits code to view the name of a principal, the scope in which it is used, and whether or not it is considered "trusted" in that scope. Malicious code can use the vulnerabilities exposed by this information to aim an attack.

❑ addIdentityCertificate

This permits code to add a certificate for an Identity's public key. Code can maliciously cause the public key to suddenly become trusted to a wider audience than it otherwise would be.

❑ removeIdentityCertificate

This permits code to remove a certificate for an Identity. Code can maliciously cause the public key to suddenly become considered less trustworthy than it otherwise would be.

❑ clearProviderProperties.{provider name}

This permits code to "clear" all the properties used to look up services implemented by the security provider. Malicious code that clears provider properties can make services implemented by the provider to be no longer accessible to other parts of the program that normally utilize the Provider.

❑ putProviderProperty.{provider name}

This permits code to set properties for the specified Provider.

❑ removeProviderProperty.{provider name}

This permits code to remove properties from the specified Provider. This permits code to remove the properties used to look up services implemented by the security provider. Malicious code that clears provider properties can make services implemented by the provider to be no longer accessible to other parts of the program that normally utilize the Provider.

❑ getSignerPrivateKey

This permits code to retrieve a Signer's private key. This permission can allow malicious code to retrieve and steal a signer's secret private key

❏   setSignerKeyPair
    This permits code to set the key pair (public key and private key) for a
    Signer. This permission can allow an attacker to substitute a target users
    keypair with a possibly weaker keypair (example, a keypair of a smaller
    keysize). Once the key is replaced the attacker can eavesdrop on encrypted
    communication between the target user and his peers. This can be done if
    the target user's peers wrap an encryption session key under the target
    user's substituted public key. This will allow the attacker (who possesses
    the corresponding private key) to unwrap the session key and decipher the
    communication data encrypted under that session key.

Action(s): none.

Example

The segment of the policy file shown below permits code to dynamically register the
provider named MyJCE:

```
grant {
  permission java.security.SecurityPermission   "insertProvider.MyJCE";
};
```

Granting this would allow somebody to introduce a possibly malicious provider (for
example, one that discloses the private keys passed to it) as the highest-priority
provider. This would be possible because the Security object, which manages the
installed providers, currently does not check the integrity or authenticity of a provider
before attaching it.

java.security.AllPermission

Granting this permission allows classes loaded from the code base specified in the
grant to have all permissions, just as if Tomcat was running without a security
manager. It is introduced to simplify the work of a system administrator, who might
need to perform multiple tasks that require all (or numerous) permissions. It would be
inconvenient to require the security policy to iterate through all permissions. Note that
AllPermission also implies new permissions that are defined in the future.

**Granting this permission leaves the system *wide open*, and
system administrators must be extremely cautious while
granting this permission to any web applications.**

Target(s): None.

Action(s): None.

Example

The segment of Tomcat's policy file shown below grants the
java.security.AllPermission to the Java system code:

```
// These permissions apply to javac
grant codeBase "file:${java.home}/lib/-" {
    permission java.security.AllPermission;
};
```

Debugging Java Security Manager Installation

Once Tomcat is operational with the Java security manager in place, the security
policies defined in the policy file will be enforced. This security policy enforcement
could cause previously working web applications, from the *non-secure* days, to fail.
This would happen when a web application attempts to execute an operation that is
prohibited by lack of a required permission. When the security manager detects this
violation, an AccessControlException or a SecurityException is thrown.

Adding the missing permissions to the policy file usually takes care of the
AccessControlException and SecurityExceptions. The systems
administrator should confirm that the web application legitimately requires the
permissions being granted.

Debugging the permission that is missing can be challenging, and one option is to turn
the *debug output* on for all security decisions that are made during execution. Setting
the java.security.debug system property will turn on the security debug output.
This system property can be set by setting the environment variable CATALINA_OPTS
for Tomcat 4.1 (TOMCAT_OPTS for Tomcat 3.2) before starting Tomcat.

 The environment variable for the security debug output is set as shown below:

For Tomcat 4.1:

```
export CATALINA_OPTS=-Djava.security.debug=access,failure (Unix)
set CATALINA_OPTS=-Djava.security.debug=access,failure   (Windows)
```

For Tomcat 3.2:

```
export TOMCAT_OPTS=-Djava.security.debug=access,failure (Unix)
set TOMCAT_OPTS=-Djava.security.debug=access,failure   (Windows)
```

It is recommended to begin debugging permission problems by setting the
java.security.debug property to "access,failure". See the Java security
documentation (http://java.sun.com/products/jdk/1.2/docs/guide/security/) for a complete list
of options.

The security debug output is sent to the *applications log file* that is found in the `logs` sub-directory under Tomcat's home directory.

> **The actual *log file*, where the output ends up, can be changed by the `logger` directive in the application context.**

The security manager generates fairly large debug output files, and aside from disk space debugging may have performance implications as well. However, it is appropriate to turn on the security manager debug output while tracking down problems and then turn the output *off* after the problem is resolved. The debug output file can be searched for the word "denied" to determine which permission is being denied.

Installation Check

The following steps can be used to check the installation and working of Tomcat's Java security manager using a simple JSP application, `SecurityTest.jsp`. This JSP application is programmed to retrieve and display the `java.home` system property.

Code for `SecurityTest.jsp` is shown below:

```
<html>
  <head>
    <title>Tomcat Security Permissions Test</title>
      <meta http-equiv="Content-Type" content="text/html;
           charset=iso-8859-1">
  </head>
  <body>
    <h1>Testing Security Permissions  </h1>
    <p><b>  java.lang.System.getProperty("java.home") returns ===>
    <%=java.lang.System.getProperty("java.home") %></b>
  </body>
</html>
```

Checking security manager installation will consist of the following steps:

1. Verifying the output of `SecurityTest.jsp` in Tomcat with *no security manager* installed.

2. Verifying that an access control exception is produced when the security manager is installed and the policy *does not permit reading* `"java.home"` property.

3. *Verifying* that granting permission to read `"java.home"` will permit the JSP to run without any security exceptions.

Step 1: We will deploy and run `SecurityTest.jsp` without the security manager installed on Tomcat. This application should display a web page such as that shown below:

82

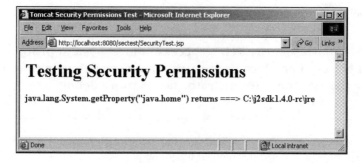

Step 2: For this step, we will edit Tomcat's delivered policy file (`catalina.policy` or `tomcat.policy`) and make sure that the permission to read the `java.home` property is removed. After editing the policy file, the section declaring web application permissions should look as below. Note that the permission to `read java.home` is commented out:

```
// ========== WEB APPLICATION PERMISSIONS ============================

// These permissions are granted by default to all web applications
// In addition, a web application will be given a read FilePermission
// and JndiPermission for all files and directories in its document
// root.
grant {
  // Required for JNDI lookup of named JDBC DataSource's and
  // javamail named MimePart DataSource used to send mail
  //permission java.util.PropertyPermission "java.home", "read";
  permission java.util.PropertyPermission "java.naming.*", "read";
  permission java.util.PropertyPermission "javax.sql.*", "read";
     ….
     ….
```

Now, Tomcat must be restarted with the `-security` switch so that the security policies in Tomcat's policy file are enforced. `SecurityTest.jsp` should produce an access control exception when executed now. The screenshot below shows the web output of the access error produced by `SecurityTest.jsp`:

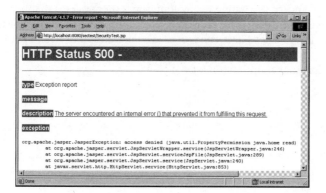

The Java call stack from the screenshot clearly illustrates the problem in this case.

> **The "-Djava.security.debug=access,failure" system property can be set to produce the security manager debug output, in case the systems administrator needs more debug information.**

Step 3: Undo the changes made in Step 2 and restart the Tomcat server and refresh the page. You should see the same screenshot from Step 1.

Summary

An important task of the systems administrator is to protect sensitive and critical system resources from outright malicious or just plain buggy Tomcat web applications. As a policy, code should not be given access to more resources than is necessary for the functioning of the web applications executing the code. Even permissions that retrieve seemingly innocent pieces of information, such as the java.home property, should be granted sparingly because hackers leverage this information to more accurately aim attacks on the system. It is not wise to divulge more information about the system than necessary.

We learned how to use the Java security manager's versatile permission-granting mechanism to control resource access by code running on Tomcat's JVM. The systems administrators have to deliberately analyze the risks involved when they grant new permissions to code by modifying Tomcat's policy file. If they find that granting of a specific permission (or set of permissions) required by an application increases the risk above the organization's agreed-upon threshold, they may have to request the application developers to modify the code. If modification of the code is not possible, they may have to take the necessary steps to ensure the exposure due to permissions cannot be exploited to mount attacks on the system. These steps may involve placing the system behind a firewall and/or separating the system from other systems that have sensitive or strategic resources that need to be protected. The job of the system administrator is not completed after the policies file is configured. The administrator has to periodically monitor Tomcat's log files to check for any security or access violations and take actions based on the violations found in the logs.

Apache Tomcat Security

Handbook

4

Security Realms

In this chapter we will see how Realms are used for adding security to Java Web Applications. We start off with an introduction to Realms, and explain where they fit in the general area of Web Application security. We then go over to Tomcat's Realms in detail and the different implementations it provides – Memory, JDBC, JNDI, and JAAS Realms. We will cover the setup and configuration for these in detail, and also how (and why) a custom implementation of a Realm can (or should) be developed.

Before starting with the chapter, let's first understand what a Realm is.

Realms

The Servlet 2.3 specification defines a Realm as a "security policy domain." In plain English, a Realm is a mechanism to protect web application resources such as HTML pages and servlets/JSPs. Realms do this by defining a security constraint for them. This security constraint consists of the following:

❑ The name of the protected web resource. This can be a URL regular expression matching the resource name. For example, /jsp, /*.jsp matches all JSP files in the jsp/ directory (the path is relative to the web application root).

❑ The permitted operations on the web resource, such as DELETE, GET, POST, PUT.

❑ A set of roles that can access these resources. The roles in turn contain users, and we can have multiple users in a role, as well as the same user in multiple roles.

❑ Requirements from the Transport layer. This relates to using either HTTP or HTTPS as the transport –we will look at this in more detail later in the chapter.

The Servlet specification does not, however, define a portable way for an application to declare its security requirements, nor does it define any API for the interaction between the servlet container and the Realm implementation. Due to this, Realm-based security (also called Container-Managed Security) is inherently non-portable. We will look at this in the *Pros and Cons of Container-Managed Security* section later in the chapter.

The term Realm is also used in the Servlet specification for the string passed in the HTTP request during BASIC Authentication. This string specifies the protection space, and does not have to match the Realm/security policy domain.

When we talk of Realms in this chapter, we refer to the former (security policy domain) and not the latter.

Security and Web Applications

Web applications consist of static content (HTML pages, images files, etc.), dynamic content (JSPs, servlets) and a deployment descriptor (the web.xml file). These are distributed as web archive files (.war files) and are deployed in a servlet container such as Tomcat. The web application then can be accessed over the Internet or intranet from web browsers.

How do we provide security for these web applications? Before we answer that, we need to understand what we mean when we talk of security. Let's revisit some of these concepts:

❑ We need to ensure that the user, as well as the web site running the web application, prove their identity to each other. This is called **authentication**.

❑ We need to ensure that only authorized user(s) can access the resources of the web application (the static/dynamic content that it provides). This is called **access control**.

❑ We need to ensure that a third party does not tamper with the data that is transmitted between the web application and the user's browser. This property is called **data integrity**.

❑ And finally, we need to ensure that a third party/unauthorized person cannot access the data while it is in transit between the web application and the user's browser. This property is called **data privacy**.

The authentication of a user can be done using four different mechanisms with varying levels of security:

❑ HTTP BASIC Authentication

❑ HTTP DIGEST Authentication

❑   FORM-Based Authentication

❑   HTTPS CLIENT Authentication

We will see each one of these in more detail in the next section. The Servlet 2.3 specification (Tomcat 4.x implements this specification) provides for two models of security that provide for access control – declarative and programmatic. We will look at these two models later in the chapter.

As far as data integrity and data privacy is concerned, it is dependant on the nature of the underlying transport – we should use HTTPS-based connections for data that is sensitive. This is covered to some extent in the *Using HTTP BASIC and FORM-based Authentication over SSL* section later in the chapter, and in greater detail in the next chapter.

Authentication Mechanisms

As we discussed earlier, there are four mechanisms for authentication.

HTTP BASIC Authentication

In HTTP BASIC Authentication, when the user tries to access a restricted resource, he/she is presented with a pop-up window by the browser asking for the username and password.

The screenshot below shows such a BASIC Authentication window – this particular one is shown when users try accessing the Tomcat `manager` Web Application. The `manager` application (accessible by default at the URL http://host:port/manager/html/list) allows for managing the deployed web applications – start, stop, reload, and remove web applications:

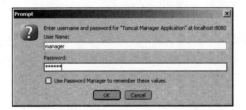

The following is an extract from the deployment descriptor of the `manager` web application (`$CATALINA_HOME\server\webapps\manager\WEB-INF\web.xml`) that shows `BASIC` authentication being specified as the means of authentication:

```
<web-app>
    ....
      <login-config>
         <auth-method>BASIC</auth-method>
         <realm-name>Tomcat Manager Application</realm-name>
      </login-config>
    ....
</web-app>
```

This mechanism is the simplest and also the least secure – the user's password is not encrypted, but instead is sent across as a standard base64-encoded string. Also, the web site is not authenticated. This means of authentication is generally not suitable for a sensitive web application accessible over the Internet, though might be acceptable in a trusted intranet environment. We can overcome this limitation if we use HTTPS as the transport instead of HTTP. Here the transport ensures that the password and all other data being transmitted is encrypted. This is described in the *Using HTTP BASIC and FORM-based Authentication over SSL* section later in the chapter.

HTTP DIGEST Authentication

DIGEST Authentication looks the same to the user as BASIC authentication – a pop-up window asking for the username and password is shown as before. However, behind the scenes things work a bit differently. In DIGEST authentication, the password is transmitted not as base64 but as a digested (encrypted) version. This is, however, not widely used, since some browsers do not support it – for example Mozilla 0.9 doesn't.

The following is an extract from the web.xml file showing the configuration for HTTP DIGEST:

```
<web-app>
    ....
    <login-config>
        <auth-method>DIGEST</auth-method>
        <realm-name>Tomcat Manager Application</realm-name>
    </login-config>
    ....
</web-app>
```

The default algorithm used for computing the digest is "MD5." An optional HTTP header also allows for an alternate algorithm to be specified.

FORM-Based Authentication

Both HTTP BASIC as well as HTTP DIGEST authentication do not allow for specifying a custom login screen or custom error handling. FORM-based authentication overcomes this limitation.

The following is an extract from web.xml that specifies FORM-based authentication. This particular example is from the deployment descriptor for the admin web application ($CATALINA_HOME\server\webapps\admin\WEB-INF\web.xml). The admin application is described in more detail later in the chapter:

```
<web-app>
    ....
    <login-config>

        <auth-method>FORM</auth-method>
        <realm-name>
            Tomcat Server Configuration Form-Based Authentication Area
```

```
            </realm-name>
        <form-login-config>
            <form-login-page>/login.jsp</form-login-page>
            <form-error-page>/error.jsp</form-error-page>
        </form-login-config>
    </login-config>
    ....
</web-app>
```

As we can see, we specify the login page (`login.jsp`) and the error-handling page (`error.jsp`) for performing the authorization and error handling in case of login failure.

The screenshot below shows the web page displayed when the user tries to access the `admin` web application (accessible at the URL http://host:port/admin):

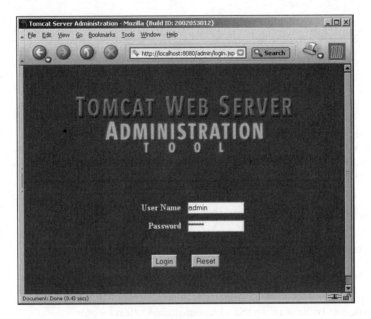

The Servlet specification requires that the username and password form fields in the login page must be named `j_username` and `j_password` respectively, and the action associated with the form must be `j_security_check`. `j_security_check` is a resource in the web container that implements authentication.

A very simple example of an HTML page for FORM-based authentication is listed below. This is taken from an example JSP for Tomcat 4.1.12 (`$CATALINA_HOME/webapps/examples/jsp/security/protected/login.jsp`):

```
<html>
  <head>
    <title>Login Page for Examples</title>

  <body bgcolor="white">
    <form method="POST"
          action='<%= response.encodeURL("j_security_check") %>' >
      <table border="0" cellspacing="5">
        <tr>
          <th align="right">Username:</th>
            <td align="left">
              <input type="text" name="j_username"></td>
        </tr>
        <tr>
          <th align="right">Password:</th>
            <td align="left">
              <input type="password" name="j_password"></td>
        </tr>
        <tr>
          <td align="right"><input type="submit" value="Log In"></td>
          <td align="left"><input type="reset"></td>
        </tr>
      </table>
    </form>
  </body>
</html>
```

This mechanism suffers from the same limitation as BASIC authentication – the password is passed as an unencrypted base64 string. We can overcome this limitation by using an HTTPS-based transport (instead of HTTP) for the login page. This is described in the *Using HTTP BASIC and FORM-based Authentication over SSL* section later in the chapter.

HTTPS CLIENT Authentication

HTTP CLIENT Authentication is not used very commonly – its use is limited to certain business-to-business scenarios, and is complex to deploy.

Deploying HTTPS CLIENT Authentication is a four-step process.

Step 1: Configure Tomcat to do SSL client authentication

The first step in using this mechanism is to configure Tomcat to authenticate the client using HTTPS. The following is a sample connector directive from `server.xml` that illustrates this:

```
<Connector
    className="org.apache.catalina.connector.http.HttpConnector"
    port="8443"
    minProcessors="5"
    maxProcessors="75"
    acceptCount="10"
    debug="0"
    scheme="https"
    secure="true">
  <Factory
```

```
                className="org.apache.catalina.net.SSLServerSocketFactory"
                clientAuth="true"
                protocol="TLS"
                keystorePass="password1"/>
    </Connector>
```

Step 2: Get a digital certificate and install it on the client machine

Users would need to obtain a digital certificate that authenticates them to the server. An organization can obtain these from a Certificate Authority (CA) and install them on all client browsers. Installing a certificate is browser specific. Here is how you do it for Mozilla 1.0 and Internet Explorer 5.0:

❑ **Mozilla 1.0**

Select the Preferences item on the Edit menu. This brings up the Preferences panel. Next, select the category: Privacy & Security. Here, select the sub-category Certificates in the window-pane on the right, and click the Manage Certificates button. Finally, click the Your Certificates tab in the displayed window. To import the certificate, click on the Import button at the bottom.

❑ **Internet Explorer 5**

Going to Tools |Internet Options| Content| Certificates| Import option allows us to import a certificate.

Step 3: Add a user matching the certificate Subject name

Next, we add a user whose username matches that Subject name in the digital certificate. The Subject field was specified while creating the certificate. Once the certificate is installed in the browser, we can view its contents using browser-specific commands. For example, on Internet Explorer 5, we can use the Tools|Internet Options|Content|Certificates option, select the required certificate, and click the Details tab.

The process of adding a user to a Realm varies with the Realm implementations – we will look at this in detail later in the chapter.

Step 4: Specify CLIENT-CERT as the authentication method

Finally, we edit the web.xml file, and add CLIENT-CERT as the authentication constraint. A sample entry is shown below.

```
    <login-config>
        <auth-method>CLIENT-CERT</auth-method>
        <realm-name>A Really Secure Realm</realm-name>
    </login-config>
```

We should choose the method of authentication that is most suitable for our application and its security requirements. The factors to consider while deciding this are discussed in the *Choosing an Authentication Mechanism* section.

Using HTTP BASIC and FORM-based Authentication over SSL

In order to make HTTP BASIC and FORM-based authentication more secure, we can use SSL as the transport instead of HTTP. To do this, we would first need to obtain a digital certificate and configure Tomcat for SSL support. This is explained in more detail in the next chapter.

Next, we specify their protection types – CONFIDENTIAL or INTEGRAL – as the user authentication method within the <transport-guarantee> elements in the deployment descriptor. We use CONFIDENTIAL when we want to prevent other entities from observing the contents of the transmission, and INTEGRAL to ensure that the data is not tampered with
during transit.

The following is an example from the deployment descriptor (web.xml) that illustrates this:

```
<!-- SECURITY CONSTRAINT -->
  <security-constraint>

    <web-resource-collection>
      <web-resource-name>MyProtectedRespource</web-resource-name>
      <url-pattern>/protected/jsp/*.jsp</url-pattern>
      <http-method>GET</http-method>
    </web-resource-collection>

    <auth-constraint>
      <role-name>some_user</role-name>
    </auth-constraint>

    <user-data-constraint>
      <transport-guarantee>CONFIDENTIAL</transport-guarantee>
    </user-data-constraint>

  </security-constraint>
```

The security constraint specified by CONFIDENTIAL and INTEGRAL applies to all requests that match the URL patterns (here /protected/jsp/*.jsp), not just to the login dialog.

Choosing an Authentication Mechanism

Some of the factors that we need to consider while choosing an authentication mechanism are listed below.

Ease of Deployment

BASIC and DIGEST authentication are both very simple to deploy. FORM-based authentication requires developing a custom login and error page. HTTPS CLIENT authentication has the most complex deployment of all four – it requires us to obtain/purchase a digital certificate, and to do setup on the client (browser) side.

Security

In both BASIC as well as FORM-based authentication, the password is sent to the server without being encrypted. These limitations of the BASIC and FORM-based authentication can be overcome if we use SSL as the transport as we explained earlier in the chapter.

DIGEST Authentication is more secure than both BASIC as well as FORM-based authentication. In this mechanism, a digest of the password is sent instead of the clear-text version. However, we should note that while the password is encrypted, the content of the web page itself is not encrypted. This is still an improvement over BASIC Authentication, where even the password is not encrypted. Thus an eavesdropper listening to the network traffic would be able to only get at the current web page, but not (unlike in BASIC and FORM-based) be able to get the other web resources protected by that password.

Is the DIGEST authentication mechanism open to replay attacks? Reply attacks (that is, repeating the request in order to repeat a web transaction) cannot be used for other web resources, because the digest contains not only the encrypted form of the password, but also of the URI being requested. It can, however, be used to "replay" a request for the same web resource. In most cases, this is not a serious problem, since the web page was not encrypted in the first place and hence the eavesdropper would have been able to access it too. However, the web resources could very well execute some action on the server side (such as a JSP/servlet), and thus we would not want such a reply attack. Some digest implementations guard against this by encoding some implementation-specific information, such as client IP address, timestamp, and so on to make such attacks more difficult.

HTTPS CLIENT Authentication is the most secure of the four authentication mechanisms.

Custom Login and Error Page

FORM-based authentication is the only mechanism that allows for custom login and error pages.

Authorization: Security Models for Web Applications

As we noted earlier, the Servlet 2.3 specification provides for two models of security – declarative and programmatic. In this section we look at both of these models and make a comparison between them to see the advantages of one over the other.

Container-Managed Security

In the declarative security model, also called the security configuration, the usernames, the access control information, and so on are stored external to the web application. The security configuration is specified in the deployment descriptor for the web application.

This model is also called Container-Managed Security since the web container manages the security. Tomcat's Realms are an implementation of container-managed security. We will talk about Tomcat Realms in this chapter in greater detail.

Programmatic Security

In programmatic security, the web application itself is aware of the security, and has logic to manage access rights. This can be used in addition to container-managed security to provide for a finer degree of control.

This model is implemented by providing methods in the `javax.servlet.http.HttpServletRequest` interface that allow servlets/JSP to get information about which user is accessing the servlet, and what his or her allowed role is.

The `HTTPServletRequest` class methods that provide this functionality are:

Method	Description
`public String getAuthType ()`	Returns the authentication string used to protect the servlet. This is one of BASIC_AUTH, FORM_AUTH, CLIENT_CERT_AUTH, or DIGEST_AUTH. In case the servlet is not protected, the method returns NULL.
`public String getRemoteUser ()`	If the user has been authenticated, this method returns the login username. Otherwise, it returns NULL.
`public boolean isUserInRole (String role)`	Returns true if the authenticated user exists in the specified role. Returns false if the user doesn't exist or if the user has not been authenticated.
`public java.security.Principal getUserPrincipal ()`	Returns a java.security.Principal object containing the name of the current authenticated user, null if the user has not been authenticated.

The following is a snippet of servlet code that shows the use of programmatic security:

```
import javax.servlet.*;
import javax.servlet.http.*;
import java.io.*;

public class ProgrammaticSecurityServlet extends HttpServlet {

    public void doGet (HttpServletRequest  request,
                       HttpServletResponse response)
    throws IOException {
```

```
String userName = request.getRemoteUser ();
if (request.isUserInRole ("role1")) {
  /* add code */
} else if (request.isUserInRole ("role2")) {
  /* add code */
} else {
  /* add code */
}
  ...
}
```

As we can see from the code above, programmatic security allows us to access information that is validated by container-managed security.

Pros and Cons of Container-Managed Security (Realms)

Why would we want to use container-managed security for our web applications?

Its chief advantages are that the security policy is decoupled from the application code. This is extremely useful, since at the time of development the security policy might be different from that at the time of deployment. Also, the security policy might change with time, or across different deployments of the web application. Keeping this policy separate from the code allows for all this, and avoids expensive and error-prone code modifications.

The chief disadvantage of container-managed security is that it is non-portable across servlet engines. Tomcat implements Realms in a particular way, and we can't just create a WAR file of the web application and distribute it, since it would not have any security policies. We would instead need to duplicate the configuration changes made in Tomcat's server.xml, and then create the required roles and users in whatever Realm implementation is being used. In case the other servlet engine is not Tomcat, this would mean that we would need to port the setup to it. Here programmatic security scores, as it has the policies as a part of its own code.

Another limitation of Realms is that we are restricted to the user management that the Realm implementation provides; for instance, if we wish to have additional attributes for a user other than just name and password.

Tomcat's Realms

Realms consist of a database of roles and the users associated with them. A role defines a set of security permissions. For example, the default Tomcat configuration has a role called manager that is used to specify access to the Tomcat manager web application (the webapp that allows us to manage all deployed web applications). If we add a user in the manager role, then that user gets access rights to run the manager web application.

This database can be stored using different implementations:

❑ **Memory Realm**
This Realm database is stored in configuration files in the file system and is loaded into memory at the time of starting Tomcat.

❑ **UserDatabase Realm**
This Realm is new to Tomcat as of version 4.1. It uses the file system to store Realm related information.

❑ **JDBC Realm**
This Realm database is stored in a relational database (for example, MySQL, Oracle, and so on) and is accessed via an appropriate JDBC driver connection.

❑ **JNDI Realm**
This Realm database is stored in a directory that can be accessed via the Java Naming and Directory Interface (JNDI) API. JNDI is typically used to access LDAP directories, but can be used to access any directory that has a JNDI provider, such as a relational database or even a file system-based resource. Tomcat 4.1 comes with a JNDI-based implementation (UserDatabase) that updates from a configuration saved on the file system.

❑ **JAAS Realm**
A Realm implementation that authenticates users using the Java Authentication and Authorization Service (JAAS). JAAS Realms are a new feature as of this writing.

❑ **Custom Realm**
In addition, developers can code a custom implementation for storing this database. We will see later in the chapter how these can be implemented. This is not usually required, except when a proprietary repository/directory is being used to store user and role information.

Protecting a web application involves two basic steps:

❑ **Add a security constraint to the web application**
This involves specifying the protected web resources, the operations permitted on them, and the roles that can perform them. The next section shows how this security constraint is specified.

❑ **Select a Realm implementation and perform the required configuration steps**
The setup step common to all the implementations is adding a <Realm> directive in the $CATALINA_HOME/conf/server.xml file. A sample directive is shown below – this is the directive for the Memory Realm.

```
<Realm className="org.apache.catalina.realm.MemoryRealm" />
```

This directive can be placed inside an `<Engine>`, `<Host>`, or a `<Context>` element in the `server.xml` file. The Realm directive has a different effect based on where it is placed, as we will see in the discussion of *Single Sign On for Web Applications*.

Tomcat comes configured with a default Realm (Memory Realm in the case of Tomcat 4.0 and `UserDatabase` in the case of Tomcat 4.1). We can avoid some of the configuration steps if we stay with the default. We will discuss each of these Realms and their configuration in detail later in the chapter. We will also see the security implications of staying with the default Realm configuration.

Adding Security Constraints to Web Applications

Before we see the configuration of these Realms, let us first go over how a web application is protected. Suppose have a sample web application and we wish to restrict access to some selective JSP files in it. Let us look at the deployment descriptor for the application listed below:

```
<?xml version="1.0" encoding="ISO-8859-1"?>
<!DOCTYPE web-app
    PUBLIC "-//Sun Microsystems, Inc.//DTD Web Application 2.3//EN"
    "http://java.sun.com/dtd/web-app_2_3.dtd">

<web-app>
    <display-name>Our sample application</display-name>
```

We define a `<security-constraint>` for the JSP files to be protected, and the `<url-pattern>` element lists all the URL patterns (here all the JSP files in `%CATALINA_HOME%/webapps/<webapp_name>/protected/`) that need to be protected:

```
<security-constraint>
    <display-name>
        Security Constraint Definition for the protected JSPs
    </display-name>
    <web-resource-collection>
        <web-resource-name>Protected Area</web-resource-name>
<!-- Define the context-relative URL(s) to be protected -->
        <url-pattern>/jsp/protected/*.jsp</url-pattern>
```

We can specify specific HTTP methods that need protection, or, if we leave out the `<http-method>` elements, all will be protected by default:

```
<!-- If you list HTTP methods, only those methods are protected -->
        <http-method>DELETE</http-method>
        <http-method>GET</http-method>
        <http-method>POST</http-method>
        <http-method>PUT</http-method>
    </web-resource-collection>
```

We now list all the roles that can access this secure area:

```
<auth-constraint>
<!-- Anyone with one of the listed roles may access this area -->
    <role-name>admin_role</role-name>
    <role-name>another_role</role-name>
</auth-constraint>
```

Finally, we can specify the requirements from the transport layer. This is done using the <transport-guarantee> element, and this can be set to CONFIDENTIAL, INTEGRAL or MISSING (that is, HTTP being used, and hence no transport guarantees for security). We discussed this earlier in the section on *Using HTTP BASIC and FORM-based Authentication over SSL*:

```
<user-data-constraint>
    <transport-guarantee>CONFIDENTIAL</transport-guarantee>
</user-data-constraint>
</security-constraint>
```

Next, the <login-config> element specifies the authentication mechanism to use. As we discussed earlier, this can be HTTP BASIC, HTTP DIGEST, FORM-based authentication, or HTTP CLIENT-authentication. Here we use FORM-based authentication.

```
<!-- Login configuration uses form-based authentication -->
<login-config>
  <auth-method>FORM</auth-method>
  <realm-name>Form-Based Authentication Area</realm-name>
  <form-login-config>
    <form-login-page>/login.jsp</form-login-page>
    <form-error-page>/error.jsp</form-error-page>
  </form-login-config>
</login-config>
```

Finally, we specify all the roles referenced in the web application (admin_role and another_role in our example below). Users in these roles are the only ones allowed to access the protected area of the web application (/jsp/protected/*.jsp in this example). In the Realm configurations (Memory, UserDatabase, etc.) that we discuss later, we will see how to create a role and add users to it.

```
<!-- Security roles referenced by this web application -->
<security-role>
  <description>
    The roles that can access the privileged area
  </description>
  <role-name>admin_role</role-name>
  <role-name>another_role </role-name>
</security-role>
    ...
</web-app>
```

Single Sign On (SSO) for Web Applications

A web site can consist of different web applications. If a user is authenticated while accessing a protected area, and then tries to access another web application, he would be required to authenticate himself all over again. This is not a good user experience, and for this reason many web sites have "Single Sign On" (SSO) features. With SSO, a user is authenticated once, and that authentication user is recognized across all equivalent web applications during the course of the session.

Let's see how we configure Tomcat for Single Sign On.

- ❑ Define the Realm directive at the `<Engine>` or `<Host>` level, and not at the `<Context>` level.

- ❑ In case the Realm directive is at the `<Context>` level, it has effect only for the particular web application. Do not define another Realm directive inside the `<Context>`. Realm directive configurations are covered starting from the next section onwards.

- ❑ Define a `<Valve>` for Single Sign On inside the `<Host>` element:
  `<Valve class="org.apache.catalina.authenticator.SingleSignOn"/>`

- ❑ Define security constraints for each of the web applications.
  This is covered in detail in the *Adding Security Constraints to Web Applications* section above.

The scope of the Single Sign On includes all the web applications registered under a virtual host.

Security Considerations for Single Sign On

The web applications configured under Single Sign On can use different authentication mechanisms. If a user is authenticated while accessing one web application, he is not re-authenticated when he tries to access another application where he has equivalent rights. This means that the level of security for the entire web site is that of the weakest link; that is, the least secure authentication mechanism. For example, if we use a less secure mechanism like HTTP BASIC for one of the web applications, it serves no purpose to use a more secure mechanism for the rest.

The web browser clients use cookies to maintain Single Sign On across the different web applications. This can be a security risk as intruders can impersonate an ongoing session. Using HTTPS as the transport can overcome this risk.

Memory Realm

Memory Realms read the data at startup time from an XML configuration file into memory. These are the default Realms for Tomcat 4.0.x (we have used Tomcat 4.0.6 for the examples in this chapter). In Tomcat 4.1 (unlike Tomcat 4.0) the default Realm is UserDatabaseRealm that uses a JNDI implementation, and not memory realm. Though this too uses the file system to store the Realm-related information, changes to this database do not require Tomcat to be restarted. We will see this in more detail in the *JNDI Realm* section.

Configuration

The first step in configuring the Memory Realm is adding a Realm entry in the $CATALINA_HOME/conf/server.xml file. The simplest variant of this is shown below:

```
<Realm className="org.apache.catalina.realm.MemoryRealm" />
```

The complete list of the Realm attributes for Memory Realm are listed below:

Attribute name	Description	Required
className	This is the className of the Java class that implements Memory Realms. This must be org.apache.catalina.realm.MemoryRealm.	Mandatory
debug	The debug level. A missing or "0" (zero) valued debug level turns off debugging. The log file that the log messages go to is specified in a Logger directive.	Optional
digest	The passwords can either be stored as clear-text or encrypted using a digest algorithm. The supported digest algorithms are those that the java.security.MessageDigest class provides – MD5 (digest value md5) and SHA (digest value sha). A missing digest attribute means that the password is stored as clear text.	Optional
pathname	The absolute or relative (from $CATALINA_HOME) pathname for the file where the Realm information (username, role name, and passwords) are stored. This defaults to conf/tomcat_users.xml if not specified.	Optional

A more complete Realm configuration directive is:

```
<Realm
    className="org.apache.catalina.realm.MemoryRealm"
    debug="5"
    digest="sha"
    pathname="conf/tomcat_users.xml" />
```

The MemoryRealm class (org.apache.catalina.realm.MemoryRealm) implements
the org.apache.catalina.Realm Java interface, as do all other Realm
implementations that we cover in this chapter.

In case we change anything in the Realm configuration, we need to restart Tomcat in
order to make it re-read it.

Adding a User

Adding a new user requires editing the $CATALINA_HOME/conf/tomcat_users.xml
file (or the file specified in the pathname attribute in the Realm directive, if so
configured). The extract from this file below shows a new role called user1 being
added in the role another_role:

```
<?xml version='1.0' encoding='utf-8'?>
    <tomcat-users>
    <user username="user1" password="secret" roles="another_role"/>
    ....
</tomcat-users>
```

Where does this role another_role come from? Remember the security constraints
that we had defined earlier in the deployment descriptor (web.xml) for the web
application? The role name another_role should match such a security role for a
web application. The following is an extract from web.xml that shows the security role
definition for another_role:

```
<security-constraint>
    ...
    <auth-constraint>
    <!-- Anyone with one of the listed roles may access this area -->
        <role-name>another_role</role-name>
    </auth-constraint>
    </security-constraint>
    ...
<security-role>
    <description>
        Description for all roles
    </description>
    <role-name>another_role</role-name>
    </security-role>
```

What happens if the role referenced in web.xml doesn't match any of the roles in tomcat-users.xml? Well, in that case nobody will be able to access that web resource. This is the case for the manager role in Tomcat 4.0. The default configuration in Tomcat 4.0 (see the default tomcat-users.xml below) does not have an entry for the manager role:

```
<!--
  NOTE:  By default, no user is included in the "manager" role
  required to operate the "/manager" web application.  If you wish to
  use this app, you must define such a user - the username and
  password are arbitrary.
-->
<tomcat-users>
  <user name="tomcat" password="tomcat" roles="tomcat" />
  <user name="role1"  password="tomcat" roles="role1"  />
  <user name="both"   password="tomcat" roles="tomcat,role1" />
</tomcat-users>
```

We therefore need to add a user in the manager role before we begin to use the manager application:

```
<tomcat-users>
  <user name="manager_user"
        password="manager_passwd"
        roles="manager" />
</tomcat-users>
```

What if one of the roles added for a user doesn't correspond to an actual role? Tomcat does not flag any error for this, and that role definition does not have any effect.

A user can belong to multiple roles, for example:

```
<user username="user1" password="secret" roles="role1,role2,role3"/>
```

Multiple users can belong to the same role.

```
<user username="user1" password="secret" roles="role1,role2,role3"/>
<user username="user2" password="secret" roles="role1"/>
<user username="user3" password="secret" roles="role1"/>
```

The user element shown above contains three attributes:

❑ username is a mandatory attribute, and contains the name of the user. This is a unique identifier for a user.

❑ password is a mandatory attribute, and contains the password for the user.

❑ roles is a mandatory attribute that contains a comma-separated list of roles that the user belongs to.

104

The password that we saw being set in the password attribute above (secret) was not the best possible choice for a password. Worse, it was stored as clear-text in the tomcat-users.xml file. For improved security, the following measures can be taken:

❑ Change the file system permissions for the configuration file, if the operating system allows for it.

❑ Use encrypted passwords. This is discussed in the next section

❑ And finally, use a better password: one that is harder to compute by brute force.

Using Encrypted Passwords

As we mentioned earlier, we can use the digest attribute for the Realm configuration in %CATALINA_HOME%/conf/server.xml to set the digest algorithm we want to use.

Note that there is a difference between using HTTP DIGEST for authentication and storing digested versions of the password. In HTTP DIGEST, the password string is "digested" on the client side by the browser before being transmitted. The server then creates a digested version of the password stored on its end and compares the two strings.

When we set the digest attribute in the Realm directive, we are specifying that the password stored in the Realm database (the tomcat_users.xml file in case of Memory, but this can be in an external application as we will see in JDBC/JNDI Realms) is stored in an encrypted form, and not as clear-text.

> **At the time of writing, Tomcat had a bug in which HTTP DIGEST authentication did not work when the passwords were stored in the digested form.**

```
<Realm className="org.apache.catalina.realm.MemoryRealm"
       debug="5"
       digest="sha"
       pathname="conf/tomcat_users.xml" />
```

We now have to generate the encrypted version of the password, using the following command:

```
$ java -classpath $CATALINA_HOME/catalina.jar
org.apache.catalina.realm.RealmBase -a sha aReal1lyG00doNe

aReal1lyG00doNe:c23e47c2003a93af2dad4dae78f5e1c4a4735732
```

Tomcat also comes with a batch file/shell script called digest that does the same thing.

```
$ cd $CATALINA_HOME/bin
$ digest -a sha aReal11yG00doNe

aReal11yG00doNe:c23e47c2003a93af2dad4dae78f5e1c4a4735732
```

In the command above, we use the SHA digest algorithm (-a sha parameter) and a better choice in passwords (aReal11yG00doNe). The output from the Java program is the original password and the digest version (in bold font) separated by a colon.

Once the digest version of the password is created, we can add this as the password in the tomcat-users.xml file:

```
<user username="user1"
      password="c23e47c2003a93af2dad4dae78f5e1c4a4735732"
      roles="role1,role2, role3"/>
```

We can also use the MD5 algorithm as shown below.

Configure the server.xml file configuration file:

```
<Realm className="org.apache.catalina.realm.MemoryRealm"
       debug="5"
       digest="md5"
       pathname="conf/tomcat_users.xml" />
```

Generate the MD5 digest version of the password:

```
$ java -classpath $CATALINA_HOME/catalina.jar
org.apache.catalina.realm.RealmBase -a md5 aReal11yG00doNe

aReal11yG00doNe:9b4e814db0df11a7d7ba37ba3c0be2ac
$
```

Add to the tomcat-users.xml file:

```
<user username="user1"
      password="9b4e814db0df11a7d7ba37ba3c0be2ac"
      roles="role1,role2, role3"/>
```

Choosing between MD5 and SHA

Both MD5 and SHA are one-way hash functions. A one-way hash function takes a variable-length message and produces a fixed-length hash. Given the hash, it is computationally "hard" to determine information about the message from it, or find another message that produces the same hash. While both SHA and MD5 are secure, SHA has a hash code of a larger size (160 bit) than MD5 (128 bit), and therefore is harder to break. Hence, use of SHA is recommended over MD5.

Deleting a User

Deleting a user is as simple as deleting the line (or commenting it out) corresponding to it in `tomcat-users.xml`. As before, deletion of a user takes effect only when Tomcat is restarted.

Pros and Cons of Memory Realms

Some important issues to be noted before deciding on using this Realm implementation are:

❑　Memory Realms is a very simple implementation and requires a minimal amount of setup. While this can be useful for development purposes, it may not be the best implementation for a production environment where security and uptime are crucial.

❑　The major limitation to using Memory Realms is that changes to the Memory Realm configuration require Tomcat to be restarted. The other Realm implementations – JDBC, JNDI, and UserDatabase Realms (new in Tomcat 4.1) overcome this limitation.

❑　The authentication is performed the first time the user attempts to access a restricted resource, and the user and his roles are cached for the duration of the session. This lasts until session timeout/invalidation for FORM-based authentication and as long as the browser window is open for BASIC authentication.

❑　The Realm database is stored on the file system in XML format. This can be a security risk if the file permissions are not set correctly.

UserDatabase Realm

Tomcat 4.1 introduces a new Realm implementation called `UserDatabase` Realm as its default Realm. Although this uses the file system to store the Realm-related information, changes to this database do not require Tomcat to be restarted if they are made through the `admin` web application.

Configuration

The first step in configuring the UserDatabase Realm is adding a Realm entry in the `$CATALINA_HOME/conf/server.xml` file.

The attributes for the `UserDatabase` Realm are listed below:

Attribute name	Description	Required
className	This is the `className` of the Java class that implements Memory Realms. This must be `org.apache.catalina.realm.UserDatabase Realm`.	Mandatory
debug	The debug level. A missing or "0" (zero) valued debug level turns off debugging. The log file that the log messages go to is specified in a Logger directive.	Optional
digest	The passwords can either be stored as clear-text or encrypted using a digest algorithm. The supported digest algorithms are those that the `java.security.MessageDigest` class provides – MD5 (digest value "md5") and SHA (digest value sha). A missing digest attribute means that the password is stored as clear-text.	Optional
resourceName	Name of the User Database resource key.	Mandatory

A sample configuration directive is shown below:

```
<Realm className="org.apache.catalina.realm.UserDatabaseRealm"
       debug="0"
       resourceName="UserDatabase"/>
```

The `resourceName` attribute refers to the key name of the `UserDatabase` that is configured in the global JNDI resources. The following is an extract from the `server.xml` file that shows the default JNDI resource configuration.

```
<!-- Global JNDI resources -->
<GlobalNamingResources>

    <!-- Test entry for demonstration purposes -->
    <Environment name="simpleValue"
                 type="java.lang.Integer"
                 value="30"/>

    <!-- Editable user database that can also be used by
         UserDatabaseRealm to authenticate users -->

    <Resource name="UserDatabase"
              auth="Container"
              type="org.apache.catalina.UserDatabase"
```

```
                    description="User database that can be updated and
                               saved">
        </Resource>
        <ResourceParams
            name="UserDatabase">

          <parameter>
            <name>factory</name>
             <value>
                org.apache.catalina.users.MemoryUserDatabaseFactory
             </value>
          </parameter>

          <parameter>
            <name>pathname</name>
            <value>conf/tomcat-users.xml</value>
          </parameter>

        </ResourceParams>

    </GlobalNamingResources>
```

> Note the `<ResourceParam>` element with the name attribute
> `UserDatabase`. This name must match the `resourceName`
> attribute in the Realm element. Also note the file
> `$CATALINA_HOME/conf/tomcat-users.xml` that is configured as
> the pathname for the user database. This path is relative to
> `$CATALINA_HOME`.

Adding a Role

Add a new role can be done using the admin application.

The admin application, as we mentioned earlier, can be accessed at the URL
http://host:port/admin. Here, host is the hostname of the machine and port is the port
number that Tomcat runs on (8080 by default). On accessing this URL, you would be
prompted for a username and password. You need to enter the valid username and
password of a user that belongs to the admin role. This is specified at install time if
you had installed on Windows using the binary installer. Otherwise, you would need to
add a user to the admin role (see below) before attempting this.

After logging in, you are presented with a number of options, including that of managing the roles. The screenshot below shows the different options available for Roles:

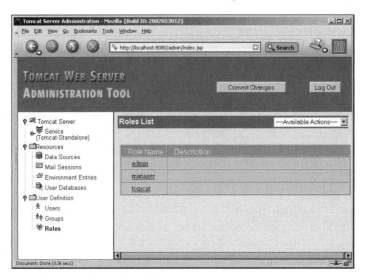

Select the Create New Role in the drop down list on the top right corner of the Roles List pane. You will then will be prompted for a new role name and description. Add a unique name for the role – say role1 – and save it using the Save button.

This application writes out the changes to the $CATALINA_HOME/conf/tomcat_users.xml file (or the file specified in the pathname attribute in the Realm directive, if so configured). The extract from this file below shows a new role called role1 being added:

```
<?xml version='1.0' encoding='utf-8'?>
   <tomcat-users>
     ....
     <role rolename="role1" description=""/>
     ...
</tomcat-users>
```

The role element takes two attributes:

❑   rolename
    This is a unique identifier for a role.

❑   description
    Optional description for a role.

We can also make changes by editing this file manually. However, if we do this, these changes take effect only when Tomcat is restarted.

Adding a User

The admin application also provides for adding users. To do this, access the admin web application as shown in the previous section and click on the Users link on the left pane of the admin home page. On selecting this, we're presented with the list of all the roles available. The screenshot below shows the different options available for managing users in the
admin application:

We choose the Create New User option. This allows us to add information about the user – the username, password, and description text, and also allows us to choose the group(s) that the user should belong to:

Adding a new user using the `admin` application also updates the
`%CATALINA_HOME%/conf/tomcat_users.xml` file (or the file specified in the
pathname attribute in the *Realm* directive, if so configured). The extract from this file
below shows a new role called `user1` has been added:

```
<?xml version='1.0' encoding='utf-8'?>
<tomcat-users>
<user username="user1"
      password="secret"
      fullName="A description of user1"
      roles="role1"/>
....
</tomcat-users>
```

The user element can have four attributes:

❏ username is a mandatory attribute, and contains the name of the user. This
   is a unique identifier for a user.

❏ password is a mandatory attribute, and contains the password for the user.

❏ fullName is an optional attribute that contains descriptive text for the user.

❏ roles is a mandatory attribute that contains a comma-separated list of
   roles that the user belongs to.

❏ The password that we saw being set in the password attribute above
   (secret) was stored as clear-text. For improved security, the following
   measures can be taken:

   ❏ Change the file system permissions for the configuration file, if the
      operating system allows for it. For example, on UNIX, the chmod
      command can be used to give read permission to only the userid that
      Tomcat starts up as.

   ❏ Use encrypted passwords.

> **Tomcat 4.1.12 (the latest version at the time of writing) has a
> bug – it ignores the digest attribute while writing out the
> password field. Due to this, only the clear-text version of the
> password is written out. We therefore need to manually edit
> the tomcat-users.xml file (see the next section "Using
> encrypted passwords"). The drawback of this workaround is
> that Tomcat would need to be restarted for changes to take
> effect – thus erasing the advantages that the UserDatabase
> Realm gave us over Memory Realms.**

Using Encrypted Passwords

As we discussed earlier for Memory Realms, we can use the digest attribute for the
Realm configuration in `%CATALINA_HOME%/conf/server.xml` to set the digest
algorithm to use.

❑ Configure the `server.xml`:

```
<Realm className="org.apache.catalina.realm.UserDatabaseRealm"
       debug="5"
       digest="sha"
       pathname="conf/tomcat_users.xml" />
```

❑ We generate the SHA digest version of the password:

```
$ java -classpath $CATALINA_HOME/catalina.jar
org.apache.catalina.realm.RealmBase -a sha aReal11yG00doNe

aReal11yG00doNe:c23e47c2003a93af2dad4dae78f5e1c4a4735732
```

❑ Add this as the password in the `tomcat-users.xml` file

```
<user username="user1"
password="c23e47c2003a93af2dad4dae78f5e1c4a4735732"
      fullName="User One"
      roles="role1,role2, role3"/>
```

> **If you add a digest attribute for the Realm directive, remember to change the password field for all the users in `tomcat-users.xml` to their digested version too. This is especially important for the `admin` user, as otherwise we won't be able to log in to the `admin` application.**

```
<user username="admin"
        password="d033e22ae348aeb5660fc2140aec35850c4da997"
        roles="admin,manager"/>
```

The extract from `tomcat-users.xml` above shows this being done.

Deleting a Role

To delete a role, select the option **Delete Existing Roles** from the drop down list on the right hand top corner of the User pane. Select the checkbox corresponding to the required role and click on Save:

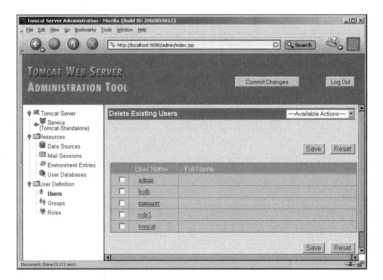

Deleting a User

Deleting a user can be done either by using the admin application (see screenshot below) or by removing the entry for the user from the tomcat_users.xml file. In the latter case the change won't take effect until Tomcat is restarted – hence the former is preferable.

More on UserDatabases: Using the UserDatabase API

The `UserDatabase` class
(`org.apache.catalina.users.MemoryUserDatabaseFactory`) implements the
`org.apache.catalina.UserDatabase` interface. This interface provides for
methods to list as well as manage the Realm users and roles. It should be noted that
this API is a Tomcat proprietary API, and not a J2EE standard.

The API methods for managing users are listed below:

Method	Description
getUsers()	Returns the set of users defined in the Realm Database.
createUser()	Creates a new user.
findUser()	Gets a user by Username.
removeUser()	Removes a user from the Realm Database.

The API methods for managing roles are listed below:

Method	Description
getRoles()	Returns the set of roles defined in the Realm Database.
createRole()	Creates a new role.
findRoles()	Gets a role by role name.
removeRole()	Removes a role from the Realm Database.

The following is a small code fragment from a servlet that shows these API methods
being used:

```
/* Tomcat classes- from CATALINA_HOME\server\lib\catalina.jar */
import org.catalina.User;
import org.catalina.UserDatabase;

/* JNDI classes */
import javax.naming.Context;
import javax.naming.InitialContext;

import java.util.Iterator;

public void doGet(HttpServletRequest request,
                  HttpServletResponse response)
throws IOException, ServletException  {

        Context initCtx =  new InitialContext();
        Context envCtx =  (Context) initCtx.lookup("java:comp/env");
```

```
    /* userDatabase is the resource name as specified in the
     * server.xml file */

    UserDatabase database =   (UserDatabase)
envCtx.lookup("userDatabase");
```

We can also add a check to ensure that users belonging to a specific role (in this case admin) are the only ones allowed to perform these privileged operations. Do we need to perform this check? No, we can instead protect this application using container-managed security. All we need to do is to add a security constraint in the deployment descriptor (web.xml) restricting access to only users of the admin role. See the *Adding Security to Web Applications* section for more information.

```
    /* Check using the isUserInRole() Programmatic Security API call
     * to see if the current user should be able to access this
     * privileged information
     */

    if (request.isUserInRole ("admin") {
    /* Validated user- now we can do operations
     * to view or manage the Realm data
     */
    Iterator allUsers       =  database.getUsers ();
    Iterator allRoles       =  database.getRoles ();
    ...
    } else {
      /* Nope- unauthorized access */
    }
```

Before we try running this servlet, we would need to edit the $CATALINA_HOME/conf/server.xml file and add a ResourceLink element in the Context declaration of web application that this servlet is a part of (myapp in this case):

```
<Context path="/myapp" docBase="examples" debug="0"
            reloadable="true" crossContext="true">
    ...

    <ResourceLink name="userDatabase"
              global="UserDatabase"
              type="org.apache.catalina.UserDatabase"/>

</Context>
```

Pros and Cons of UserDatabase Realms

UserDatabase Realms are an improvement over Memory Realms in the following ways:

❑   Changes made to the UserDatabase take effect immediately, and therefore Tomcat does not need to be restarted if a new user or role is added or removed.

❑ User Database Realms expose a Tomcat proprietary Java API that can be used to build applications that access as well as manage the data stored in the Realm. We will look at this API in the *More on UserDatabases: Using the UserDatabase API* section later in the chapter.

❑ Tomcat comes with an `admin` web application to manage the Realm data. This uses the above Java API.

❑ There are some other issues that we should note while deciding on using this Realm implementation:

❑ The Realm database is stored on the file system like memory Realms, and hence the same security concerns apply – change the file system permissions for the configuration file, if the operating system allows for it.

❑ The authentication is performed the first time the user attempts to access a restricted resource, and the user and his or her roles are cached for the duration of the session. This lasts till session timeout/invalidation for FORM-based authentication and as long as the browser window is open for BASIC authentication.

❑ The default Tomcat 4.1 installation comes with the `admin` and `manager` web applications that are protected using UserDatabase Realms. Unlike Tomcat 4.0, however, the Tomcat 4.1 installer on Windows enables access to these web applications. While this is helpful, it can be a security risk – the password for this user is stored as clear-text on the file system.

❑ The `manager` web application (accessible at http://host:port/manager/html/list) allows for managing the web applications instance – listing, starting, stopping, and restarting them. The `admin` web application (accessible at http://hostserver:port/admin) allows for managing the Tomcat configuration and adding/removing users and roles.

JDBC Realm

A JDBC Realm, as the name suggests, stores Realm data in a relational database and accesses it using a JDBC connection. We can use any database that has a JDBC driver, such as Oracle, MySQL, or DB2. In this chapter we will use MySQL version 3.23 as our database.

Configuration

Configuring a JDBC Realm is more complex than Memory or User Database Realms. The configuration involves a five-step process as explained below. The prerequisite to performing this setup is that a JDBC-compliant database (MySQL in our example) needs to be installed and running. As we mentioned earlier, the procedure for this is not explained in this chapter – please refer to MySQL documentation at http://www.mysql.com/ for more information.

Step 1: Install the Database Driver

The JDBC driver for MySQL can be downloaded from http://www.mysql.com/. Place the JAR file in the $CATALINA_HOME/server/lib directory (if you do not need it visible to web applications) or the $CATALINA_HOME/common/lib directory.

Step 2: Create the Realm Database

We need to create two tables – users and user roles. The names of these tables and the column names are not important, and we specify these to Tomcat via the Realm configuration.

The users table contains the username and password mapping. The following table shows the required schema for this table:

Column name	Description	Type
user_name	Name of user	varchar (15) NOT NULL
user_pass	Password of user	varchar (32) NOT NULL

The users roles table contains the username and role mapping. The following table shows the required schema for this table:

Column name	Description	Type
user_name	Name of user	varchar (15) NOT NULL
user_role	Password of user	varchar (32) NOT NULL

The following SQL script (create_realm_database.sql) creates this database (realmdatabase) and the required tables:

```
create database realmdatabase;

use realmdatabase;

create table users (
  user_name varchar (15) not null primary key,
  user_pass varchar (32) not null
  );

create table user_roles (
  user_name varchar (15) not null references users (user_name),
  role_name varchar (15) not null,
  primary key (user_name, role_name)
  );
```

Save the script above as `create_realm_database.sql` and execute it using the `mysql` command:

```
$ mysql -u rootuser -p < create_realm_database.sql
```

Here `rootuser` is the privileged user allowed to create databases, and the `-p` option causes `mysql` to ask for a password. In case we run this command remotely, we would need to specify the hostname using an `-h host` option.

Step 3: Create User for Accessing the Realm Database

We now need to create a user for accessing the Realm database. This user will be used by Tomcat to view the Realm data, and hence it needs `SELECT` privileges only.

```
$ mysql -u rootuser -p

mysql> GRANT SELECT ON realmdatabase.*
    -> to 'realmuser'@'localhost' identified by 'realmpass';

mysql> FLUSH PRIVILEGES;
```

Here `realmuser` and `realmpass` are the username and password of the database user that Tomcat connects as, and since we are connecting to the database from the same machine as MySQL, we specify localhost as the hostname.

The database user is different from the Realm user that we talk about elsewhere in the chapter – the database user controls access to the MySQL database, while the Realm user controls access to the Realm.

The `FLUSH PRIVILEGES` directive causes Tomcat to update the privileges table. Another way to do the same thing is to use the MySQL `admin` tool:

```
$ mysqladmin reload
```

MySQL should store the password for the realmuser database user in an encrypted form. We can check this using the following SQL command:

```
mysql> SELECT * from mysql.user where user="realmuser";
```

Older versions of MySQL may store the password as clear-text and not in an encrypted form. In those versions, we can use the `PASSWORD()` MySQL function to make the database encrypt it:

```
mysql> GRANT SELECT ON realmdatabase.*
    -> to 'realmuser'@'localhost' identified by PASSWORD
('realmpass');

mysql> FLUSH PRIVILEGES;
```

We can change a database user's password in the following way:

```
mysql> SET PASSWORD for 'realmuser'@'localhost' = PASSWORD
('a_new_password');

mysql> FLUSH PRIVILEGES;
```

Finally, we can revoke (remove) a database user's privileges by using the REVOKE database clause as shown below:

```
mysql> REVOKE SELECT ON realmdatabase.* from 'realmuser'@'localhost';

mysql> FLUSH PRIVILEGES;
```

Step 4: Populate the Realm Database

Next, we need to populate the Realm database with the roles and users required for the admin and manager web applications.

In our deployment, we create a user called admin, with password admin_pass. Adding the username and password to the users table does this:

```
$ mysql -u rootuser -p

mysql> USE realmdatabase

mysql> INSERT INTO users (user_name, user_pass) VALUES ('admin',
'admin_pass');
```

We can then add this user to the admin and manager roles in the user_role table:

```
mysql> INSERT INTO user_roles (user_name, role_name) VALUES ('admin',
'admin');

mysql> INSERT INTO user_roles (user_name, role_name) VALUES ('admin',
'manager');
```

Adding users and roles in JDBC realms is discussed in more detail later in the chapter.

Step 5: Configure the Realm

The final step in configuring the JDBC Realm is adding a Realm entry in the $CATALINA_HOME/conf/server.xml file.

You would need to first remove or comment out the existing entry, if any, for the Memory Realm (the default for Tomcat 4.0) or the UserDatabase Realm (the default for Tomcat 4.1).

The Realm attributes for JDBC Realm are listed below:

Attribute name	Description	Mandatory/Optional
className	This is the class name of the Java class that implements memory realms. This must be org.apache.catalina.realm.JDBCRealm.	Mandatory
connectionName	The database username for establishing the JDBC connection.	Mandatory if the connectionURL doesn't include it.
connectionPassword	The database password for establishing the JDBC connection.	Mandatory if the connectionURL doesn't include it.
connectionURL	The database URL for establishing the JDBC connection.	Mandatory
debug	The debug level. A missing or "0" (zero) valued debug level turns of debugging. The log file to which the log messages go is specified in a Logger directive.	Optional
digest	The passwords can either be stored as clear-text or encrypted using a digest algorithm. The supported digest algorithms are those that the java.security.MessageDigest class provides – MD5 (digest value md5) and SHA (digest value sha). A missing digest attribute means that the password is stored as clear-text.	Optional
driverName	The fully qualified java class name of the JDBC driver.	Mandatory
roleNameCol	The name of the column in *user roles* database table that stores the name of a role assigned to this user.	Mandatory

Attribute name	Description	Mandatory/Optional
userCredCol	The name of the column in *users* database table that stores the password for this user. The password can be either in clear-text or in an encrypted digest form depending on the value of the *digest* attribute.	Mandatory
userNameCol	The name of the column in *users* and *user roles* database table that stores the username for this user.	Mandatory
userRoleTable	The name of the database table that contains one row for each role assigned to a particular username. This table must contain the columns named in the userNameCol and roleNameCol directives – it can contain additional columns too, but these are ignored.	Mandatory
userTable	The name of the database table that contains one row for each username that Tomcat needs to recognize. This table must contain the columns named in the userNameCol and userCredCol directives – it can contain additional columns too, but these are ignored.	Mandatory

Based on the Realm database we created earlier, our Realm directive would now look like the following:

```
<Realm
    className="org.apache.catalina.realm.JDBCRealm"
    driverName="org.gjt.mm.mysql.Driver"
    connectionURL="jdbc:mysql://localhost/realmdatabase"
    connectionName="realmuser"
    connectionPassword="realmpass"
    userTable="users"
    userNameCol="user_name"
    userCredCol="user_pass"
    userRoleTable="user_roles"
    roleNameCol="role_name"
/>
```

The `className` attribute is set to `org.apache.catalina.realm.JDBCRealm` – this is the class for the JDBC Realm, and like all Realms classes, it implements the `org.apache.catalina.Realm` interface. The `driverName` attribute is set to the JDBC driver class – this is `org.gjt.mm.mysql.Driver` for the MySQL JDBC driver.

The `connectionName` contains the JDBC connection string. In this case, because the MySQL database is running on the local machine on the default port and the database name is `realmdatabase`, the connection string is `dbc:mysql://localhost/realmdatabase`. The `connectionName` and `connectionPassword` are set to the name and password of the user that Tomcat connects as. Finally, the `userTable`, `userNameCol`, `userCredCol`, `userRoleTable`, and `roleNameCol` attributes are set to the respective values bases on the database tables created.

Finally, we need to restart Tomcat in order to make it re-read the Realm configuration.

Adding a User

In the *Populate the Realm database* section, we saw how a user is added to the JDBC realm.

```
mysql> INSERT INTO users (user_name, user_pass)
    -> VALUES ('newuser', 'user_pass');
```

Adding a user in a JDBC Realm does not require a Tomcat restart, unlike in Memory Realms.

The user password above was added as clear-text. We can restrict `SELECT` privileges for this database to prevent unauthorized users from reading this data. Another precaution that can be taken is storing the digested version of this password in the database. The security benefits of doing this are twofold: even if the database table is compromised, the passwords cannot be read. The transmission of passwords between Tomcat and the relational database is more secure since we don't have clear-text passwords being sent. Many web sites are hosted on shared hosting machines, and there could be users on these machines or on the network that are able to monitor the traffic.

To enable digested passwords, we would need to set the digest attribute in the Realm configuration in the `server.xml` file to the required digest algorithm (SHA or MD5). SHA is more secure than MD5, as explained in the section on Adding Users in *Memory Realms*.

```
<Realm
    className="org.apache.catalina.realm.JDBCRealm"
    driverName="org.gjt.mm.mysql.Driver"
    connectionURL="jdbc:mysql://localhost/realmdatabase"
    connectionName="realmuser"
    connectionPassword="realmpass"
```

```
        userTable="users"
        userNameCol="user_name"
        userCredCol="user_pass"
        userRoleTable="user_roles"
        roleNameCol="role_name"
        digest="md5"
/>
```

We can then add the digest value of the password instead:

```
mysql> INSERT INTO users (user_name, user_pass)
    -> VALUES ('newuser', MD5 ('user_pass'));
```

Here MD5 () is a MySQL function that converts a string to its MD5 digest value. Other relational databases would have equivalent methods.

> **If we change the Realm configuration and start using digests for the password, we would need to change all password entries to their digest values. We would also need to restart Tomcat – this is required in order to make it re-read the Realm configuration changes in server.xml.**

The username is the primary key of the users table. Therefore, if we have to change the password, we need to either delete the entry and create a new one, or use the UPDATE database clause to change it:

```
mysql> UPDATE users SET user_pass="newpass" where user="newuser';
```

Adding a Role

We saw earlier how a user could be added to a role:

```
mysql> INSERT INTO user_roles (user_name, role_name) VALUES
    -> ('newuser', 'role1');
```

A user can belong to more than one role – this is configured as shown below:

```
mysql> INSERT INTO user_roles (user_name, role_name) VALUES
    -> ('newuser', 'role2');
```

The primary key in the user roles table is (user_name, role_name), and hence we can have multiple entries for the same user.

Deleting a User

Deleting a user is done as shown below. Here we are deleting the user newuser that we just created:

```
mysql> DELETE FROM users WHERE user_name="newuser";
```

Deleting a Rrole

Deleting a role is done in a manner similar to deleting a user.

```
mysql> DELETE FROM user_roles WHERE user_name="newuser" AND
role_name="role1";
```

Here we are deleting the user to role mapping for user newuser and role role1.

Pros and Cons of JDBC Realms

JDBC Realms are an improvement over Memory Realms for the same reason the UserDatabase realm are:

❑   Changes made to the JDBC Realm take effect immediately, and therefore Tomcat does not need to be restarted if a new user or role is added or removed.

❑   JDBC Realms do not expose a custom API like User Database Realms. This is not required, however, as the data is stored in a relational database and we can easily build a custom application using the JDBC API to access as well as manage the data stored in it.

❑   There are some other issues that we should note while deciding on using this Realm implementation:

    ❑   The Realm database is stored in a relational database. The access rights to the tables used for the Realm data should be limited to valid, authorized users. We will later see in the *Create User to Access Realm Database* section how this can be done.

    ❑   The authentication is performed the first time the user attempts to access a restricted resource, and the user and his or her roles are cached for the duration of the session. This lasts till session timeout/invalidation for FORM-based authentication and as long as the browser window is open for BASIC authentication.

    ❑   The default Tomcat 4.1 installation comes with the admin and manager web applications that are protected using User Database Realms. Tomcat 4.0 has the manager application protected by Memory Realms. In case we switch over to using JDBC Realms, we would need to populate the Realm with data for the admin and manager roles – we show how this is done in the *Populate the Realm Database* section later in the section.

    ❑   Unlike UserDatabase Realms, Tomcat does not provide any application to administer the realms data to add/remove users and roles. We would thus need to do this ourselves, either by issuing SQL commands (shown earlier in this chapter) or by developing custom applications.

❑ At the time of writing, JDBC Realms do not use connection pooling to connect to the backend database. This impacts performance if a large number of users try and authenticate at the same time.

JNDI Realm

JNDI, or Java Naming and Directory Interface is a standard Java API that provides applications a unified interface to a number of different naming and directory services.

The JNDI architecture has two components – an API that is used by client-side applications to access the naming/directory services and a Service Provider Interface (SPI) that allows vendors to develop custom "providers" for their naming/directory servers. These providers allow different directory servers to be "plugged in" transparent to the client application. LDAP, or Lightweight Directory Access Protocol is one such directory protocol. OpenLDAP (http://www.openldap.org/) and Netscape Directory Server (http://enterprise.netscape.com/products/identsvcs/directory.html) are two popular implementations of LDAP:

Figure 1

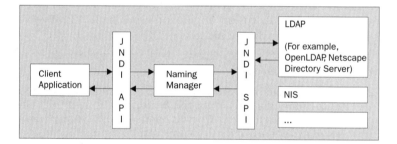

Further information on JNDI can be found at http://java.sun.com/products/jndi/docs.html.

A JNDI Realm stores data in an LDAP directory server (such as Netscape Directory Server, OpenLDAP, etc.) and accesses it using a JNDI provider. In this chapter we will use OpenLDAP as the directory server. OpenLDAP can be downloaded from http://www.openldap.org/software/download/ and is available in Open Source under the OpenLDAP Public License (http://www.openldap.org/software/release/license.html). We will not cover OpenLDAP in detail in this chapter. You can find information on LDAP from the book *Implementing LDAP (ISBN 1-861002-21-1) Wrox Press*, and information on OpenLDAP at the following web sites:

OpenLDAP: A quick start guide	http://www.openldap.org/doc/admin/quickstart.html
OpenLDAP 2.1 Administrator's Guide	http://www.openldap.org/doc/admin/

Configuration

Configuring a JNDI Realm is more complex than Memory or User Database realms. The configuration involves a five-step process as in the case of JDBC Realms.

Step 1: Install the JNDI driver

Place the JNDI driver JAR file in the `$CATALINA_HOME/server/lib` directory (if you do not need it visible to web applications) or the `$CATALINA_HOME/common/lib` directory. The JNDI driver JAR file is typically named `ldap.jar` and can be downloaded from http://java.sun.com/products/jndi/.

Step 2: Create the LDAP schema

After installing the JNDI driver, we create the LDAP schema for storing the user and role data. This step is different for each directory server; refer to your LDAP server documentation for further information.

Before creating the schema, there are some design issues to be considered. These are:

Connection to the Directory

Connections to the directory server can be made either anonymously or by using the username and password specified in the Realm configuration by the `connectionName` and `connectionPassword` properties (see the *Configure the Realm* section below).

An anonymous connection is sufficient in most cases.

Authenticating the User

Authentication of a user by a directory server can be done in two "modes" – the bind mode and the comparison mode.

❑ **Bind Mode**

In the bind mode, user authentication is done by "binding" to the directory server using the Distinguished Name (DN) of the user and the password presented by the user. If the bind succeeds, the user is considered authenticated.

Thus, in the bind mode, the directory server does the actual authentication. The directory server saves a digested version of the user's password, and it converts the user's password to its digested version before comparing it. Due to this, the digest attribute in the Realm configuration in server.xml is ignored. This does, however, mean that the password is transmitted as clear-text from Tomcat to the directory server. This is not the same as transmitting the password from the user's browser to the Tomcat end – here mechanisms like HTTP Digest or even HTTPS may be used. Several LDAP servers support SSL connections, so this can be used to protect the transmission of the password as clear-text.

❑ **Comparison Mode**

In the comparison mode, the Realm retrieves the password from the directory and does the comparison of the passwords itself. For enabling the comparison mode, we need to specify the userPassword attribute of the Realm directive to the directory attribute that contains the user's password.

❑ **Choosing between the two modes**

The bind mode is the more secure way, since in the comparison mode the configuration allows the Realm to read the user's password.

Another disadvantage of the comparison mode is that the Realm implementation must handle password digests (in case the directory server stored the digested version of the password) and all the variations of the digest algorithms.

Step 3: Assign Roles to the User

There are two approaches to storing roles in the JNDI directory:

❑ **Explicit directory entries**

Roles can be represented as explicit directory entries. In this case the roleBase, roleSubtree, roleSearch, and roleName attributes in the Realm directive are used. These are discussed in more detail in the *Configure the Realm* section.

❑ **Attributes of the user entry**

Alternatively, roles can also be represented as attributes in the user's LDAP directory entry. In this case the userRoleName attribute (discussed later) in the Realm configuration should be set appropriately.

Step 4: Populate the Directory

We now need to populate the LDAP directory with the users for the admin (Tomcat 4.1 only) and manager roles. This is required if we wish to use the admin and manager web applications

The following shows sample entries for the admin and manager roles, and a user (user1) that is listed in both roles:

```
# Top-level entry
    dn: dc=companyname,dc=com
    objectClass: dcObject
    dc:companyname

# Entry to contain people
# The searches for users are based on this entry.
    dn: ou=people,dc=companyname,dc=com
    objectClass: organizationalUnit
    ou: people

# User entry for role "admin" and "manager"
    dn: uid=user1,ou=people,dc=companyname,dc=com
```

```
        objectClass: inetOrgPerson
        uid: user1
        sn: user1
        cn: super user1
        mail: root@companyname.com
        userPassword: secret

# Entry to contain LDAP groups
# The searches for roles are based on this entry.
        dn: ou=groups,dc=companyname,dc=com
        objectClass: organizationalUnit
        ou: groups

# Entry for the "manager" role
        dn: cn=manager,ou=groups,dc=companyname,dc=com
        objectClass: groupOfUniqueNames
        cn: manager
        uniqueMember: uid=user1,ou=people,dc=companyname,dc=com

# Entry for the "admin" role
        dn: cn=admin,ou=groups,dc=companyname,dc=com
        objectClass: groupOfUniqueNames
        cn: admin
        uniqueMember: uid=user1,ou=people,dc=companyname,dc=com
```

The data above is in LDIF format, and it can be uploaded into OpenLDAP using the ldapadd tool.

```
$ ldapadd -f tomcat.ldif -x -D "cn=LDAPRootuser,dc=companyname,dc=com"
-w password
```

In the example above, tomcat.ldif is the file that contains the data about the roles and users in LDIF format. The value passed via the -D flag is that of the Distinguished Name (DN used to bind to the directory server. This is the DN of a superuser that has the right to update the LDAP directory, and it authenticates itself via a password (the -w option). This superuser was configured in the rootdn directive in slapd.conf. The following is a sample entry:

```
database ldbm
suffix dc="companyname",dc="com"
rootdn "cn=LDAPRootUser,dc=companyname,dc=com"
rootpw password
```

Step 5: Create a User to Access the Directory

Next, we need to create an OpenLDAP user that has read access to the data published in the LDAP directory. The default OpenLDAP configuration gives read access to all users (except the super-user who has write access too). This is a security risk, especially if the passwords are being stored as clear-text. The following is a sample from the OpenLDAP configuration file that shows access to the userPassword (the name of the attribute, in this configuration, that contains the Realm user password) attribute being restricted:

```
access to attr=userPassword
    by dn="cn=tomcatuser,dc=companyname,dc=com" read
    by * none
```

Attributes of the JNDI Realm

The Realm attributes for the JNDI Realm are listed below:

Attribute name	Description	Mandatory/Optional
className	This is the className of the java class that implements Memory Realms. This must be org.apache.catalina.realm.JNDIRealm.	Mandatory
connectionName	The username used to authenticate against the directory service via JNDI.	Optional if an anonymous JNDI connection is sufficient
connectionPassword	The password used to authenticate against the directory service via JNDI.	Optional if an anonymous JNDI connection is sufficient
connectionURL	The URL for establishing the JNDI connection. The format of this URL is defined by the JNDI provider, and is usually an LDAP URL (ldap://host:port/dnname) that specifies the domain name of directory server to connect to, the (optional) port number, and the distinguished name (DN) of the root naming context.	Mandatory
contextFactory	The fully qualified name of the java class used to create the context for the JNDI connection.	Optional

Table continued on following page

Attribute name	Description	Mandatory/Optional
debug	The debug level. A missing or "0" (zero) valued debug level turns off debugging. The log file that the log messages go to is specified in a Logger directive.	Optional
digest	The passwords can either be stored as clear-text or encrypted using a digest algorithm. The supported digest algorithms are those that the `java.security.MessageDigest` class provides – MD5 (digest value "md5") and SHA (digest value "sha"). A missing digest attribute means that the password is stored as clear-text.	Optional
roleBase	The base directory entry for role searches. If not specified, it defaults to the top-level element in the directory context.	Optional
roleName	The LDAP directory attribute that contains the Realm role name. In addition we can use the `userRoleName` to specify the name of the attribute in the user's entry that contains additional role names. In case the `roleName` attribute is missing, role searches are not performed and roles are taken from only the user's entry.	Optional
roleSearch	The LDAP pattern (called a LDAP filter) for searching the directory for roles. The format for the LDAP pattern is that of the `java.text.Message` class, and {0} gets substituted by the distinguished name (DN) of the user, and {1} by the username. In case the `roleSearch` is not specified, searches are not performed and the roles are taken from the user's entry as in the case of roleName.	Optional

Attribute name	Description	Mandatory/Optional
roleSubtree	If set to true, the entire sub-tree of the element specified by roleBase is searched for role entries. The default is false – this causes only the top-level entries to be searched.	Optional
userPassword	Name of the attribute in the user's entry that has the password for the Realm user.	Optional
userPattern	The LDAP pattern for the distinguished name (DN) of the Realm user's directory entry. As before, the format for the LDAP pattern is that of the java.text.Message class. The pattern {0} gets substituted by the username.	Optional
userRoleName	The name of an attribute in the user's directory entry that contains the values of the role names for the user.	Optional
userSearch	The LDAP filter expression to use for searching for a user's directory entry. Again, the format for the LDAP pattern is that of the java.text.Message class and the pattern {0} gets substituted by the username.	Optional
userSubtree	If set to true, the entire sub-tree of the element specified by userBase is searched for user entries. The default is false – this causes only the top-level entries to be searched.	Optional

The Realm directive would be different based on how users bind to the LDAP directory. The sample configuration shown below is for an LDAP server running on the same machine (hence the localhost in the connectionURL) and has users logging in using their user id (see the userPattern attribute specifying this):

```
<Realm    className="org.apache.catalina.realm.JNDIRealm"
          connectionURL="ldap://localhost:389"
          userPattern="uid={0},ou=people,dc=companyname,dc=com"
          roleBase="ou=groups,dc=companyname,dc=com"
          roleName="cn"
          roleSearch="(uniqueMember={0})"
    />
```

Finally, we need to restart Tomcat in order to make it re-read the Realm configuration.

Adding Roles and Users

Adding a role or a user can be done using the ldapadd command as we saw earlier in the *Populate the Directory* section. Other LDAP implementations, such as Netscape Directory Server, have GUI-based interfaces that make this simpler.

Remove a Role or a User

The ldapremove command is used to remove a user or role from the LDAP database.

```
$ ldapremove  "uid=user1,ou=people,dc=companyname,dc=com" -x -D
"cn=LDAPRootuser,dc= companyname,dc=com" -w password
```

Here uid=user1,ou=people,dc=companyname,dc=com is the Distinguished Name of the user that is being deleted. The same command works for removing a role – we just specify the DN of the role to be deleted.

As before, the value passed via the – D flag is that of the Distinguished Name used to bind to the directory server. This is the DN of a super-user that has right to update the LDAP directory, and it authenticates itself via a password (the –w option).

Pros and Cons of JNDI Realms

JNDI Realms are an improvement over Memory Realms for the same reason the UserDatabase realm are:

❑ Changes made to the JNDI Realm take effect immediately, and therefore Tomcat does not need to be restarted if a new user or role is added or removed.

❑ JNDI Realms do not expose a custom API like User Database Realms. This is however not required, as the data is stored in a directory and we can easily build a custom application using the JNDI API to access as well as manage the data stored in it.

❑ There are some other issues that we should note while deciding on using this Realm implementation:

   ❑ The Realm database is stored in a directory. The access rights to this data should be limited to valid, authorized users. Please refer to the documentation of your directory server on how this can be done.

   ❑ The authentication is performed the first time the user attempts to access a restricted resource, and the user and his or her roles are cached for the duration of the session. This lasts till session timeout/invalidation for FORM-based authentication and as long as the browser window is open for BASIC authentication.

❑ The default Tomcat 4.1 installation comes with the admin and manager web applications that are protected using User Database Realms. Tomcat 4.0 has a manager application protected by Memory Realms. In case we switch over to using JNDI Realms, we would need to populate the Realm with data for the admin and manager roles.

❑ Unlike UserDatabase Realms, Tomcat does not provide any application to administer the Realms data; that is to add/remove users and roles. We would thus need to do this ourselves, either by issuing LDAP server-specific commands or by developing custom applications using the JNDI API.

JAAS Realm

JAAS Realms are a new Realm implementation in Tomcat 4.1, and lack documentation. They use JAAS (Java Authentication and Authorization Service) to authenticate a user and provide access control.

JAAS allows for Pluggable Authentication Modules (PAM). With PAMs, the authentication technology is abstracted out, and thus the backend authentication technology can be changed transparent to the application making the request.

Some of the basic terminology relevant to JAAS Realms is introduced below. This is not a tutorial on JAAS, and further information, including javadocs and downloads, can be found at http://java.sun.com/products/jaas/.

❑ **Subject:**
The Subject (`javax.security.auth.Subject` class) is the identity that we wish to authenticate.

❑ **Principal**
The Principal (`java.security.Principal`) represents the interaction of a Subject with an authenticating authority.

❑ **LoginContext**
This is the Java class that acts as session with the authentication Provider. It also loads the Provider class after reading its configuration file.

❑ **Provider**
This is a class that implements the `javax.security.auth.spi.LoginModule` interface, and has the code for the actual authentication strategy.

JAAS is packaged along with JDK 1.4, though there is an optional download available for JDK 1.3 from http://java.sun.com/products/jaas/.

Configuration

Configuring JAAS Realms is a five-step process.

Step 1: Set up the Actual Authentication Technology

JAAS provides an API interface to the authentication technology. We first need to perform setup steps, if required, for this. For example, if we were using JNDI at the backend, we would need to install and configure a JNDI directory server.

Step 2: Write or Obtain a Provider for the Authentication Technology

The Provider, as we discussed earlier, is a java class that implements the `javax.security.auth.spi.LoginModule` interface. A provider needs to implement the methods of this interface, namely:

Method	Description
initialize	Initialize the `LoginModule`
abort	Abort the authentication process
commit	Commit the authentication process
login	Authenticate a Subject
logout	Log out a Subject

The Provider would also make use of a `Principal` class (an implementation of the `java.security.Principal` interface) that represents users and roles in this particular implementation. For example, JAAS comes with implementations for Windows NT users and domains (`com.sun.security.auth.NTUserPrincipal` and `com.sun.security.auth.NTDomainPrincipal`).

JAAS also provides some Provider implementations as a part of the `jaasmod.jar` JAR file. These include a JNDI provider (`com.sun.security.auth.module.JndiLoginModule`), NT Login provider (`com.sun.security.auth.module.NTLoginModule`), and a Solaris Login provider (`com.sun.security.auth.module.SolarisLoginModule`).

In some cases third-party vendors also provide Providers for their products.

Step 3: Configure the Provider

We have to add configuration statements for the Provider in a configuration file. For some providers, such as the Solaris and NT Login providers, this is a very simple setup. The following is a sample of the JAAS provider configuration for Solaris Login Provider:

```
SolarisLogin {
  com.sun.security.auth.module.SolarisLoginModule required;
};
```

Other Providers, such as the JNDI Provider, have a more complex setup (see sample below). In general, the configuration attributes are Provider-specific.

```
JNDILogin {
  com.sun.security.auth.module.JndiLoginModule required
  user.provider.url="ldap://localhost:389/ou=People,
                                     dc=companyname,
                                     dc=com"
  group.provider.url="ldap://localhost:389/ou=Group,
                                     dc=companyname,
                                     dc=com";
};
```

The configuration for the Providers (the ones we saw above) is passed to the JRE through the `java.security.auth.login.config` environment parameter.

Step 4: Make Changes in Java Security Policy, if Required

The JAAS authentication provider class is a trusted part of the system, and hence requires special access permissions. The following is a sample Java policy file that shows the kind of
permissions required.

```
//trust the provider
grant codeBase "file:./provider/" {
  permission java.security.AllPermission;
};


//trust JAAS
grant codeBase "file:/path/to/jaas.jar" {
  permission java.security.AllPermission;
};

//these permissions are needed by the client
grant codeBase "file:./client/" {
  permission javax.security.auth.AuthPermission
                             "createLoginContext";
  permission
          javax.security.auth.AuthPermission "doAs";
  permission java.util.PropertyPermission
                             "user.home", "read";
};
```

This policy file is passed to the JRE through the `java.security.policy` environment parameter. In addition, JAAS has a format for specifying access rights for the authenticated user. In the following example, the user user1 has read permissions in the user.home directory:

```
grant Principal com.sun.security.auth.NTUserPrincipal "user1" {
    permission java.util.PropertyPermission
                            "user.home", "read";
};
```

This policy file is passed to the JRE through the `java.security.auth.policy` environment parameter. From JDK 1.4 onwards, we don't need a separate policy file for this, and we can combine it with the previous security policy file.

Step 5: Configure the Realm Directive

The list of configuration attributes for the JAAS Realm element are shown below:

Attribute name	Description	Required
className	This is the `className` of the java class that implements JAAS realms. This must be `org.apache.Catalina.realm.JAASRealm`.	Mandatory
debug	The debug level. A missing or "0" (zero) valued debug level turns of debugging. The log file that the log messages go to is specified in a Logger directive.	Optional
appName	The application name passed to the JAAS `LoginContext`, which uses it to select the set of relevant `LoginModules`. This name should match the name of the enclosing block in the JAAS provider configuration.	Mandatory
roleClassNames	Comma-delimited list of `javax.security.Principal` classes that represent security roles.	Mandatory
userClassNames	Comma-delimited list of `javax.security.Principal` classes that represent individual users.	Mandatory

A sample configuration directive from `server.xml` is shown below:

```
<Realm className="org.apache.catalina.realm.JAASRealm"
       appName="Tomcat"
       roleClassNames="com.wrox.APrincipalImpl"
       userClassNames="com.wrox.AnotherPrincipalImpl"/>
```

Tomcat would need to be restarted for the Realm configuration changes to take effect.

137

Adding or Deleting Users and Roles

Adding or removing users and roles in the JAAS Realm is specific to the back-end technology being used for authentication. For example, if we use NT Realms, adding a user would be equivalent to creating a new NT login account.

Developing Custom Realms

Tomcat provides a number of Realm implementation, from those that read from a configuration file on the file system (`Memory`, `UserDatabase`) to those that use external programs for storing the Realm database (relational database in the case of JDBC Realms, directory server in the case of JNDI Realms).

So would we want to write our own Realm implementation? In most cases, we would not need to do so. However, there are use cases, for instance, when user and role information is stored in a custom application or enterprise directory, and the same set of permissions needs to be used to provide access to web applications.

Again, if this application or enterprise directory has a JNDI interface (as is the case with most packaged directory servers), we can use the JNDI Realm implementation instead of writing our own.

Writing a custom Realm implementation involves the following steps:

❑ Write a class that implements the `org.apache.catalina.Realm` interface. Tomcat provides a class called RealmBase (`org.apache.catalina.realm.RealmBase`) that implements this interface and also has code common to all Realm implementations. All other Realm implementations extend that class, and we should do the same.

❑ Any parameters that need to be passed to our Realm implementation can be specified as attributes to the Realm directive. These attributes should have corresponding set/get methods in the Realm implementation. For example, the JDBC Realm has attributes for the JDBC connection URL (`connectionURL`) and corresponding set/get methods (`setConnectionURL()`, `getConnectionURL()`).

❑ Implement the methods of the Realm interface. The primary method that needs to be implemented is the `authenticate()` method. Refer to the source code of existing Realm implementation (downloadable with the rest of the Tomcat code from http://www.apache.org).

❑ Configure the Realm directive, and set the className to the custom Realm class (called `OurCustomRealm` here):

```
<Realm
    className="org.apache.catalina.realm.OurCustomRealm"
    ...
/>
```

As before, any Realm configuration changes would require Tomcat to be restarted.

An alternative to writing a Realm implementation is to write a JAAS LoginModule for it. This is preferable, because it provides a standard configuration mechanism as a JAAS Realm.

Choosing a Realm Implementation

How do we choose between the different Realm implementations we discussed so far? Some of the factors that we should consider are listed in this section.

Performance

For all implementations other than Memory Realms and User Database, each authorization requires calls to external software, such as a database call in case of JDBC Realms, or a JNDI call for JNDI Realms. However, this validation check is performed the first time the user attempts to access a restricted resource, and the user and his or her roles are cached for the duration of the session. This lasts till session timeout/invalidation for FORM-based authentication and as long as the browser window is open for BASIC authentication.

Security

Memory Realms and User Database Realms store their passwords as clear-text (by default) or as an encrypted "digest" in an XML configuration file. This may not seem very secure, since the file system permissions may allow for this to be read. However, permissive database configurations are equally a security risk, as the database table that stores the username/password may allow for read access for everyone.

Add/Change Users, Roles Without Restarts

In case of Memory Realms, adding/removing or changing a user or role does not take effect until Tomcat is restarted – the configuration file that stores this information is read only at start-up time. In case of User Database, JDBC, JNDI and JAAS Realms, new users and roles can be assigned and existing ones removed or changed without requiring Tomcat to be restarted.

Managability

In case we use the User Database Realm (Tomcat 4.1 only) we have a web application (the admin application) that allows us to add/remove users and roles using a GUI. We do not have such an application for the other Realms.

Custom Management Applications

UserDatabase Realms expose a Java API that can be used to build custom applications for accessing as well as modifying the Realms data. In case of JDBC realms, the data is stored in a relational database; hence we can use SQL calls or the JDBC API to build a custom application for managing the Realm data. Similarly, we can use the JNDI or JAAS API to build custom management applications for the JNDI and JAAS Realms respectively.

Summary

In this chapter we covered Tomcat's Realms and how they provide security for web applications.

We got an overview of web application security – both Container-Managed Security (implemented by Tomcat Realms) and Programmatic Security. We then covered the different Realm implementations (Memory, JDBC, JNDI, and JAAS), specifically:

- ❑ Their configuration
- ❑ How to add and remove users and roles
- ❑ The pros and cons of each implementation and known problems

At the end of this chapter, we should be able to decide if we need to use Realms for protecting our applications, know how to configure and administer them, and also choose which Realm implementation to use.

Apache Tomcat Security

Handbook

5

Secure Sockets and Tomcat

The ability to securely transmit information over public and private networks has become critical to the long-term success of e-commerce. Not only do web site visitors expect their private information to be protected, they demand it. As a web site administrators and application developers we have the responsibility of doing everything we can to protect a visitor's privacy. This means that when a consumer gives us his or her credit card information, we must ensure that it is transmitted securely as it passes over not only the public Internet, but also through our own internal network.

Recently, the debate on what is considered personal privacy has been expanded to include financial information, health records, and travel itineraries, among other things. This chapter proposes one method of protecting this information. However, an environment's security is only as good as the weakest link in the chain.

The **Secure Socket Layer (SSL)** protocol provides us with a technical means of encrypting data as it passes over a network. Through the use of certificate-based identification and strong encryption algorithms we can ensure that the data is transmitted securely between two known parties. Therefore, encryption and authentication are mentioned in the same breath when referring to SSL. When correctly implemented with a strong algorithm, SSL provides us with a reasonable degree of confidence that the data has not be intercepted, read, or modified in any way while in transit.

This chapter starts with a background discussion of PKI and an overview of SSL and then describes in detail how we can configure our Tomcat server to fully utilize SSL. We will then take a look at how to configure the Apache web server to act as an SSL front-end to Tomcat. This will provide us with the ability to protect the parties involved in data transactions with our web site. The chapter concludes with a discussion of how to encrypt communication between an Apache and Tomcat server using an SSH tunnel.

PKI

To provide a little background, we will begin by taking a look at what constitutes a **Public-Key Infrastructure (PKI)** and what it is comprised of. If you are familiar with the concepts of PKI and SSL you may skip this section and the next. These sections are only meant to provide some background for better understanding the Tomcat configurations.

What is PKI?

A **Public Key Infrastructure (PKI)** is comprised of encryption technologies, services, and software that an organization employs to protect its data transactions and other business interactions from being compromised. The key components of any PKI are the *encryption methodologies* used and *identity management* using digital certificates. Let's take a closer look at what these terms mean.

Encryption

Encryption refers to the process of taking clear, readable information and transforming it to a state that is unintelligible. Encryption algorithms are mathematical functions that perform the transformation, and are referred to as **cryptographic algorithms**, or **ciphers**. Most encryption algorithms provide a mechanism for decryption as well. Decryption is the process of transforming the unintelligible information back into readable, usable information.

More recent cryptographic algorithms rely on the use of a **key** to encrypt the data. A key is a large number used in the algorithm to produce the encrypted result. As a general rule, the larger the number, the key's length, the stronger the encryption as long as the algorithm itself is good. Key lengths are measured in the number of bits required to form that number. A 128-bit key is significantly stronger than a 40-bit key.

There are mainly two types of keys: **symmetric** and **asymmetric**. Let's look at the difference between the two.

Symmetric

Symmetric-key encryption refers to an algorithm where the same key is used for encryption and decryption. This encryption process is shown in the following diagram:

Figure 1

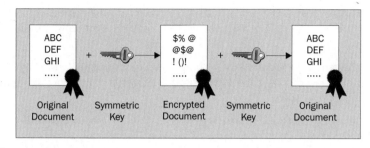

Most symmetric algorithms will utilize the same key for encryption and decryption. In this scenario, both parties in the conversation will know the secret key. This is referred to as a **shared secret**.

As long as the key is kept a secret by the two parties this form of encryption can be fairly effective. However, if the key is comprised and obtained by a third party, that party will be able to decrypt any information encrypted with the key.

Asymmetric

Public-key encryption, also known as **asymmetric encryption**, uses two keys, a **public-key** and a **private-key** to identify a particular entity that wishes to sign or encrypt data. Each entity in this scenario is associated with two keys where one key is made public, or published, known as the *public key* and the other key is kept secret, called the *private key*. As discussed in the next section, public keys can be published through the use of digital certificates. Information that is encrypted using a particular entity's public key can only be decrypted using the secret, private key associated with that entity. This ensures that only the entity for which the information was intended can view the information. The following diagram demonstrates how public-key encryption works:

Figure 2

Digital Certificates

Digital certificates provide the means by which the client and server present their identities and authenticate themselves. They are a very important part of any PKI.

Certificates are primarily comprised of the following items:

- ❑ **The subject** – The name of the entity to which the certificate has been issued. In the case of web servers, this would be the fully qualified domain name of the server (e.g. www.wrox.com).

- ❑ **The subject's public key** – The public-key of the entity identifying itself with the certificate. This key is used during public-key encryption as described earlier.

- ❑ **Issuing certificate authority** – The entity that issued the certificate. This is sometimes a chain of issuing authorities. We will talk about certificate authorities in the next section.

- ❑ **Validity timestamps** – The *issue date* and *expiration date* of the certificate, which establish the validity period of the certificate. The certificate authority typically sets the expiration date.

Because your digital certificate is considered to provide proof of you or your web site's identity, it is critical that it is protected from being obtained by external entities that could misuse the certificate. The most important aspect of this protection is that the private-key matching the public-key contained in the certificate must be adequately secured. If someone were to obtain your private-key he would be able to present himself as you or your organization, and would also be able to decrypt and view any information intended for you.

Certificate Authorities

A **Certificate Authority**, or **CA**, is an entity that issues certificates. A certificate authority can be anything from an individual, in the case of self-signed certificates, to a large, well-known, and globally recognized organization. When a **Certificate Signing Request** is submitted to the CA, the CA will verify the identity of the requestor and issue the certificate. If the identity of the requestor cannot be verified, the CA will reject the request. Therefore, if the certificate has passed the verification process and the CA has issued (or **signed**) the certificate, the CA at the least gives some guarantee that the entity presenting the certificate is who it says it is. We will see how to generate a certificate signing request later in the chapter.

Clients and servers that are configured to trust the issuing CA will accept the certificate as valid identification. For example, if a web server presents a certificate issued by a CA that the web browser is configured to trust, the browser will accept the identification and allow the SSL handshake to continue. However, if the browser does not trust the issuing CA, it will typically ask the user to decide whether or not to proceed. By default, many web browsers and other SSL clients come pre-configured to trust a set of known certificate authorities. If you have **self-signed** your certificate or have used a CA internal to your organization to issue the certificate, you must configure the browser or SSL client to trust the CA.

Examples of well-known and trusted certificate authorities are:

- ❑ Verisign (http://www.verisign.com/)

- ❑ Thawte (http://www.thawte.com/)

- ❑ Entrust (http://www.entrust.com/)

To view the list of trusted root certificate authorities in your Mozilla browser click on the Edit menu and select Preferences as shown below:

The Preference window appears. On this window under Privacy and Security in the tree select Certificates. In Certificates press the Manage Certificates... button as shown below:

In the Certificate Manager window, select the Authorities tab. Your window should look something like the following:

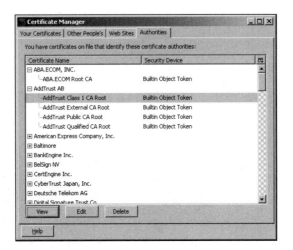

This list shows all of the certificate authorities that are considered trusted by your web browser. You can use the View button to see more details on each certificate. It should contain the fields that we discussed earlier.

Certificate Chains

Certificates that have been signed and issued by a CA can be looked at as a chain of certificates. The certificate that the CA used to sign your certificate becomes the first link in this chain. This first link is referred to as the **root certificate**. If the certificate used by the CA to sign your certificate was itself a root certificate (or its own), the certificate chain will be made up of only two certificates as shown below:

Figure 3

In this scenario, trusting the root CA certificate will be sufficient to trust the CA. However, in some cases yet another CA signs the issuing CA's root certificate. This certificate chain is shown below:

Figure 4

In this scenario, both the root CA certificate and the intermediate CA certificate must be trusted. We will look at trusting a CA and importing certificates later in the chapter.

Digital Signatures

Like hand-written signatures, digital signatures identify a document, piece of software, or transaction as having been issued, approved, or accepted by a particular person or entity. When a digital certificate is applied to a document or transaction, that document or transaction has been digitally signed. The certificate is used in place of a pen to sign the document. Because the certificate provides proof of your or your organization's identity, it is critical that it be protected.

SSL

In this section we will discuss the Secure Socket Layer (SSL) protocol. We will begin by looking at what SSL is and why it is needed. Then we will examine how it works.

What is SSL?

The term Secure Socket Layer is used to refer to the SSL protocol. SSL is a network protocol that can be used to encrypt data as it is passed between a client and server. SSL utilizes various components of *public-key encryption* to provide encryption as well as client and server *authentication*. Because encrypting data is a relatively costly process, SSL-enabling your web server can impact the site's *performance*, since every document has to be encrypted by the server and then decrypted by the browser. Later in the chapter, we will discuss ways to improve this performance.

SSL does not perform the same function as Unix sockets or WinSock. SSL establishes a layer of abstraction that sits on top of these lower-lever socket APIs. The latest version of the SSL protocol is 3.0. More information about the SSL specification can be found here: http://wp.netscape.com/eng/ssl3/3-SPEC.HTM.

Why is SSL Needed?

Most of the Internet's traffic is over public networks. It is possible that someone has been able to gain access to the network that your information is passing over. SSL prevents that person from being able to read the information that you are transmitting by using strong algorithms to encrypt the data.

SSL also provides the ability for a client and server to authenticate each other. When a user connects to an SSL-enabled web server using a browser, the server presents its identification to the browser. The browser inspects the identification and ensures that the server is who it claims to be. This layer relieves web application developers from coding encryption, decryption, and authentication processes into their applications.

How it Works

The public Internet and most private networks utilize the Transmission Control Protocol/Internet Protocol (TCP/IP) as the basis for communication. Application layer protocols such as HTTP, SMTP, and LDAP run on top of TCP/IP. The SSL protocol utilizes TCP/IP on behalf of these higher-level protocols by running between the two network layers.

The following diagram of the standard 7-layer OSI protocol stack offers a pictorial representation of where the SSL protocol lies.

Figure 5

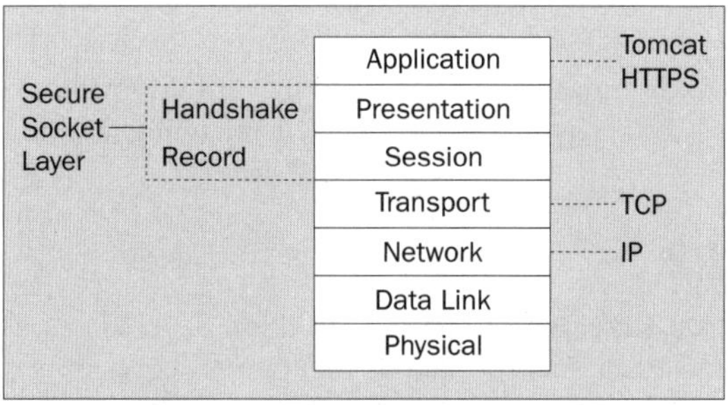

The lowest levels of the OSI protocol stack shown above are responsible for managing the physical aspects of passing data along a network circuit. The Network and Transport layers handle routing and flow control as well as breaking the transmission into multiple pieces and ensuring their error-free delivery. Many protocols, including SSL, perform connection management and message partitioning in the Session layer. The Presentation layer is typically used for translation, encryption, and compression. The Application layer's responsibilities vary depending on the particular protocol.

The SSL protocol is broken down into two key sub-protocols: a **record protocol** and a **handshake protocol**. The **SSL record protocol** is layered directly on top of the Transport layer, as shown in the diagram above, and defines how the transmitted data should be organized. The SSL record protocol encapsulates the higher-level protocols within SSL. The **SSL handshake protocol** defines how the SSL conversation should begin when a connection is established. The handshake protocol is a series of initial messages that establish the identities of the two parties and set up the encryption. The handshake accomplishes the following objectives:

- ❏ **Server authentication** – Using public-key based cryptography, the server presents its *Digital Certificate* to the client. The client inspects the server's certificate and verifies that it came from the expected server, was issued by a trusted certificate authority, and that the certificate has not expired.

- ❏ **Encryption algorithm chosen** – The client and server decide which encryption algorithm they will use for the conversation based on their mutual abilities.

- ❏ **Client authentication** – If the server is set up to require client authentication, it will ask the client for its certificate. The client will send its certificate to the server using techniques similar to those employed during server authentication. The server inspects the client's certificate and looks into a certificate data store such as a local file, system registry, or LDAP server to see if the client is authorized to access the server's resources. Client authentication is optional and is typically found in highly secure applications like banking and other financial web sites.

- ❏ **Shared secrets** – A *secret key* is exchanged between the client and server that only they know. This secret, symmetric key is used to encrypt and decrypt the messages between the two parties for that session.

- ❏ **Encrypted connection established** – Using the secret key and **Message Authentication Code (MAC)** techniques, a method for encrypting the entire conversation is established. The MAC is a piece of data that is computed from the secret key and some of the transmitted data. It is used to verify the identity of the entire message.

Now that we know what PKI and SSL are, let's see why Tomcat uses SSL.

Why Tomcat and SSL?

A typical insecure network transaction begins with the server starting up and listening for clients to establish connections. When a client initiates a connection with the server, the server will often times force the client to provide some means of authentication, usually by providing username and password credentials. If the authentication succeeds, the client will be allowed to issue requests and the server will respond to those requests. The key problems with this scenario are as follows:

❏ **No server authentication** – Even though the client had connected to a particular address and found that a server was listening, it never received any proof from the server that it was who the client believed it to be. A malicious server may have interceded between the client and the expected server and is now masquerading as that server.

❏ **No client authentication** – Just as the client received no authentication from the server, likewise, the server received no proof of identification from the client beyond a weak, one-time username and password mechanism. This form of authentication is not as robust due to the relatively limited number of possible password combinations and the use of weak passwords by your environment's users.

❏ **No data encryption** – Any data passed between the client and the server was sent as clear text, including the authentication credentials. Any program watching the connection between the two parties would have been able to listen in on the conversation and possibly view the contents. This describes another limitation of the use of usernames and passwords for authentication as described above.

❏ **Easy to repudiate** – In this environment, there is no method that guarantees that the user that digitally signed the transaction was the one in question. This makes it easy, from a legal point of view, for users to refute the claim that they purchased a particular product or executed a stock trade.

The SSL protocol provides mechanisms for overcoming these shortfalls. So how do we get Tomcat with SSL?

Tomcat provides an excellent standards-based platform onto which you can deploy your web application. Tomcat is packaged with, among other things, a stand-alone Hypertext Transfer Protocol (HTTP) server. This HTTP server can be configured as a **Secure Hypertext Transfer Protocol (HTTPS)** server, which is a secure HTTP server utilizing the SSL protocol. The Java Secure Sockets Extension (JSSE) is an API that can be used to securely transmit data between a client and server. JSSE can be used with any network application protocol like HTTP, Telnet, LDAP, and so on, over TCP/IP. It is designed for use as an addition to the standard networking components of the Java programming language. Because these networking components are at the foundation of Tomcat's HTTP server, JSSE can easily be employed to SSL-enable the server.

Configuring Tomcat and SSL

Now that you have an SSL foundation on which to build, we will take a look at how to configure Tomcat to encrypt its communication. There are several areas where SSL can work to encrypt communication between the Tomcat engine and other components of its architecture. We will discuss two such ways:

❑ When Tomcat is acting as a stand-alone web server, the web server can be configured to accept HTTPS connections from an SSL-enabled client, like a web browser. This scenario is shown in the following diagram:

Figure 6

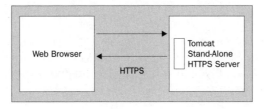

❑ If an Apache web server is handling communication with the web browser and then is using the **Apache JServ Protocol (AJP)** to forward requests to Tomcat, SSL can be utilized to encrypt the communication with the web browser and the Tomcat application server as shown in this diagram:

Figure 7

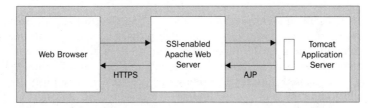

In the remainder of this chapter we will discuss how to configure Tomcat to utilize SSL in order to encrypt communication in both the scenarios discussed above.

JSSE Install

The first step to SSL-enabling your Tomcat installation is installing the **Java Secure Socket Extension (JSSE)** v1.0.2 or higher. JSSE has been integrated into the J2SE v1.4 JRE and SDK distributions. Therefore, if you are using J2SE v1.4 or higher, JSSE has already been installed for you. If you are using J2SE 1.2.x or 1.3.x, this section will cover how to install JSSE on your system. It is recommended that you do not use JSSE v1.0.2 because the HTTPS handler is not fully implemented and has some usability problems with certain versions of J2SE.

Download the latest version of JSSE from http://java.sun.com/products/jsse/index-103.html. The software is distributed in two forms: domestic and global. The domestic distribution is restricted to the United States and Canada. If you live outside of these two countries you must download the global distribution. You will be required to register in order to download this software.

JSSE is distributed in the form of a ZIP file. Unzip the file to a temporary location. The distribution will contain a docs, lib, and samples directory. The JSSE JAR files can be installed as extensions to the JDK/JRE on the system or as additions to the CLASSPATH for the application. To install the JARs as extensions, place the jcert.jar, jnet.jar, and jsse.jar into the following directory:

```
$JAVA_HOME/lib/ext/
```

For the remainder of this document, $JAVA_HOME will refer to the location of the JRE. For example, if you installed JRE 1.2.2 in /usr/local/, $JAVA_HOME would refer to /usr/local/jre1.2.2/. If you installed JDK 1.2.2 in /usr/local/, then $JAVA_HOME would refer to /usr/local/jdk1.2.2/jre/.

Installing the JSSE JARs in the $JAVA_HOME/lib/ext/ directory will allow any Java process using $JAVA_HOME to use JSSE. If you wish to limit the scope of availability to a single application, then consider bundling the JSSE JARs with the application and including them in the CLASSPATH for the application's runtime environment. This may be a necessity if your server is running in an environment where you have no control over the overall system configuration. This may also be useful for deploying your application onto systems where you are unsure of their configuration.

The next step to installing JSSE is to register the SunJSSE **Cryptographic Service Provider (CSP)**. A CSP is a piece of software that provides a software API the ability to encrypt information. The provider is registered within the runtime environment so that any software component that needs this service will be able to use it seamlessly. The JSSE CSP can be registered statically by editing the java.security properties file or by dynamically adding the provider at runtime. To register the CSP statically, edit the properties file at the following location:

```
$JAVA_HOME/lib/security/java.security
```

The property contained in the security properties file that is used for registering providers is security.provider.n where n is the order of priority used when loading more than one provider. The value for this property is the fully-qualified class name of the Java class containing the provider implementation. The name appears to be inverted because it follows the standard package naming mechanism used in Java whereby the degree of granularity increases from left to right.

Add the CSP bundled with the JSSE distribution by adding the following property to the java.security file:

```
security.provider.1=com.sun.net.ssl.internal.ssl.Provider
```

To register the CSP dynamically at runtime, add the following line of code to your program:

```
Security.addProvider (new com.sun.net.ssl.internal.ssl.Provider ());
```

This is useful when you do not have access to the `java.security` file or you are unsure of how the deployment environment will be configured. The `Security` class can be found in the `java.security` package.

The JSSE distribution comes packaged with a URL handler for the HTTPS protocol. This provider allows programs using the `java.net.URL` class to use the HTTPS protocol. The runtime environment searches a list of packages for handlers that can service a given protocol. To add the handler for the HTTPS protocol to the runtime environment, you should add the following property and value via the `java` command-line as shown here:

```
$ java -Djava.protocol.handler.pkgs=
                        com.sun.net.ssl.internal.www.protocol
```

The property can also be added to the runtime environment via the `java.lang.System` class as shown below:

```
System.setProperty ("java.protocol.handler.pkgs",
                        "com.sun.net.ssl.internal.www.protocol");
```

If the CSP and protocol handler package are registered dynamically at runtime you must take steps to ensure the registration is performed prior to any attempt to establish an SSL connection. For more information and support queries, go to Sun's support page at http://www.sun.com/developer/support/.

JDK keytool Utility

The Java environment and many of the JSSE components use a facility referred to as a **keystore** to hold keys and certificates. This keystore can be anywhere on your system but is usually maintained in a particular user's home directory or a directory accessible to all of the users on the system. As such, there can be one or many keystores present on the system.

The **keytool** utility allows you to create and manage a keystore for use within your Java environment. It also gives you the ability to create certificate requests that can be sent to a CA for verification and issuance. The keytool utility is distributed with the Java JRE and SDK. This section will cover several important functions that the keytool can perform for you. Many of the command line parameters and other functions of the keytool have remained unchanged between versions of the JDK.

Creating a New Keystore from Scratch

A new keystore is created whenever you use the options `-genkey`, `-import`, or `-identitydb` if the keystore does not exist already. For example, we can issue the following command to create a *self-signed* certificate, which is stored in the keystore:

On Unix:

```
$ $JAVA_HOME/bin/keytool -genkey -alias MySelf -keyalg RSA
```

On Windows:

```
%JAVA_HOME%\bin> keytool -genkey -alias MySelf -keyalg RSA
```

You will be prompted to enter a password for the new keystore unless you include the -storepass parameter. The keytool program echoes passwords back to the screen when entered, so care should be taken to avoid unwanted exposure while entering the password.

After entering the store password, you will be prompted for general information about the certificate, such as your name, your organization's name, and your geographic location. This information is put together to form the subject of the certificate. As discussed earlier, the subject is the identity of the entity presenting the certificate.

Once the subject information has been collected, the keytool will generate the public and private keys and create the certificate. Depending on the speed of your processor, this may take some time. Once this process is completed, the keytool will prompt you for a key password. Just as the keystore has a password, the key itself can also have a password. To use this key and certificate with Tomcat, you must use the same password. Enter the same password that you used for the keystore or press ENTER to automatically use this password. The execution of this command on a Windows platform is demonstrated here:

```
%JAVA_HOME%\bin>keytool -genkey -alias MySelf -keyalg RSA
Enter keystore password:  mykeypass
What is your first and last name?
  [Unknown]:  John Doe
What is the name of your organizational unit?
  [Unknown]:  Apache Tomcat Security
What is the name of your organization?
  [Unknown]:  Wrox Press Ltd.
What is the name of your City or Locality?
  [Unknown]:  Louisville
What is the name of your State or Province?
  [Unknown]:  Kentucky
What is the two-letter country code for this unit?
  [Unknown]:  US
Is CN=John Doe, OU=Apache Tomcat Security, O=Wrox Press Ltd.,
L=Louisville, ST=Kentucky, C=US correct?
  [no]:  yes

Enter key password for <MySelf>
        (RETURN if same as keystore password):  mykeypass
```

This command will create a keystore in the home directory of the user that executed the command. On Windows, this will be in the directory identified by the USERPROFILE environment variable. By default, the keystore's filename will be .keystore. Through the use of the –alias parameter, the keystore entry is given the alias MySelf. This allows you to refer to the entry using an alias. The ability to use different aliases for entries is useful when multiple servers are running in the same environment. The key algorithm is indicated by using the –keyalg parameter. In this case, the algorithm used to generate the key is RSA. More information on the RSA encryption algorithm can be found at http://www.rsasecurity.com/.

If you would like for the keystore file to be created somewhere other than the user's home directory, you can specify the keystore location using the –keystore parameter as shown below:

```
$ $JAVA_HOME/bin/keytool –genkey –alias MySelf –keyalg RSA –keystore
    $CATALINA_HOME/.keystore –storepass mykeypass
```

This command will create the keystore in the Tomcat installation directory with the filename .keystore. This assumes that the user executing the command has the necessary permissions to create files in and write to the installation directory. The –storepass parameter can be used to set the password for the keystore. In this case, the password will be set to mykeypass.

The Cacerts Keystore

A special keystore, **cacerts**, contains the list of certificate authorities trusted by the Java environment by default. This keystore is distributed with the JDK/JRE and resides in the following location:

```
$JAVA_HOME/lib/security/cacerts
```

To print a list of the trusted certificate authorities run the following command:

```
$ $JAVA_HOME/bin/keytool –list –keystore
    $JAVA_HOME/lib/security/cacerts
```

You will be prompted for the keystore password. By default, the keystore password is set to changeit. As the password implies, you should change it for all of your Java environment installations to protect the cacerts keystore from tampering. It is important to note that keystore passwords are *case-sensitive*. To change the password of your cacerts keystore run the following command:

```
$ $JAVA_HOME/bin/keytool –storepasswd –keystore
    $JAVA_HOME/lib/security/cacerts
```

This command will change the password for the cacerts keystore. You will be prompted for the current keystore password and will be required to enter the new password twice. This command can be used to change the password for any keystore.

Generating a Certificate Signing Request

You have now succeeded in creating a new keystore by generating a self-signed certificate. This certificate can be used with your SSL-enabled Tomcat server. However, since this certificate was self-signed, SSL clients (including most web browsers) will not trust this certificate, because a trusted certificate authority did not issue it. To obtain a certificate issued by a trusted CA, we must first generate a *Certificate Signing Request (CSR)* that can be submitted to the CA for issuance.

The self-signed certificate can be removed by deleting it from the keystore. This is done by using the –delete parameter as follows:

```
# $JAVA_HOME/bin/keytool -delete -alias MySelf -keystore
    $CATALINA_HOME/.keystore -storepass mykeypass
```

To generate the CSR, we first need to generate the key that will be used for the certificate. Use the following command to generate the key:

```
# $JAVA_HOME/bin/keytool -genkey -alias mysite -keystore
    $CATALINA_HOME/.keystore -storepass mykeypass
```

You will be prompted for the subject details for the certificate. Instead of responding with your first and last name as prompted, give the fully qualified domain name of your web site. Doing so will allow the web server to identify itself with the certificate. Many CAs require that you include at least the state and country in the subject identifier. Therefore, it is recommended that you answer these questions appropriately. The following example shows this command run for the web server named www.mysite.com owned by MySite, Inc. in Louisville, Kentucky:

```
# $JAVA_HOME/bin/keytool -genkey -alias mysite -keystore
        $CATALINA_HOME/.keystore -storepass mykeypass
What is your first and last name?
  [Unknown]:  www.mysite.com
What is the name of your organizational unit?
  [Unknown]:  IT
What is the name of your organization?
  [Unknown]:  MySite, Inc.
What is the name of your City or Locality?
  [Unknown]:  Louisville
What is the name of your State or Province?
  [Unknown]:  Kentucky
What is the two-letter country code for this unit?
  [Unknown]:  US
Is <CN=www.mysite.com, OU=IT, O="MySite, Inc.", L=Louisville,
ST=Kentucky, C=US> correct?
  [no]:  yes

Enter key password for <mysite>
        (RETURN if same as keystore password):  mykeypass
```

The certificate that is generated will be self-signed and can be used temporarily until you receive a certificate issued by a trusted CA. However, your users will receive browser security warnings when connecting to the server. You will replace this certificate with the CA signed certificate in a later step.

Now that the key has been generated, you can create a CSR that can be submitted to a trusted CA. The following command generates the CSR:

```
$ $JAVA_HOME/bin/keytool -certreq -alias mysite
    -keystore $CATALINA_HOME/.keystore -file
    /tmp/mysite.csr -storepass mykeypass
```

The CSR is placed in the /tmp/mysite.csr file. The contents of the file will be similar to what is shown here:

```
-----BEGIN NEW CERTIFICATE REQUEST-----
MIICdzCCAjQCAQAwcjELMAkGA1UEBhMCVVMxETAPBgNVBAgTCEt1bnR1Y2t5MRMwEQYDVQQHEwpM
b3Vpc3ZpbGxlMRUwEwYDVQQKEwxNeVNpdGUsIEluYy4xCzAJBgNVBAsTAklUMRcwFQYDVQQDEw53
d3cubX1zaXR1LmNvbTCCAbcwggEsBgcqhkjOOAQBMIIBHwKBgQD9f1OBHXUSKVLfSpwu7OTn9hG3
UjzvRADDHj+At1EmaUVdQCJR+1k9jVj6v8X1ujD2y5tVbNeBO4AdNG/yZmC3a51QpaSfn+gEexAi
wk+7qdf+t8Yb+DtX58aophUPBPuD9tPFHsMCNVQTWhaRMvZ1864rYdcq7/IiAxmd0UgBxwIVAJdg
UI8VIwvMspK5gqLrhAvwWBz1AoGBAPfhoIXWmz3ey7yrXDa4V7l51K+7+jrqgvlXTAs9B4JnUV1X
jrrUWU/mcQcQgYCOSRZxI+hMKBYTt88JMozIpuE8FnqLVHyNKOCjrh4rs6Z1kW6jfwv6ITVi8fti
egEkO8yk8b6oUZCJqIPf4VrlnwaSi2ZegHtVJWQBTDv+z0kqA4GEAAKBgFFVpKaIgj5UCk5Br1P8
N1m8ZJmdKRLG5Mm1tCip1Sypr6U4tM0ObeZO8O2ieP1GtGBI2qjO0dUtRBqVmSVvoWuPjBdW175s
oi4G0RL1THzB/GKgiOV0Je+3Ncs/p+cjTtGdPBNSZdeR7i/y0joX6tBuTGPKy443DWPEW/Pknzwv
oAAwCwYHKoZIzjgEAwUAAzAAMC0CFBg3gSPmaffN2RWY9LuUwcu4UWUAAhUAkEsypwiit6b6wYA5
+j6IqNZEAk8=
-----END NEW CERTIFICATE REQUEST-----
```

This file, in its entirety, comprises the certificate signing request and should be submitted to a trusted CA so that the issued certificate can be returned. The process for submitting a CSR varies depending on the CA. Most CAs will accept CSR submissions through their web site or via e-mail. Once you receive the certificate from the CA, it should be imported into the keystore. If you received a certificate from a CA that is not trusted by default, you will need to add the root CA certificate to the keystore.

Trusting a Certificate Authority

You can configure your system to trust the issuing CA by importing the root CA certificate into your keystore or into the cacerts keystore. If you import the root certificate into the cacerts keystore, then trust is added globally for any process using that JDK/JRE installation.

You can obtain the root CA certificate by contacting the CA. This is usually done by visiting the CA's website and requesting the root CA. If you are using a CA that was set up internally within your organization, contact the CA administrator to obtain the root certificate.

To import the root CA certificate into your keystore, use the following command:

```
$ $JAVA_HOME/bin/keytool -import -alias rootca
        -keystore $CATALINA_HOME/.keystore -file
        /tmp/cacert.cer -storepass mykeypass
```

This command assumes that you have saved the root CA certificate into the file `/tmp/cacert.cer`. The alias given to this root CA certificate will be `rootca`. You will need to change the alias as appropriate for your installation.

To import the root CA certificate into you cacerts keystore, use the following command:

```
$ $JAVA_HOME/bin/keytool -import -alias rootca
    -keystore /usr/local/tomcat/.keystore -file /tmp/cacert.cer
    -storepass mykeypass
```

This will assign trust to this root CA certificate for the entire system. Repeat these commands as necessary, using a different alias each time, to complete the certificate chain.

> **It is extremely important that you are certain that a CA should be trusted when you add it as a trusted CA in your environment. Trusting a malicious CA can lead to undesirable results including distribution of private information and data loss through program execution.**

Importing a Certificate into a Keystore

To import the certificate issued to you by the CA, all of the root and intermediate CA certificates must have been trusted either by default of by following the procedure discussed in the previous section.

Typically the CA will notify via e-mail when your certificate has been issued and will provide you with the information necessary for picking up the certificate. The certificate you receive from the CA will be a text file similar to the one shown earlier.

Save this file to your system. For this exercise, it is assumed that the certificate has been placed in a file named `/tmp/mysite.cer`.

To import the certificate into your keystore, thus replacing your self-signed certificate, use the following command:

```
$ $JAVA_HOME/bin/keytool -import -alias mysite
        -keystore $CATALINA_HOME/.keystore
        -storepass mykeypass -file /tmp/mysite.cer
```

You must use the same alias so that the self-signed certificate already existing in the keystore will be replaced. Once this certificate has been imported into your keystore, you are ready to proceed with configuring Tomcat to use SSL.

Configuring an HTTPS Connector

For Tomcat to run as a stand-alone SSL-enabled web server, you must configure a Tomcat connector that will handle the communication. You can configure the connector by manually editing the configuration file or by using the administration interface.

Editing the Tomcat Configuration File

HTTPS connectors can be added to your configuration by editing the $CATALINA_HOME/conf/server.xml file. Since this configuration file underwent many changes between Tomcat 3.2.x, 3.3.x and 4.x, this section will cover each version individually. To enable the HTTPS connector, uncomment and modify the following entries from the server.xml file as shown below:

For 3.2.x:

```
<Connector className="org.apache.tomcat.service.PoolTcpConnector">
  <Parameter name="handler"
     value="org.apache.tomcat.service.http.HttpConnectionHandler"/>
  <Parameter name="port" value="8443"/>
  <Parameter name="socketFactory"
     value="org.apache.tomcat.net.SSLSocketFactory" />
  <Parameter name="keystore"
     value="$CATALINA_HOME/.keystore"/>
  <Parameter name="keypass" value="mykeypass"/>
  <Parameter name="clientAuth" value="false"/>
</Connector>
```

For 3.3.x:

```
<Http10Connector port="8443" secure="true"
   keystore="$CATALINA_HOME/.keystore"
   keypass="mykeypass"
   clientAuth="false"/>
```

For 4.1:

```
<Connector className="org.apache.coyote.tomcat4.CoyoteConnector"
   port="8443" minProcessors="5" maxProcessors="75"
   enableLookups="true" acceptCount="10" debug="0" scheme="https"
   secure="true" useURIValidationHack="false">
   <Factory
      className="org.apache.coyote.tomcat4.CoyoteServerSocketFactory"
      clientAuth="false" protocol="TLS"
      keystoreFile="$CATALINA_HOME/.keystore"
      keystorePass="mykeypass"/>
</Connector>
```

In these examples, $CATALINA_HOME must be replaced with the path to your Tomcat installation directory.

> **Notice that this file contains the password for your keystore. Read permissions for this file should be limited to the appropriate set of users.**

Using the Administration Interface

Tomcat 4.x comes packaged with a browser-accessible administration interface. Among other things, it allows you to create a connector. As is the case with any administration interface, care must be taken to limit its use to authorized persons. You must also ensure that the file in which the password for the admin user account is contained has appropriate access permissions.

> **One caveat about using the administration GUI is that once you save your changes, the server.xml file will lose all of the comments and formatting present when the server is installed. You should consider keeping a copy of the original for future reference.**

To add a connector, follow these steps:

1. Log in to the administration application by pointing your browser to http://<YourServerName>/admin/. If you haven't configured your admin user, do so according to the documentation.

2. Click on Service (Tomcat-Standalone).

3. From the drop-down box in the right-hand frame choose Create New Connector.

4. In the Type box, choose HTTPS. This will add a couple of extra fields at the bottom of the page.

5. Fill out the page using the values similar to those used when editing the server.xml configuration file.

6. Click Save.

The following screen shot shows the Create New Connector form filled in:

The Type field indicates what type of connector you will be creating. In this case, you're creating an HTTPS connector. The Port Number field indicates what network port the server will listen on. The standard SSL port is 443. In this example, we will use 8443 in case you have another SSL server already running in your environment. The Keystore Filename and Keystore Password fields are used to indicate the location of the keystore and its password.

Installation Caveats

There are some issues that one faces after generating and installing a certificate. In this section we look at these caveats.

No Such Algorithm Exceptions

This usually indicates that the JRE is not able to locate the JSSE JAR files. For the JSSE JAR files to be found by the JRE, they must be either in the $JAVA_HOME/lib/ext directory or in the CLASSPATH for the JRE.

Keystore Files Not Found

By default, the keytool utility and Tomcat will look for the keystore in the home directory of the user running the JRE. If you have placed your keystore in a location other than the user's home directory you will have to be sure that the keystore has been indicated using the keystoreFile parameter.

Keystore Tampering and Incorrect Passwords

The keytool utility and Tomcat may log a message similar to `Keystore was tampered with, or password was incorrect`. This usually indicates a problem with the password specified in the parameter or when prompted. Check to make sure that you are correctly specifying the password via the keystore command-line argument – `storepass` or by adding the `keypass/keystorePass` attribute to the elements in `server.xml`. Remember that the keystore password is case-sensitive.

Known Issues

The following are a couple of known issues with respect to Tomcat's use of the keystore:

❑ **Keystore and alias passwords must be equal**
The keystore and the alias password must be the same for the Tomcat connector to use the certificate in the keystore.

❑ **Multiple certificates in the keystore**
There is currently no method for instructing Tomcat to use one certificate or another in the keystore. This is necessary while handling multiple sites in Tomcat, and you can create multiple keystores to get around this issue or use Apache as an SSL front-end as described earlier in this chapter.

SSL Web Resource Protection

The **Java 2, Platform Enterprise Edition (J2EE)** specification provides a mechanism for protecting the resources available within your web application. The protection is accomplished through the use of **security constraints** that are placed on **resource collections**. The resources within your web application can be described in terms of the URLs and the HTTP methods used to gain access to those resources. For example, you may want to protect access to any URL containing the pattern `/checkout/*`. The set of URLs matching this pattern is referred to as a resource collection. Security constraints can be placed on these resource collections to ensure that a certain level of security access has been obtained before the resource can be accessed.

There are several different types of security constraints that can be placed on your resource collections. A common security constraint used is that of *authentication*. Constraints can be placed on a resource to require authentication in one of the following forms: **Basic**, **Form-based**, and **Client-certificate**:

❑ **Basic** – The web server will attempt to authenticate the client using **HTTP Basic Authentication**. The browser will prompt the user for a username and password, which will then be compared against a security database. HTTP Basic Authentication uses realms of access and HTTP headers to manage the authentication state.

- ❑ **Form-based** – Login pages can be customized to request authentication credentials in the form of a username and password. Like HTTP Basic Authentication, this form of authentication is not particularly safe due to the fact that the username and password, though sometimes Base64 encoded, are essentially sent across the public Internet in plain text. A third party could intercept these usernames and passwords during transmission.

- ❑ **Client-certificate** – This form of authentication is more secure than the previous two methods. Client-certificate authentication is performed during the *SSL handshake* discussed earlier in this chapter. The web server will ask the client to send its certificate for authentication and then will search for the certificate in a database of trusted client-certificates. If the certificate is trusted, the authentication will succeed and access to the resource will be permitted.

Another commonly used security constraint is to require that the resource be accessed using HTTP over SSL (HTTPS). If a web browser attempts to access a resource collection that is protected in this way, it will be redirected to the SSL server. If you do not have an SSL-enabled web server configured you must configure one to use this constraint. This form of security constraint strengthens basic and form-based authentication, since the username and password will be encrypted via SSL when transmitting them across the public Internet. The sort of constraint is a *must* when your web site visitors are asked to provide private information like credit card numbers as part of the check-out process.

WidgetWorld

Let's look at an example web application called WidgetWorld that requires that its process for completing a purchase be done using SSL. At the WidgetWorld web site you can place and order from a selection of four different types of widgets and proceed to the checkout.

Looking at web.xml

The WidgetWorld online catalog has been developed in Java as a J2EE application. The WidgetWorld has been packaged as a WAR to allow for quick, convenient deployment to the application server. The web.xml file contained in the WEB-INF directory is shown here:

```
<?xml version="1.0" encoding="ISO-8859-1"?>

<!DOCTYPE web-app
    PUBLIC "-//Sun Microsystems, Inc.//DTD Web Application 2.3//EN"
    "http://java.sun.com/dtd/web-app_2_3.dtd">

<web-app>

    <display-name>Widget World</display-name>
    <description>Online Widget Ordering System</description>
```

```
<security-constraint>
  <display-name>Widget World Check Out</display-name>
  <web-resource-collection>
     <web-resource-name>Protected Area</web-resource-name>
     <url-pattern>/jsp/checkout/*</url-pattern>
  </web-resource-collection>
  <user-data-constraint>
     <transport-guarantee>CONFIDENTIAL</transport-guarantee>
  </user-data-constraint>
</security-constraint>
</web-app>
```

A security constraint has been placed on any resource that matches the pattern
/jsp/checkout/. The <transport-guarantee> element contains the word
CONFIDENTIAL. This means that any access to that resource must be encrypted. If the
server receives a request for the resource through HTTP, it must be configured to
redirect to an HTTPS server so that the data transfer will be encrypted.

Looking at server.xml

WidgetWorld has selected Tomcat as its J2EE application server and uses the stand-
alone web server bundled with Tomcat for communication with web browsers. The
server.xml has the following entry for the stand-alone HTTP connector:

```
<Connector className="org.apache.coyote.tomcat4.CoyoteConnector"
    port="8080" minProcessors="5" maxProcessors="75"
    enableLookups="true" redirectPort="8443"
    acceptCount="10" debug="0" connectionTimeout="20000"
    useURIValidationHack="false" />
```

If the connector receives a request for a resource that has a data encryption security
constraint placed on it, the connector will redirect the request to port 8443. In order for
this to be successful, you must have configured an HTTPS connector running on this
port as discussed earlier in the chapter.

The welcome page for WidgetWorld is shown here:

Clicking on the See Our Catalog link will submit a request for the resource /jsp/catalog.jsp. Since the resource is not protected access will be allowed:

When the user clicks the Checkout button, the form is submitted to the /jsp/checkout/index.jsp. This URL matches the /jsp/checkout/* resource pattern defined in the web.xml file. The server will redirect the browser to the port defined in the server.xml file. As you can see from the following screenshot, the address protocol and port have changed to HTTPS and 8443, respectively.

When the user has completed reviewing the order, he/she can click on the Complete Check Out button. This button takes the user to a Thank You page:

167

Once the user has been redirected to the HTTPS server, it is a good idea to have the user access that server for the remainder of the visit to your web page. Directing the browser from a non-secure to a secure and back to a non-secure resource can sometimes confuse users and cause them to become alarmed due to browser security messages. In addition to that, information added to the session while in the secure environment can become compromised if the browser is returned to the non-secure environment.

SSL and Apache

An excellent alternative to using the stand-alone web server packaged with Tomcat is to use Apache in conjunction with the **mod_ssl** module or **Apache-SSL**. These add-ons to Apache provide strong encryption for the web server. Commercial versions of Apache like **StrongHold** (http://www.redhat.com/software/stronghold/) also provide this functionality. In this scenario, as discussed earlier, the Apache web sever handles the SSL communication with the web browser on behalf of the Tomcat application server. The web server, leaving the job of executing the dynamic Java code to the Tomcat server, can serve requests for static files like HTML and images. Another advantage of using an SSL-enabled Apache server is that it leaves the Tomcat server to handle dynamic content without increasing the load due to encryption. Network devices called **SSL accelerators** can also provide this service.

When the Apache server receives a request for a context that will be serviced by Tomcat, it forwards the request to the application server via the AJP connector. This architecture allows for separation of the application tiers, making the overall application more secure and scalable. For example, in many installations you'll find that the web server is separated from the application server by a firewall. This is shown in the diagram below:

Figure 8

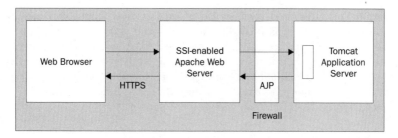

In many architecture implementations you will find two or more web servers as front-ends for one or more Tomcat instances as shown here:

Figure 9

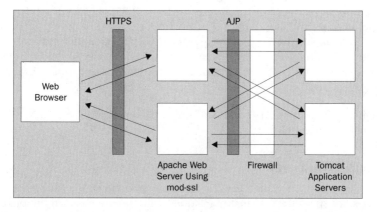

In the configuration shown in this diagram, a DNS round-robin can be set up to send some clients to one server or another. In this way the load can be balanced between the two servers. A more sophisticated setup could employ network load-balancers or content server switches to provide this same functionality and more redundancy.

Using Apache as a front-end to Tomcat provides a secure, scalable environment giving us the ability to add more web servers or Tomcat servers as our web site's usage grows.

There are two suitable alternatives for SSL-enabling your Apache server: **Apache-SSL** (http://www.apache-ssl.org/) and **mod_ssl** (http://www.modssl.org/). Both of these implementations provide strong encryption to the Apache web server. The mod_ssl code was originally derived from the Apache-SSL and has been considerably re-engineered since the split. The Apache-SSL code focuses on performance and overall security while mod_ssl provides more features. The mod_ssl module abstracts SSL functionality into a separate module, making it easy to upgrade independently of Apache. The next section will cover how to SSL-enable your Apache web server using mod_ssl.

Installing mod_ssl

The first step to installing mod_ssl is to download the latest OpenSSL release from http://www.openssl.org/. OpenSSL provides the underlying encryption mechanism used by mod_ssl. For the purposes of installing mod_ssl, it is a good idea to download and unpack all of the components in a common directory like /usr/local/tmp or C:\temp\. Leave each installation component in its own subdirectory. Once you've downloaded the distribution, unpack the distribution and follow the installation instructions to configure, build, test, and install OpenSSL.

Obtaining the Source Code

The next step is to obtain the mod_ssl source files so that they can be compiled. If you are using Apache 2.x you will not need to download the mod_ssl source files, because they are included in the distribution. The latest mod_ssl distribution can be downloaded from http://www.modssl.org/. To install mod_ssl you will patch the source code for Apache 1.3.x; therefore, you must download the version of mod_ssl with the appropriate second version identifier. For example mod_ssl-2.8.12-1.3.27 will be for only Apache version 1.3.27, as the second version identifier indicates. Unpack the distribution into the same base directory in which you placed the OpenSSL source distribution. This will make the task of configuring the various components more straightforward.

If you are going to be using Apache 1.3.x, download and unpack the latest source code from http://www.apache.org/.

Configuring mod_ssl

If you are using Apache 2.x, then there is no need to configure the mod_ssl distribution, since the source is already included with the Apache distribution, and you can move on to the next section. If you are using Apache 1.3.x, this section will help you to configure the mod_ssl distribution.
To configure mod_ssl you will need to have downloaded and unpacked the packages described above. If you used a common directory to unpack your files, the contents of the directory should look something like this:

```
apache_1.3.x
mod_ssl-2.8.x-1.3.x
openssl-0.9.x
```

The next step is to configure mod_ssl. Change the directory to mod_ssl-2.8.x-1.3.x and run the following command:

```
$ ./configure --with-apache=../apache_1.3.x
```

This will apply the necessary patch files to the Apache *source tree*. Essentially, this means copying the files that make up the source code portion of the mod_ssl distribution to the Apache directory indicated in the `--with-apache` parameter. Now that you've patched the Apache distribution, you are ready to move on to compile Apache.

Compiling Apache

Change the directory to the Apache distribution directory, `apache_1.3.x`. Configure Apache by executing the following:

```
$ SSL_BASE=../openssl-0.9.x ./configure --enable-module=ssl
```

This command sets the `SSL_BASE` environment variable to `../openssl-0.9.x` so that the `configure` script knows where the OpenSSL distribution can be found. The configure script then proceeds with configuring the Apache source tree and enabling the mod_ssl patch.

The next step is to compile the Apache source tree. Run the `make` command in the Apache distribution directory. Once the `make` process has completed compiling the Apache source tree and the mod_ssl module, the next step is to create a certificate to be used for testing the installation. To make a test certificate, run the following command:

```
$ make certificate TYPE=test
```

The process of creating a certificate is broken down into several steps:

1. First, choose the **signature algorithm**. Choose the default, RSA. RSA is supported by versions 2.0 and 3.0 of the SSL protocol. After choosing the signature algorithm the RSA private key is generated.

2. Next, you will be asked to enter information about the subject of the certificate, also referred to as the certificate's **Distinguished Name**. This process is similar to generating a certificate using the `keytool` utility discussed earlier. Enter the appropriate information for the requested components. When asked for the **Common Name**, be sure that you enter the fully-qualified domain name of the host on which you'll be running this web server.

3. The certificate generation tool will now ask you to specify the certificate **version**. Choose the default, 3.

4. The certificate will now be generated and signed with a CA certificate included with the distribution for testing purposes. Once the certificate generation is completed, you will be asked if you would like to **encrypt the private key** for the certificate. To maintain the appropriate level of security over your SSL environment you must answer *Yes* to this question.

5. Once you answer *Yes*, you will be asked to a enter **passphrase** (which is a very long password) for this server's private key. Use a strong passphrase that will be difficult to guess but easy for you to remember. Once you have entered the passphrase you have completed creating the test certificate.

The following files have been created as part of this process and will be installed with Apache when you run the `install` program. A description of the files is as follows:

❏ `conf/ssl.key/server.key` – The file which contains the server's private key.

❏ `conf/ssl.key/server.crt` – The certificate for the server.

❏ `conf/ssl.key/server.csr` – A CSR that you can use to send to a recognized CA for issuance as discussed earlier.

> **For the certificate files mentioned above, make sure that permissions on the $APACHE_HOME/conf directory are set so that they don't compromise the security of the certificate.**

To complete the installation of your new SSL-aware Apache server, run the `make install` command in the root of the Apache source tree. The `install` program will now copy all of the files to the appropriate places on your system. When the `install` command is finished, you're ready to start the server. Change the directory to the `<Apache Prefix>/bin/` directory and run the following command:

```
$ ./apachectl startssl
```

Before the server starts up, you will be required to enter the private key passphrase. Enter the passphrase you specified when generating the certificate. Your server will start up and begin accepting SSL requests on port 443, the default HTTPS port. To test your installation, direct your browser to https://<YourServerName/. Modifying the following definition in the `httpd.conf` file can change the port number:

```
<IfDefine SSL>
Listen 80
Listen 443
</IfDefine>
```

This definition tells the web server to listen on port 443 while running in SSL mode. Change the definition for 443 to the port number on which you wish to run the server. You will also need to modify the `VirtualHost` directive to use a different port. By default, the SSL virtual host is defined as follows:

```
<VirtualHost _default_:443>

...
</VirtualHost>
```

This VirtualHost directive defines the configuration parameters for the SSL server. Change 443 to reflect the same port number that you used above.

SSL and AJP

Now that we have learned how to install an SSL-aware version of the Apache web server, we will take a look at how to connect this web server to the Tomcat application server using **mod_jk**. Then we will look at encrypting that communication using an *SSH tunnel.*

Overview Of AJP

The Apache JServ Protocol (AJP) defines a method for allowing web servers such as Apache to communicate with a Java servlet container like Tomcat. The protocol uses a binary format and compression routines to improve performance. The most recent versions of the protocol will maintain persistent connections to the servlet container in order to reduce connection overheads by reusing already established connections. Once a connection has been assigned to a particular request, it will be used exclusively for that request until a response is returned.

Earlier versions of AJP had a limited ability to send SSL-related information to the servlet container as required by the servlet specification and specifically related to the section on protecting web resources. Beginning with AJP version 1.3, SSL information – including connection information and client certificates – is now being sent to the servlet container.

Overview of mod_jk

Mod_jk is an implementation of the AJP protocol for use with Apache and Tomcat. It handles communication between the Apache web server and the Tomcat application server. While mod_jk is primarily used with Apache, it can also be used with other web servers, including iPlanet and IIS.

Installing mod_jk

Mod_jk is distributed in two forms: binary and source. If binaries are available for your architecture, it is recommended that you use them. If you need to build mod_jk from the source, refer to the installation instructions included with the source distribution.

The mod_jk source and binary distributions are available from
http://jakarta.apache.org/builds/jakarta-tomcat-connectors/jk/. Download the latest version
from the release/<version>/bin/<architecture>/ directory. The primary file to
download is the mod_jk.x file. Depending on your operating system, the file
extension will be .so, .dll, .nlm, and so on. The filename also contains the version
of Apache that you will be using. To use mod_jk with an SSL-enabled Apache server,
download a file with -eapi in the file name. Once you have downloaded the module
file, rename the file mod_jk.so and place it in the $APACHE_HOME/libexec/
directory where $APACHE_HOME is the location in which you installed Apache.

Load the mod_jk module by adding the following line to your httpd.conf:

```
LoadModule jk_module              libexec/mod_jk.so
```

Then include the following IfModule directive:

```
<IfModule mod_jk.c>
        JkWorkersFile    /usr/local/apache/conf/workers.properties
        JkLogFile        /usr/local/apache/logs/mod_jk.log
        JkMount /WidgetWorld/* WidgetWorld
</IfModule>
```

These directives tell the mod_jk module where to load the workers properties from,
where the log file should be placed, and which URL Tomcat should service. In this
example, any request to http://<YourServerName>/WidgetWorld/ will be passed on to the
Tomcat Servlet engine for processing. The following is an example of the
workers.properties file with the configuration details for the
WidgetWorld worker:

```
worker.list=WidgetWorld

worker.WidgetWorld.port=8009
worker.WidgetWorld.host=localhost
worker.WidgetWorld.type=ajp13
worker.WidgetWorld.lbfactor=1.0
```

This worker is configured to connect to localhost port 8009 using the ajp1.3
protocol. If your installation were using a different host or port, you should change
these values appropriately.

With this configuration in place, the web server can begin working as a front-end to
the Tomcat application server. While the data passing between the web server and
the application server will be somewhat obfuscated by the AJP protocol, the data is
still being sent without any encryption. For some installations this is unacceptable,
due to the sensitivity of the data. The following section discusses a method for
encrypting this communication.

SSH Tunneling

Secure Shell (SSH) is a suite of network tools that provides strong encryption to many types of traditional network protocols. For example, ssh is a secure version of RSH and SCP is a secure version of RCP. The advantage of using SSH is that all of the network communication, including usernames and passwords, are encrypted when transmitted. This is also referred to as tunneling.

One feature of SSH is the ability to forward ports over a secure connection. *Port forwarding* is the process of accepting a connection on one port and passing the data on to another server. This ability can be used in your architecture to securely transmit the data between the web server and the Tomcat application server. SSH can be used to forward many application protocols like Telnet, FTP, SMTP, and so on.

Consider the following architecture diagram:

Figure 10

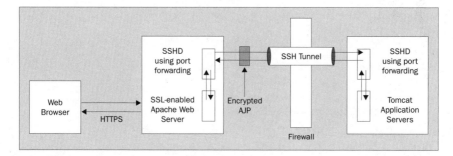

This diagram shows how SSH port forwarding can be used to encrypt the AJP data while passing through the firewall. The remainder of this section will cover how to configure SSH to provide this ability.

OpenSSH (http://www.openssh.org/) is a free version of the SSH tools. Download the latest SSH distribution from OpenSSH and install it according to the installation instructions.

For this example we will refer to the web server (to the left of the firewall) as server A and the Tomcat application server (to the right of the firewall) as server B. The AJP connector on server B has been configured to accept connections on port 8009. A user has been set up on server B named tomcat. This user will be used to establish the connection with server B.

Establishing the Tunnel

The tunnel is established by having a user on server A initiate an SSH connection to server B with a few special parameters. From server A, run the following command:

On Unix:

```
someuser@serverA$ ssh -l tomcat serverb -L 10203:serverb:8009
```

On Windows:

```
C:\> ssh -l tomcat serverb -L 10203:serverb:8009
```

This command tells SSH to connect to server B as the user tomcat. The user will be forced to authenticate to server B like normal. Once the connection has been established, the -L parameter tells SSH to establish a tunnel from port 10203 on the local host (server A) to port 8009 on server B. In other words, server A will begin listening for connections on port 10203. When it receives a connection, it will forward that connection through this SSH session to the SSH daemon running on server B. The SSH daemon on server B will then establish a connection to port 8009 on the localhost. A good way to see if the tunnel has been established is to run netstat on server A as shown below:

On Unix:

```
someuser@serverA$ netstat -l | grep 10203
```

On Windows:

```
C:\> netstat -na -p TCP
```

This netstat command should show that the server is listening for connections on port 10203 as shown in the screen output:

On Unix:

```
tcp        0        0 servera:10203              *:*                    LISTEN
```

On Windows:

```
TCP    0.0.0.0:10203            0.0.0.0:0              LISTENING
```

Configuring mod_jk

Now that the tunnel has been established the last step is to configure mod_jk to use the tunnel instead of connecting directly to server B. This change is made in the workers.properties file, which is shown below:

```
worker.WidgetWorld.host=serverb
worker.WidgetWorld.port=8009
```

Change this file to the following:

```
worker.WidgetWorld.host=localhost
worker.WidgetWorld.port=10203
```

Now restart the web server. The next time you access the WidgetWorld application, the request will be sent through the SSH tunnel to server B.

Caveats

The SSH session from server A to B is critical to this infrastructure. If the session is closed, access to the application server will be denied until the session is re-established. A good way to monitor this process is by using the `netstat` command as shown above. If the listening port is not found, the process should be restarted. A monitoring script could be used that does the same.

There will be at least some *performance degradation* since encryption will be taking place between the two servers. However, the need for encrypting this communication typically outweighs the loss in performance.

Ongoing SSL Management

One aspect of your SSL environment that is often overlooked is a plan for ongoing maintenance and management. You should develop a plan now to avoid problems in the future. As is often true in the realm of Internet security, *an ounce of prevention is worth a pound of cure.*

An important part of your plan will be to ensure that your software is kept up to date. Occasionally SSL-related bugs/exploits will be found and need immediate attention to prevent your web site from being compromised. Regardless of what web server you will be using, it is a good idea to subscribe to your web server vendor's notification mailing lists so that you'll be notified when issues like this arise.

It is critical that your method for storing keys and certificates, in this case your keystore, is protected from being stolen, tampered with, or accidentally corrupted. This means ensuring proper file system permissions and keeping a backup somewhere safe in the event of a corruption or hardware failure. All of your private key and certificate storage facilities should be protected with a passphrase. Make sure you can remember your passphrases or keep them in a safe location. Many SSL-enabled web servers require that you enter the keystore passphrase when starting the server. Losing your digital certificate will cause at least several hours of down time, which translates to lost revenue.

Since certificates are usually issued for one or two year validity periods, the day will come when your certificate expires. Choose a certificate authority that will notify you via e-mail when your certificate is getting ready to expire. If you have many web servers each with its own certificate, consider developing a certificate validity monitoring and alerting process.

177

Summary

In this chapter we looked at SSL-enabling your Tomcat application server. We began with an overview of PKI and SSL. We learned about the makeup of digital certificates and how they can be used to provide a means of confirming a server's of some user's identity. We examined how certificate authorities issue certificates and essentially vouch for the entity presenting the certificate. We also talked about how SSL works, and what takes place when an SSL client connects to an SSL server.

Next we began exploring how SSL can be enabled in a Java environment through the use of JSSE. We looked at how the keytool utility can be used with a keystore to generate self-signed certificates and to request a certificate from a certificate authority.

With this foundation to build on we learned how to configure a stand-alone HTTPS web server using a Tomcat connector. Enabling this connector can be accomplished by editing the Tomcat configuration file for Tomcat 3.2, 3.3 and 4.x. Tomcat 4.x provides an administration interface for enabling these connectors, among other things. We then looked at some installation caveats for SSL-enabling Tomcat.

We then covered how the J2EE specification provides for a means of placing security constraints on certain portions of your application, thereby providing added security to these resources. We looked at an example application, WidgetWorld, and learned how it requires SSL communication when completing the checkout process.

Next, we learned about how the Apache web server can be used as an SSL front-end to Tomcat and the advantages this can have for performance, security, and maintenance. The Apache mod_ssl module provides an excellent source of strong encryption for an Apache server. This scenario allows Apache to handle communication with the web browser and forwards the necessary requests to the Tomcat application server via AJP. We looked at how the AJP communication with the Tomcat application server can be encrypted by using the tunneling feature of SSH.

Finally we discussed ongoing management of your SSL environment and ways to ensure that your SSL-enabled web server remains available in the future.

References:

- ❏ PKI:
  http://developer.netscape.com/docs/manuals/security/pkin/index.html

- ❏ Introduction to SSL:
  http://developer.netscape.com/docs/manuals/security/sslin/contents.htm
  http://wp.netscape.com/eng/security/SSL_2.html
  http://wp.netscape.com/eng/ssl3/3-SPEC.HTM

- ❏ OSI Protocol Stack:
  http://ei.cs.vt.edu/~wwwbtb/fall.96/ClassNotes/Protocols/basics.html
  http://www.interoute.com/pda/osichart.html

Apache Tomcat Security

Handbook

6

Application Security

Security is the topic that receives the most emphasis in the computing and technology industry. As the need for application and systems interoperability increases, the number of potential entry points for an attacker increases as well. Some application developers consider security a server or a network issue, something that only concerns systems and network administrators. Still others feel that a simple username and password scheme coupled with SSL (Secure Sockets Layer) encryption is sufficient security for their application. Many systems rely on securing the server or using a firewall for primary security duties, while neglecting other parts of the system such as databases and the applications themselves. The security of a given system is only as strong as its weakest link, and in today's heterogeneous environment, *application security* is just as important as proper server configuration or using a firewall.

What is Application Security?

Web applications have unique characteristics that deserve attention when considering security. Chief among them is the concept of **state**. A web application, by its very nature, does not maintain state amongst the clients that access it. A web server has no guarantee that the request coming in is from an approved client unless the system is designed to support authentication, roles, and to track activity across requests using *sessions*. Even then, there are many possible options for an attacker. For example, a typical attack against a web application is to repeatedly send various packets of data to a web server as if the packets were originating from approved clients and analyze the response. A spoof or masquerade scenario might involve an approved client that instead switches to unapproved behavior, or attack mode, once the first level of security has been passed. From a server perspective, the client is an approved client, even though its actions once approved are unacceptable from an application point of view.

Another technique for securing your application is minimizing the data sent to and managed by the client. A poorly designed application will use hidden form fields or cookies to hold sensitive data, such as key values, usernames, control flags, and even passwords. A well-designed application will minimize the data contained in an HTML form or cookie sent to the client. By keeping more data on the server, less data is visible to and available for analysis by an attacker. For example, storing variable values as session-scope variables on the server, instead of using hidden form fields or URL parameters, will keep an attacker from seeing anything but a session key and normally visible form field values. A well-implemented application will keep specific details such as version numbers and other information hidden from users.

In general, application security means:

❑ Programs are not intrusive – they don't interrogate private information on a user's computer.

❑ Users are authenticated – wherever possible, take steps to determine who is using your application and limit them to the minimum permissions they need to accomplish their task.

❑ Data is encrypted – wherever possible, use only encrypted links to transmit information.

❑ Information is validated – information received by an application is validated and verified as much as possible.

❑ Programs behave correctly – application problems such as exceptions and overflows are caught and handled and do not cause problems for users or other applications in the same environment.

In this chapter, a variety of application security techniques will be discussed that deal with web application security issues and how they can be addressed in the design of your web application:

❑ Form and protocol validation

❑ Cookies and session IDs

❑ Structured Query Language (SQL) and database access security

❑ Java package security

All of the techniques fall squarely to the developer to implement as desired. They serve to enhance any security efforts by a system or network administrator, and can provide an extra layer of protection in most scenarios.

Validation

Probably the most obvious place for an attacker to attempt an exploit is within HTML forms, which have a number of vulnerabilities. Since a web server must generate HTML as a response to a browser's request, viewing that source HTML is a trivial exercise. One thing of interest in the source of an HTML form is the form's action handler. This provides an attacker with a glimpse of the internal application structure, and the action handler values can be used externally in an exploit script as the target of repeated requests. At the very least, this presents a possible denial of service (DoS) attack opportunity. At the worst, repeated requests can cause buffer overflows, race conditions, and response synchronization problems that bring the server down.

Other items of interest to an attacker in an HTML form are the form values. A typical application design that pays little attention to security uses form values as direct inputs to system commands, SQL queries and commands, and file system directives without any direct validation. This type of application design is made to order for an attacker, because the attacker can easily craft an HTML POST request to a web server using any values they wish, hoping that the web server will accept them and behave incorrectly. Such type of attacks are generally labeled as **Injection Attacks**, SQL Injection Attack being one of them.

Let's take a closer look at how these form values are used by attackers. In the following sub-sections we look at three validation areas:

- ❑ Regular expressions
- ❑ Obscure form values
- ❑ SSL protocol

Using Regular Expressions

One way to validate HTML form (input) values is through the use of **regular expressions**. Regular expressions are a way to match patterns and perform substitutions to validate or replace a given string of characters. The string of characters can come from anywhere, including a file, an e-mail message, or in this case, an HTML form. In a regular expression, characters like ?, *, and ^ have special meaning when used as a pattern.

For example, * means "match zero or one occurrences of the preceding character," while ^ indicates that the regex processing is anchored at the start of the string. Some examples of regular expressions include:

```
/app*/   matches "apple", "apply" and "application", but not "able"
/^root/  matches "root" but not "taproot"
```

Regular expressions easily support many other comparisons. You can check a string of characters for patterns that are all numbers, all uppercase, all lowercase, a mix of letters and numbers, or even whitespace characters such as tab and carriage return. A list of some common regular expressions is shown in the examples section below.

Regular Expression Examples

Consider the following HTML form variable:

```
<select name="user">
  <option value="Bob">Bob</option>
  <option value="Alice">Alice</option>
  <option value="Sue">Sue</option>
</select>
```

What would happen to the application if an attacker submitted a request where the form value user equaled root or admin? What kind of response would the attacker receive: an error message, or something unexpected and possibly damaging to the application or server? By using a regular expression, we can check for field values that might cause problems for our application. Let's assume that in our application, we consider users root and admin to be privileged users, and those usernames should never be allowed as values for form variables in any of our forms. In the example above, if we wanted to check to see if the form variable user contained root or admin; this regular expression, when applied to the contents of the form variable, would do the trick:

```
root|admin    matches any string consisting of "root" or "admin"
```

Using J2SE's `java.util.regex`, such a check might look like this:

```
/*
 * Checks for root or admin user in form variable
 */
String checkInput = request.getParameter("user");
Pattern p = Pattern.compile("root|admin");
Matcher m = p.matcher(checkInput);
if (m.find()) {
    System.err.println("An invalid user was entered.");
}
```

Of course, you could always use nested if statements to do the same check, but what if you had a need for something a little more powerful? You might want to remove control characters or directives from a text field, for example:

```
/*
 * Returns a version of a form text field with control characters
 removed
 */
public static CharSequence removeCNTRLChar(CharSequence inputStr) {
    String patternStr = "{cntrl}";
```

```
    String replaceStr = "";
    Pattern pattern = Pattern.compile(patternStr);
    Matcher matcher = pattern.matcher(inputStr);
    return matcher.replaceAll(replaceStr);
}
```

Regular Expressions for Older JDKs

If, for some reason, you are unable to take advantage of the `java.util.regex`
provided by version 1.4 of the Standard Edition of the Java 2 Platform (J2SE), the Apache
Jakarta project provides two regular expressions libraries for use. One is the Jakarta
Regexp package, and the other is the **Jakarta-ORO** library. Both are distributed under
the Apache license. ORO is considered the more robust solution, though both are quite
usable. ORO provides Java classes that support Perl5-compatible regular expressions,
AWK-like regular expressions, glob expressions, and utility classes for performing
substitutions, splits, and filtering filenames. Jakarta Regexp, a 100% pure Java package,
includes fewer classes that provide essential regular expression pattern matching.

Jakarta Regexp can be found here: http://jakarta.apache.org/regexp/index.html, while
Jakarta-ORO can be found here: http://jakarta.apache.org/oro/index.html. The Javadocs for
both packages are available online.

Obscure Form Data Values

One of the nice things about web applications is that it can be easy to figure out why the
page that is created by your JavaServer Page or Java servlet is not appearing in your
browser properly. Barring an error message from the server, you can simply use your
browser's View Source option to get a look at the exact HTML the browser is attempting to
render. Unfortunately, that's also one of the *bad* things about web applications and
pages. Anyone receiving content from your web server has the ability to view the source
that contributes to making your application work. In one of our regular expression
examples, we considered the scenario where an attacker would submit a form that
contained a field called `user` with a value of `root` or `admin`. Other usernames might be
just as bad, the point being that you want to avoid giving anyone more information than
they absolutely need. In the case of your application's users, they have no need to see
the values of such HTML form fields as the `OPTION` tag used within the `SELECT` tag.

Consider a scenario where you have a list of users in a drop-down list on a form. You don't
want your users to have access to the actual username value needed by your application;
you instead would like to present them with a form that lists first names. For example, you
might have a form with a drop-down list box that looks something like this:

```
Choose a username from the list:
<SELECT name="username">
    <option value="joe01">Joe</option>
    <option value="sally01">Sally</option>
    <option value="mike01">Mike</option>
</SELECT>
```

That's fine, but now you're allowing anyone who can view the HTML source of the form using their browser's View Source function to get a list of usernames. An alternative way to handle such a form would be to obscure the values in it. This can be accomplished by mapping unique keys to the real value on the server side and storing it in the user's session:

```
Choose a username from the list:
<SELECT name="username">
    <option value="34534534">Joe</option>
    <option value="54645675">Sally</option>
    <option value="97686786">Mike</option>
</SELECT>
```

Likewise, you might want to do the same thing to protect things like inventory IDs, user IDs, server names, phone numbers, or any other information that could be used in a number of different ways by an attacker. Don't forget that protecting information that can be used in a social engineering scenario is just as important as protecting information that can be used in an automated script attack scenario.

A solution, then, might be to set up two lists, one for the hidden or obscured values, and one for the value the user will see. The position of one element in the list will be equal to the index in the other list. That is, if abc is the first value obscured and is stored in a list that's kept private, then the companion or obscured value will also be first in the second list, which would be a public list used to create the actual HTML form. On the server, you can store both lists in the user's session. Then, when the form is submitted, you can match up the selected value, retrieve the actual value, and use it accordingly.

When the user views the form, the actual usernames will be replaced with hash codes of their value. Since hash codes of matching strings may or may not be the same, this is one way to obscure values in a form from prying eyes. Other schemes and key generation methods, such as message digests, may be used as well, the considerations being performance and application maintenance. An extremely paranoid developer might choose to hide values using a randomly- generated string that is 128 characters long, or some other method. There's no right or wrong method for generating the public values; it's up to you. Just remember that the public values should be unpredictable, as random as possible, and have little or no obvious relationship to the private values.

Once the form is submitted, you would check the session variable and do two things: verify that the value returned was actually a value sent, and retrieve the private value using the public value as the index or key. In the form above, the form processor is a JSP called `list2.jsp`, which might look something like this:

```
<%

// setup two lists, one public and one private
List listPublic = new ArrayList();
List listPrivate = new ArrayList();
```

```
// assume a list of 3 users
// add them to the private list
listPrivate.add("joe01");
listPrivate.add("sally01");
listPrivate.add("mike01");

// iterate over the private list and get a hash code to use
// in the public list
int listHashCode;
Iterator iterPrivate = listPrivate.iterator();
while (iterPrivate.hasNext()) {

  // get the hash of the private value
  listHashCode = iterPrivate.next().hashCode();

  // add the hash code to the public list in the same order
  listPublic.add(Integer.toString(listHashCode));

}

// store both lists as session variables for validation later
request.setAttribute("listPrivate", listPrivate);
request.setAttribute("listPublic", listPublic);

// write out the form
ListIterator iterPublicHTML = listPublic.listIterator();
int listIndex = 0;
String pubString = new String();
String privString = new String();

out.println("<form action='list2.jsp' method='post'>");
out.println("<select name='username'>");

// loop over the public list to fill the form list
while (iterPublicHTML.hasNext()) {

  // retrieve the next item in the public list for display
  listIndex = iterPublicHTML.nextIndex();
  pubString = iterPublicHTML.next().toString();
  privString = listPrivate.get(listIndex).toString();

  // create the form option tag
  // we know that usernames contain first names and a number
  // starting with zero, so use substring() to display the actual
  // value the user will see in the list box
  out.println("<option value='" + pubString + "'>");
  out.println(privString.substring(0,privString.indexOf("0")));
  out.println("</option>");

}

out.println("<input type='submit' name='submitButton'
value='Submit'>");
out.println("</form>");

%>
```

SSL Protocol Validation

Another validation that can be performed is a check for the correct request protocol. If you've got some or all of your application using Secure Sockets Layer (SSL), you will want to verify that requests are encrypted using SSL (HTTPS), and are not unencrypted HTTP. By incorporating SSL with an authentication scheme, you can control access to your application such that only authenticated users are sent to the SSL portion of your application, and anyone else is sent to a generic index page or allowed to submit a request for access to the protected portion of your application. Thus, in the portions of your application protected by SSL, you will want to check that the requests are actually using SSL. While an attacker can initiate an SSL session just like anyone else, performing the validation adds one more layer to your application's security by preventing anyone from accessing that portion using unencrypted requests.

The following code uses the `isSecure()` method to check the request type, as well as the port that received the request:

```
/*
 * check for SSL
 */
if ((request.isSecure()) && (request.getServerPort() == 443) ) {
  // SSL
} else {
  // Not SSL - redirect to login page or error page
}
```

Typically, separating your SSL-protected content from your static content is good practice. You might have a directory structure something like this:

```
/webapp/index.jsp
/webapp/public/public.jsp
/webapp/ssl/private.jsp
```

Sometimes, however, your directory structure might allow the same content to be served both with SSL and without SSL. You might have a corporate newsletter page that is available to all employees, even after they've logged in. By checking that the request is secure using `isSecure()` and that the request port in your protected JSP pages is 443, you can add an additional layer of verification to keep your users from accessing any SSL-protected page without authenticating themselves first.

Cookies and Session IDs

As mentioned previously, the one thing application developers can do to minimize security problems is to minimize the amount of information that is sent to the client. Even in a secure environment, the most (though not totally) secure resource is the server itself, not somebody's web browser, even if they've been authenticated. It's foolhardy to design your application such that once someone logs in, they have unlimited access to anything they wish to see and your security model goes wide open. To be serious about security, you must consider that *even an authenticated user is an intruder*. Just because someone has a valid username and password doesn't mean they have good intentions. Ideally, you as a developer want to minimize as much as possible the information sent to your users. So, in addition to authentication, you must develop an access control model that limits even authenticated users to the portions of the application they need; a simple authentication should not equal total access.

The client should only receive exactly what it needs to receive to do its job, which is essentially rendering pages to a specific format and providing information and options to the user. The information provided, however, should be sanitized, and only necessary as material used by the user to make a decision. For example, one of the last things you want to do is send privileged information to the client in the form of hidden Form variables, or as URL parameters on a GET or POST request, or as cookies. The only thing that should be sent to the client is a session ID and the information needed by the browser to render the page. Anything else is unnecessary and might cause problems, large or small, in the future.

Minimize Cookie Usage

Let's admit it – cookies are pretty handy. They're easy to use, they can be set and retrieved using a variety of technologies including Javascript, and they have built-in security such that only cookies belonging to a particular server can be viewed by that server. The very nature of cookies, though, makes them risky solutions in a secure environment. Used improperly, they can provide privileged information or a glimpse into an application's inner workings when analyzed closely. The last thing you want to do as a developer is start putting things like database names, social security numbers, or other types of privileged information into cookies stored on a client.

In a perfect world, your application would never use cookies. When you think about it, there's really no reason to ever use cookies, especially if you've got an application that is backed by a database. Anything you can put in a cookie you can put in a database, and by tagging the information in the database with a user's username or session ID, you can easily retrieve the information as needed once the user is authenticated. For example, lots of web sites use cookies to identify people who return at a later date. This information can easily be stored in a database, and once the user is authenticated, retrieved.

Another use for cookies is the dreaded "remember me" that you see on so many web sites these days. People get tired of typing in their usernames and passwords, or they forget them, or they use a different one on each site and don't want to track them. From a security point of view, the "remember me" function should be avoided in your application. You'll never have a guarantee that the person sitting at the computer on the other end of the request is who they say they are, and putting "remember me" functionality into your application using cookies makes the odds of that guarantee even worse. If you have to use cookies, consider using an encryption scheme to at least hide their contents from analysis.

Cookie Validation

OK, so cookies don't scare you. You're determined to use them, and you feel that the way they're being used by your application is an acceptable trade-off in security. If you're going to use them, then the least you can do is validate them and make sure they contain the information they should contain and that you think they contain.

Some validations you might consider when using cookies in your application:

- ❑ Are the dates really valid ones?
- ❑ Does the information stored in a cookie match the information stored elsewhere?
- ❑ Does the information stored in a cookie seem reasonable?
- ❑ Is the request coming at an odd time of day?
- ❑ Is the information in the cookie suspicious?

For example, if, for some reason, last month's sales were stored in a cookie, does that number seem reasonable 30 or 60 days later? A developer can gauge whether a number seems reasonable. If the highest sales in your organization in any month, ever, were $200,000.00, then seeing a cookie value of $2,000,000.00 might be an indicator someone was trying to artificially inflate their sales. Each application will be different; it is up to the developer to determine which business rules can be used to indicate suspicious activity.

Another indicator that something might be wrong would be if the information in a cookie changed to something unusual or if the request is coming at an odd time of day. For example, let's say your application uses a cookie that holds some information used by accounting staff when running payroll. Payroll is only run on the 15th and the 30th of every month. Is your application seeing a request with that cookie on the 5th or 21st of the month? Since there might be cases where payroll has to be run at an odd time of the month, it might not be plausible to refuse to process the request entirely. Even so, the request and the request parameters should at least be logged if they seem suspicious, and an administrator alerted via e-mail or some other means. As with all security issues, the degree of alarm should be proportionate to the degree of risk.

Using Sessions with JSESSIONID

Probably the easiest way to keep privileged or confidential information from being transmitted to the client is to use a session. By using variables with session scope, you can store information particular to that session right there on the server. When the user leaves, the session variables eventually time out and are cleared. If your application provides log out functionality, you can clear the session variables yourself when the user triggers the log out function.

By default, Tomcat enables sessions and all JSP have access to the implicit `session` object. Tomcat sends a value known as JSESSIONID on each response to a client. The JSESSIONID is unique and is generated by a random number so that the session ID typically cannot be predicted. This stops a malicious user from hijacking someone's session and receiving information that was destined for them. Whenever possible, only use the JSESSIONID cookie to tie a remote client to its session data, avoiding other cookies. Because JSESSIONID is there automatically, you can use this as a convenient link to a `Session` object on the server that stores information that shouldn't be stored on the client in a cookie, hidden form variable, or exposed on a GET or POST URL.

In your JSP, you can disable sessions, and in some cases it makes sense to do so. In many cases, you will want to keep sessions enabled. If you'd like to disable sessions, you can do it like this in your JSP page:

```
<%@ page session="false" %>
```

Keep in mind that this does not disable sessions for the server itself. This only keeps the `session` object from being visible to that particular JSP page. The advantages to this include a slightly faster run time for your pages, and less memory used. However, in most cases the disadvantages of disabling sessions outweigh the advantages.

To store data in a session variable, you call the `setAttribute()` method of the `session` object:

```
String stringA = new String();
String stringB = new String();

stringA = "foo";
stringB = "bar";

// store two variables as session variables for use later
session.setAttribute("myVarA", stringA);
session.setAttribute("myVarB", stringB);
```

In the `setAttribute()` method, the first parameter is the name of the variable, and the second parameter is the variable whose contents should be stored in the session variable. So, in the example above, the contents of `stringA` would be stored in a session variable called `myVarA`, and the contents of `stringB` would be stored in session variable `myVarB`.

To retrieve the contents of those same session variables, you call the corresponding get() method:

```
String myVarA = new String();
String myVarB = new String();

// retrieve the contents of two session variables stored previously
myVarA = session.getAttribute("myVarA");
myVarB = session.getAttribute("myVarB");
```

The session object can take other actions, as well. For example, if you wanted to remove a particular variable from a client's session, instead of just making it null or 0, you would call removeAttribute():

```
// delete myVarA from session
session.removeAttribute("myVarA");
```

One other aspect of sessions is checking to see if the session is new. This becomes important if your application needs to store information across multiple requests. If, for example, the client browser has disabled cookies, then the cookie storing JSESSIONID can't be set. This would make every session new, on every request, preventing your application from storing information as session variables from one request to the next. Normally, a server-side process has little or no ability to interrogate the configuration of a client browser, but in this case you can call the isNew() method of the session object to see if the request has generated a new one. If it is new, and your application expects to be able to retrieve information from the session object that was stored previously, then you throw an error.

```
If (session.isNew()) {
   // take action
} else {
   // retrieve session variables
}
```

Session variables provide an ideal way to minimize the information sent to the client browser and keep confidential information on the server. They're not perfect, though. While easy to use, enabled and available by default, and able to store just about anything within reason, a developer still has to consider performance and resource issues when using them just like any other technology. You don't want to store a record set with 5,000 1024-byte records in it as a session variable, nor do you want to force the overhead of dozens of different session variables onto the memory available to your application. Managed wisely, however, session variables can go a long way towards helping your application maintain its security model and good behavior.

SQL Security

Like validation, SQL and *database security* is one of those topics that many developers overlook, for various reasons, whether it be time or other resource constraints, or lack of familiarity with the topic. A database, however, is one of the most important information and knowledge resources an organization can have, and in many cases an organization's entire value resides in one or more databases. Faced with that environment, making your database connection information and your SQL statements as foolproof as possible should be a primary concern.

A developer typically has no control over some of the more administrative tasks related to databases. For example, a developer may not have control over things like sernames and access or modification privileges. Those matters are usually left to a database administrator (DBA). A developer does have control over other matters, such as:

- ❑ Security of database connection parameters and other information
- ❑ Validation of SQL queries, especially INSERT, UPDATE, and DELETE
- ❑ An application's use of stored procedures where possible

By doing their part, developers can keep their applications from being the entry point for database mischief.

Securing Connection Parameters

To use any database in your application, the first thing you have to do is connect to it. The database can be on the same server as the web server serving your application, or it can be on a dedicated database server or some other server that is reachable over a network. Either way, to interact with the database, you will have to make a database connection. How you make your database connection can be the difference between keeping your database secure and exposing it to an attacker.

The easiest way to connect to a database in your application is by using a Connection object and the getConnection() method of the DriverManager class. Consider the following JSP code, which connects to MySQL:

```
<%@ page contentType="text/html;
   charset=iso-8859-1" language="java"
   import="java.sql.*,java.util.*" errorPage="" %>
<%

// String defining database connection
String dbURI = "jdbc:mysql:///test";
String dbUser = "admin";
String dbPassword = "tomcat";

// Connection reference
Connection conn = null;
```

```
try {

    // Load database driver
    Class.forName("org.gjt.mm.mysql.Driver");

    // Make connection
    conn = DriverManager.getConnection(dbURI, dbUser, dbPassword);

} finally {

    // Close connection

    if (conn != null) {
      try {
        conn.close();
      } catch (SQLException sqle) {
          // ignore
      }
    }
}
%>
```

It looks pretty good, and it will make a connection to MySQL just as it should. However, the username, connection URL, and connection password are contained within the JSP itself. This is definitely a potential security hole. If a vulnerability were found in the JSP compiler that somehow displayed the source of the JSP instead of the dynamic output, your database connection information would be there for all to see. While MySQL has the ability to restrict connections based on hostnames and IP addresses, other database systems may not have that ability, or MySQL's restrictions might be misconfigured. In any case, with a connection URL, username, and password, trying to connect to your database and cause mischief would be a target few attackers could ignore.

A better way to handle your database connection information is through the use of JNDI. With JNDI, a server administrator will configure a database connection at the server level, in the server configuration files such as Tomcat's server.xml file and your application's web.xml file. That way, sensitive information like usernames and passwords isn't in your JSP. JNDI uses the concept of a Context to store information for all sorts of resources. While you can use JNDI for things like JavaMail configuration and Bean configuration, you can also use it for DataSource information. To use the connection information, you retrieve a reference to a Context object that matches your datasource, and make your connection that way.

Assuming your server administrator has configured server.xml appropriately, a corresponding entry in your application's web.xml file might look like this:

```
<resource-ref>
  <description>
    Resource reference to a factory for java.sql.Connection
    instances for accessing a MySQL database configured in server.xml
  </description>
  <res-ref-name>
```

```
      jdbc/myAppDB
   </res-ref-name>
   <res-type>
      javax.sql.DataSource
   </res-type>
   <res-auth>
      Container
   </res-auth>
</resource-ref>
```

To use this entry in web.xml and its corresponding Context in server.xml in your application, you would set up your connection like this:

```
Context initCtx = new InitialContext();
Context envCtx = (Context) initCtx.lookup("java:comp/env");
DataSource ds = (DataSource) envCtx.lookup("jdbc/myAppDB");

Connection conn = ds.getConnection();
... use this connection to access the database ...
conn.close();
```

The difference here is that your connection information such as URL, username, and password are stored in server.xml. Your JSP, servlets, and other Java classes don't need to have that information in them; all they need to do is grab a reference to the appropriate DataSource context. Server.xml can be protected from casual browsing using built-in file system permissions.

If, for some reason, you can't make changes to your server.xml file to configure a JNDI Datasource or convince your server administrator to do so, an alternative to putting connection information into your JSP might be to create a class that makes connections to your database, and returns references to those connections. The database connection information would be in the class itself, and not in your JSP. Since classes are compiled and are stored in the WEB-INF folder, which can't be viewed, the possibility of someone getting your database's connection information is minimized.

Drawbacks of doing this include having to recompile every class that makes a connection every time connection information changes, and the need to have different classes for different database tasks, or some sort of custom database query engine library. By using JNDI, your connection information is in one place, and changing it causes the change to be distributed to all resources automatically. As a developer, you can acquire references to these connections directly without having to bother with maintaining usernames, passwords, and other deployment-specific details. For more information on JNDI Datasources and some example configurations for popular database systems, see Tomcat's JNDI Datasource HOW-TO, available here: http://jakarta.apache.org/tomcat/tomcat-4.1-doc/jndi-datasource-examples-howto.html.

Prepared Statements

Another entry point for mischief where databases are concerned is in the SQL statements themselves. After all, the primary use for JSP and servlets is generating dynamic content based on a set of criteria, with the content itself coming from some resource such as a database or file. Many developers write code that accepts actions from forms with little or no validation, and in turn uses the values of the fields in those forms as direct input to SQL statements.

Consider the following SQL statement construct:

```
String query = "SELECT * from test WHERE id = " +
request.getParameter("id");
```

Or, even worse:

```
String query = "DELETE FROM test WHERE id = " +
request.getParameter("id");
```

What would happen to those queries, and the information stored in the database, if id contained something it shouldn't, such as a list of numbers that were never included on the form that generated the request, a specially crafted SQL query itself, or a value like TRUE or 9999? SQL allows nested statements, too. What would happen if the contents of id were something like SELECT * FROM test? That might trigger the following scenario, or something similar, once the SQL statement was sent to the database:

```
String query = "DELETE FROM test WHERE id = " + "SELECT * from test";
```

This is definitely not a desirable behavior. Validation of the values used in your SQL statements is good practice, so that you can at least trap values that might be harmful and you want to avoid constructing your query string directly from HTML form input. You have no control over what someone might type into a text field on a form, or whether they might use a script to craft bogus values for form fields and then repeatedly submit them to your application.

The good news is that there's already a mechanism for validating your SQL statements and for helping to make sure the only content in your SQL statements is the content you expect. The mechanism for doing this is the PreparedStatment interface found in java.sql. A **prepared statement** is a SQL statement that's been compiled into a form that your database management system can understand. Think of it as the difference between a Java source code file and a Java class file. A prepared statement is similar: you take a regular SQL statement, and ask the compiler to prepare it for processing. On the way, preparing the statement causes different rules to be applied to the statement such as *strong typecasting*, detection of spoofed SQL statements, and automatic handling of special characters in strings.

A SQL statement that will be used with `java.sql.PreparedStatement` looks like this:

```
"SELECT * FROM myTable where CustomerName = ? "
```

The key here is the ? character. The ? character acts as a placeholder. In the statement above, there's only one ?, which means the SQL statement only takes one parameter. That parameter has to be there for the `PreparedStatement` action to be successful. You can prepare a SQL statement that doesn't take any variables, but that doesn't do much beyond saving some processing time when the statement is actually sent to the database.

So how do you use a prepared statement? The code shown below uses a JNDI datasource as well as a prepared statement to update some sales information for a given salesperson's ID number. Note the use of two ? characters in the SQL statement being prepared:

```
Context initCtx = new InitialContext();
Context envCtx = (Context) initCtx.lookup("java:comp/env");
DataSource ds = (DataSource) envCtx.lookup("jdbc/myAppDB");
Connection conn = ds.getConnection();

PreparedStatement getSales;

String updateSalesSQL = "UPDATE SALES SET MonthlyTotal = ? WHERE
SalesPersonID = ? ";
updateSales = conn.prepareStatement(updateSalesSQL);

try {
  // update the monthly sales total
  updateSales.setBigDecimal(1, request.getParameter("salesTotal");
  updateSales.setInt(2, request.getParameter("salesID");

  // execute the SQL statement
  updateSales.executeUpdate();

} catch (SQLException sqle) {
  System.err.println("Unable to execute SQL: " +
                                  sqle.printStackTrace();
} finally {
  conn.close();
}
```

Thus, using a `PreparedStatment`, the validation is done for us. If something other than an int or a `BigDecimal` were the values of `salesTotal` and `salesID`, a `SQLException` would be thrown and our SQL statement would never even reach our database.

Stored Procedures

Yet another way to prevent or at least decrease database problems via your application is to use a stored procedure. **Stored procedures** are a special feature supported by many available relational database systems, and allow database administrators to restrict how queries are sent to database systems and even which queries are allowed. To provide an example of a stored procedure, we'll have to assume that our application's database username has the privileges to create stored procedures on the fly. Normally, a database administrator would be the only person allowed to create a stored procedure. The process for creating stored procedures is different for different database systems, and so is the exact syntax, but they all look similar.

Consider the code shown below. This code creates a stored procedure using `java.sql.CallableStatement`, and then executes the stored procedure:

```
// get a connection
Context initCtx = new InitialContext();
Context envCtx = (Context) initCtx.lookup("java:comp/env");
DataSource ds = (DataSource) envCtx.lookup("jdbc/myAppDB");

Connection conn = ds.getConnection();

// create the stored procedure
String createProcedure = "create procedure SHOW_SUPPLIERS " + "as " +
"select SUPPLIERS.SUPPLIER_NAME, " + PRODUCTS.PRODUCT_NAME " + "from
SUPPLIERS, PRODUCTS " + "where SUPPLIERS.SUPPLIER_ID = " +
PRODUCTS.PRODUCT_ID " + "order by SUPPLIER_NAME";

Statement stmt = conn.createStatement();
stmt.executeUpdate(createProcedure);

// now use the procedure
CallableStatement cs = conn.prepareCall("{call SHOW_SUPPLIERS}");
ResultSet rs = cs.executeQuery();

// do something with rs here
```

The `ResultSet` that would be returned would have all of the rows that were returned by the SQL statement contained in `createProcedure`.

Not only does a stored procedure allow a database administrator to restrict which queries are executed, it even prevents the application developer from knowing any details about the database structure itself, such as table names. In an ideal scenario, a database administrator would create stored procedures for all queries, and then publish the names of the stored procedures as well as what would be returned in the `ResultSet`, if anything.

Securing Your Java Package

As a developer, you know you've been extremely diligent when considering the security of your application. You've taken steps to protect your databases, you've taken steps to obscure and hide the information that client applications can see, and you've designed your application so that privileged and confidential information is always kept on the server. There's another aspect of security, however, that still needs to be addressed from an application perspective, and that's the topic of protecting your Java packages themselves.

Both the Tomcat and Java security managers are discussed in Chapter 3. The following sections complement the chapters on the security managers, and in particular take advantage of the Java Security Manager's security policy file to add another layer of security to your application.

Java.security

To use Java's built-in security manager, you have to start a Java application with the security manager enabled. The security manager is not automatic. Since Tomcat is itself a Java application, it's critical that Tomcat be started with the security manager enabled. Without the security manager, none of its features are available to Tomcat or to applications running within the Tomcat environment. Since the security manager is discussed in Chapter 3, we won't go into too much detail here. Simply, if you want to start Tomcat with the security manager enabled, you would add -security to your Tomcat startup command:

```
$CATALINA_HOME/bin/catalina.sh start -security    (Unix)
%CATALINA_HOME%\bin\catalina start -security       (Windows)
```

Protecting Packages

The packages and Java classes that make up your Java application can be targeted by an attacker just as your JSP and servlet code can be targeted. The goal here is to protect your packages and their classes from access by untrusted code. Potential exploits include package insertion and package access.

In **package-insertion scheme**, untrusted code will try to gain access to package-protected class members by attempting to define new classes of its own within the targeted package. This can allow the untrusted code access to the protected members. There are two ways to protect against a package-insertion attack:

❑   One is to use what is known as a *sealed JAR file*.

❑   Another way is to use the security properties file.

Using the Security Properties File

In this method to protect against package-insertion attacks, we add a line to the java.security properties file that looks like this:

```
package.definition=Package#1 [,Package#2,...,Package#n]
```

Where Package#1 is the name of your package. By defining your packages in the java.security properties file like this, you can protect against a package-insertion attack because any attempt to define a new class in one of the listed packages will cause the class loader's defineClass method to throw an exception. You can avoid the exception thrown by the defineClass method if you grant the code the following permission:

```
RuntimePermission("defineClassInPackage."+package)
```

In a package-access scheme, untrusted code can be prevented from accessing particular packages by explicitly restricting access to the package and granting access permissions only to trusted code. To explicitly declare permissions for accessing a package, put the following line in your java.security properties file:

```
package.access=Package#1 [,Package#2,...,Package#n]
```

Where again Package#1 is the name of your package. By declaring access restrictions in your properties file, you can prevent code from accessing any class in that package unless it has been granted the following permission:

```
RuntimePermission("accessClassInPackage."+package)
```

If untrusted code attempts to access a package where it has no permission to do so, the class loader's loadClass method will throw an exception that can be caught.

Using a Sealed JAR File

If you can't modify your java.security properties file for some reason, you still have a method of protecting your packages. This method is known as a **sealed JAR file**, and it can protect all of the packages within the JAR file, or specific permissions can be applied to distinct packages without applying to the whole JAR file. When creating a JAR file, part of its contents is known as a **manifest**, which is essentially a list of everything inside the JAR file, as well as different parameters and options that might apply to the contents. In a JAR manifest, the following attributes can be defined:

Attribute	Description
Implementation-Title	Title of the package
Implementation-Version	Version number

Attribute	Description
Implementation-Vendor	Vendor's company or organization
Specification-Title	Title of the specification
Specification-Version	Version number
Specification-Vendor	Vendor's company or organization
Sealed	Whether the package or JAR is sealed

As an example, let's look at the JAR manifest for the `java.util` package:

```
Manifest-version: 1.0
Name: java/util/
Specification-Title: Java Utility Classes
Specification-Version: 1.2
Specification-Vendor: Sun Microsystems Inc.
Implementation-Title: java.util
Implementation-Version: build57
Implementation-Vendor: SunMicrosystems. Inc.
```

All well and good, but how do you designate a package as sealed? You do this with an additional parameter in the manifest called `Sealed`. `Sealed` takes one argument, either `true` or `false`, without regard to case. Here's our previous manifest with the new parameter:

```
Manifest-version: 1.0
Name: java/util/
Sealed: true
Specification-Title: Java Utility Classes
Specification-Version: 1.2
Specification-Vendor: Sun Microsystems Inc.
Implementation-Title: java.util
Implementation-Version: build57
Implementation-Vendor: SunMicrosystems. Inc.
```

When creating your JAR file, a default manifest is included. In order to add additional information to your manifest, such as the `Sealed` attribute and other attributes like `Implementation-Version`, you need to use the JAR tool's –m command line switch. For example, the following command would create a JAR file called `myJarFile` and would merge the manifest in `myManifestFile` into the default manifest:

```
jar -cmf myManifestFile myJarFile *.class
```

Inside `myManifestFile` is where you would list your `Sealed` attributes, as well as any others that you wanted to include. For more information on the Manifest file portion of creating JAR files, consult the following documentation:
http://java.sun.com/docs/books/tutorial/jar/basics/manifest.html.

Let's take a look at how Sealed applies to packages and JAR files. A package sealed within a JAR means that classes defined in that package must originate from the same JAR file. If it doesn't, a SecurityException is thrown. If the JAR file itself is sealed instead of an individual package, then all packages defined by that JAR are sealed unless overridden specifically on a package-by-package basis. So, if you want to seal your packages, you don't need to tag each one with Sealed; you only need to tag the JAR file as sealed. If the Sealed attribute is missing from a package, then it defaults to the Sealed attribute of the JAR file itself. If the Sealed attribute is missing from the JAR file, then the JAR file is treated as unsealed, in order to support backwards compatibility. At that point, the system will interrogate specific package headers to determine if any of the packages are sealed individually, even if the JAR file itself is not.

The main benefit to package sealing is that it restricts access to package-protected members only to classes that are defined in the package from the same JAR file. As an example, the rt.jar file, all of the standard core Java packages, with the exception of the sun.io and java.text.resources packages, are sealed.

The Sealed attribute is checked for installed as well as downloaded extensions. If an action is attempted that violates the attribute, a SecurityException is thrown. In addition, the null package is not sealable. So, if you have a class that you want to seal, you must place that class into a package (or its own package) and seal the package, or place the package in a sealed JAR file.

Known Issues

Like any application, bugs and other issues will come up. Tomcat is certainly no different, nor is Java. The advantage both have is that both are relatively easy to analyze for possible problems, and Java's robust security features and security model make it less susceptible than some other technologies to common problems like buffer overflows. With that in mind, what follows is a discussion of some known issues that have cropped up that affect applications using Tomcat as their environment.

The Default Invoker Servlet

Recently, a problem was discovered with Tomcat's default invoker servlet. By default, versions of Tomcat earlier than 4.1.12 would allow a visitor to view the source code of any JSP by using a specially crafted URL that passed the name of the JSP to the invoker servlet. Obviously, you don't want your JSP source visible to anyone who wants it, especially if you're using confidential information like database connection URLs and other information in your pages. The workaround is pretty easy if you're using one of the earlier versions of Tomcat, but if you aren't, then you don't need to worry about it, since the default invoker servlet is disabled by default in Tomcat versions 4.0.5 and up, as well as 4.1.12 and later.

Just for discussion, here's how the exploit works. Let's say you have a JSP called inventory.jsp. Normally, your users would access that JSP with a URL that might look like http://www.site.com/inventory.jsp. Accessed with that URL, the page compiles and behaves accordingly. However, a specially crafted URL can instead deliver the source of the JSP to the user instead of the results of the source. To do that, you would use a URL that looked like this:

```
http://www.site.com/servlet/org.apache.catalina.servlets.DefaultServle
t/inventory.jsp
```

By using that URL, the source of inventory.jsp would be displayed to the user.

Workarounds

How do you protect against this exploit if you can't run a recent version of Tomcat? There are a couple of different ways:

1. If you're using Tomcat in conjunction with a web server like Apache, you can filter all requests for /servlet/org.apache.catalina.servlets.DefaultServlet using whatever mechanism is available to your web server.

2. If you're using Tomcat with Apache and a connector like mod_jk.so (mod_jk.dll on Windows), then make sure you only map valid requests and URLs you know your application uses to Tomcat using JkMount.

3. If you're using Tomcat as a stand-alone web server, or even if you're not and still want to add another way to block this exploit, then disable the default invoker servlet in your application's web.xml file like this:

```xml
<security-constraint>
  <display-name>Default Servlet</display-name>
  <!-- Disable direct calls on the Default Servlet -->
  <web-resource-collection>
   <web-resource-name>Disallowed Location</web-resource-name>
   <url-pattern>
/servlet/org.apache.catalina.servlets.DefaultServlet/*
   </url-pattern>
     <http-method>DELETE</http-method>
     <http-method>GET</http-method>
     <http-method>POST</http-method>
     <http-method>PUT</http-method>
  </web-resource-collection>
  <auth-constraint>
     <role-name></role-name>
  </auth-constraint>
</security-constraint>
```

That will disallow any requests that attempt to use the DefaultServlet to view your application's content.

Symbolic Links

In Tomcat 4.1.12 and up, symbolic links are disabled by default. In general, Tomcat is restricted to its own directory tree, commonly known as CATALINA_HOME or CATALINA_BASE in some cases. There's no real reason applications running in Tomcat's environment need access to anything outside of that structure, since one of the primary features of Tomcat is that it is a reference implementation for the servlet specification, which means that anything Tomcat does must be portable across operating systems. If symbolic links were necessary for Tomcat to operate, that would break Tomcat's interoperability with platforms that don't support symbolic links like Windows and others.

Nevertheless, there are many applications out there that require symbolic links regardless of portability concerns. The symbolic links issue tends to crop up when developers upgrade from older versions of Tomcat and have an application that requires symbolic links. They go to upgrade to a recent version, and suddenly find that their application doesn't work because Tomcat will not honor the symbolic links they were using with their earlier environment.

At first glance, symbolic links seem pretty harmless. However, on closer scrutiny, it can be seen that using them and allowing applications to use them can be dangerous under some circumstances. For example, in a UNIX or Linux environment, if you're using Tomcat as a stand-alone web server on port 80, then Tomcat is running as root, or superuser. That means Tomcat and applications running within Tomcat have the operating system privileges to do anything anytime. Imagine a symbolic link within your application's directory structure linking to a critical operating system file outside of Tomcat's directory environment, and that file being read by a rogue class or application or being overwritten with something else, such as a Trojan horse, and you can see why symbolic links might be a bad idea.

Workarounds

If you need to use symbolic links in your application in a Tomcat environment using recent versions of Tomcat, you can. To do it, add a Resources tag to Tomcat's server.xml in the application Context where you want to enable symbolic links. The Resources tag needs to specify the allowLinking parameter. For example:

```
<Context path="/examples" docBase="examples" debug="0"
        reloadable="true" crossContext="true">

   <!--add a context logger -->
   <Logger className="org.apache.catalina.logger.FileLogger"
           prefix="localhost_examples_log." suffix=".txt"
           timestamp="true"/>

   <!--add a resource to allow symbolic links -->
   <Resources className="org.apache.naming.resources.FileDirContext"
           allowLinking="true" docBase="examples" />
</Context>
```

JK Synchronization

Another issue was discovered when using Tomcat in conjunction with the Apache web server, and the JK connector. The JK connector acts as the conduit between Apache and Tomcat for the purposes of serving responses and receiving requests. If you're using a version of mod_jk earlier than 1.2.1, your system is susceptible to this exploit.

How does it work? A malicious user can submit multiple requests to Apache for a URL mapped via JK to Tomcat, and by deliberately modifying the size of the data packets being sent to Apache can cause desynchronization of the requests and responses between Apache and Tomcat over the JK conduit. What does this mean, exactly? It means that by causing JK to get out of synch, responses from Tomcat meant for one user might end up being transmitted to a different user. This could lead to one user seeing confidential information meant for someone else entirely. In addition, the desynchronization can cause problems for both Apache and Tomcat from a server resources point of view.

Workarounds

The solution is to upgrade your version of mod_jk to version 1.2.1 or later. Keep in mind that this is only necessary if you're using Tomcat in conjunction with the Apache web server, and are using mod_jk instead of mod_jk2. You can find the source to mod_jk 1.2.1 and later, as well as binaries of the Apache modules, here: http://jakarta.apache.org/builds/jakarta-tomcat-connectors/jk/release/.

Protecting WEB-INF

By default, Tomcat will refuse to serve content for requests specifically trying to access the WEB-INF folder of your application Context, as well as all of its subfolders. This is by design, and is desired behavior. Java decompilers are readily available, and it wouldn't be very secure if your Java class files could be retrieved by anyone who wanted them and decompiled at their leisure. However, many people use Tomcat in conjunction with Apache for various reasons, and unless told to protect WEB-INF explicitly, Apache will merrily attempt to serve content from that folder and the folders under it if possible, completely bypassing Tomcat's security measures. This is due to Apache having potential access to CATALINA_HOME. Tomcat can only monitor requests coming at it, and cannot monitor requests answered by other applications, including Apache.

Workarounds

It's easy to protect WEB-INF when you are using Apache, and if you're using Tomcat's ApacheConfig auto-generation function to generate Apache configuration directives for mod_jk, then the protection is already there. The auto-generation function creates the appropriate Apache directives for every Context found in server.xml when Tomcat starts. Directives to protect WEB-INF and META-INF directories under each Context are included by default. If you're not using the auto-generation function, then you can protect your application's WEB-INF and META-INF folders and their subfolders by adding the following to Apache's httpd.conf file for each virtual host, and for each application URL:

```
# Tell Apache to deny direct access to WEB-INF and META-INF
# for /myApp
<Location "/myApp/WEB-INF/*">
        AllowOverride None
        deny from all
</Location>

<Location "/myApp/META-INF/*">
        AllowOverride None
        deny from all
</Location>
```

The Apache directives shown above will prevent Apache from serving any requests that try to access files in WEB-INF and META-INF directly for a given URL like /myApp, and for a given Apache VirtualHost.

Summary

In this chapter, we've seen how application security can play a critical part in the overall security model of a system. Server-based security tools and techniques such as restricting file permissions and managing users are only one part of the solution. Likewise, network and protocol-based tools like firewalls are only part of the total solution. In conjunction with security policies, server configuration, the Java security sandbox, and technologies like SSL, a developer can contribute significantly to the overall security of the system. As any security professional will tell you, a security model is only as strong as its weakest participant. It does no good to have the best firewall in the world in place if your application repeatedly broadcasts confidential information in the clear, or fails to adequately authenticate and validate information sent to it.

A few key points to remember would be:

❑   Most important of all, an application developer should take steps to *minimize the information transmitted* to a client as much as possible. Any information given to a client accessing your application is information that can potentially be used in an attack against it.

❑ When possible, use *SSL encryption* to encrypt information transmitted back and forth between your application and its users. If you do use SSL, don't mix protected and unprotected information in the same request, and don't allow your users to flip back and forth between protected and unprotected information. Once authenticated in an SSL session, all activity should be by SSL until the user logs out or the session times out.

❑ *Validation* plays a key part in protecting your application from mischief and attack. Assume by default that everything sent to your application by a client is suspect, since even an attacker can have a username and password. Don't succumb to assuming that everything is OK once someone is authenticated.

❑ If you can't use an encryption scheme like public and private key encryption, or message digests, do what you can to *obscure or hide information* sent to the client as long as it doesn't adversely affect performance or user experience. Only you as the developer can determine an acceptable trade-off between performance and risk in your application.

❑ Respect security precautions set up by systems administrators, network administrators, and database administrators.

❑ Pay close attention to protecting information about other *resources* in your application's environment, especially things like database connection URLs, file locations, and access information. Avoid putting privileged information in application source code like a JSP that might fall prey to some future vulnerability.

❑ Take advantage of the security functionality available by default in Tomcat and Java.

❑ Realize that security can never be 100% perfect. Humans will always make errors. Subscribe to various mailing lists such as the `bugtraq` list and the `tomcat-user` list. Monitor security-oriented web sites like CERT (`www.cert.org`) and SecurityFocus (`online.securityfocus.com`). Even if you don't want to be or can't be active on the lists, at the very least set them to digest mode and monitor the posts every couple of days so that you can be aware of potential issues and exploits that may compromise your application.

Application development is a daunting and complex task, with many decisions to make and alternatives to consider. By understanding how your application fits into a system's security model, taking steps to support and fortify that security model, and being vigilant for ways to make your application more secure, you can go a long way towards designing, building, and maintaining a stable, secure, and robust application.

Apache Tomcat Security

Handbook

Appendix

Support, Errata, and Code Download

We always value hearing from our readers, and we want to know what you think about this book and series: what you liked, what you didn't like, and what you think we can do better next time. You can send us your comments either by returning the reply card in the back of the book, or by e-mailing us at feedback@wrox.com. Please be sure to mention the book title in your message.

How to Download the Sample Code for the Book

When you log on to the Wrox site, http://www.wrox.com/, simply locate the title through our Search facility or by using one of the title lists. Click on Download Code on the book's detail page.

The files that are available for download from our site have been archived using WinZip. When you have saved the attachments to a folder on your hard-drive, you will need to extract the files using WinZip, or a compatible tool. Inside the Zip file will be a folder structure and an HTML file that explains the structure and gives you further information, including links to e-mail support, and suggested further reading.

Errata

We've made every effort to ensure that there are no errors in the text or in the code. However, no one is perfect and mistakes can occur. If you find an error in this book, like a spelling mistake or a faulty piece of code, we would be very grateful for the feedback. By sending in errata, you may save another reader hours of frustration, and of course, you will be helping us to provide even higher quality information. Simply e-mail the information to support@wrox.com; your information will be checked and if correct, posted to the Errata page for that title.

To find errata, locate this book on the Wrox web site (http://www.wrox.com/books/1861008309.htm), and click on the **Book Errata** link on the book's detail page:

E-Mail Support

If you wish to query a problem in the book with an expert who knows the book in detail then e-mail support@wrox.com, with the title of the book, and the last four numbers of the ISBN in the subject field of the e-mail. A typical e-mail should include the following:

- ❑ The name, last four digits of the ISBN (8309), and page number of the problem, in the Subject field

- ❑ Your name, contact information, and the problem, in the body of the message

We won't send you junk mail. We need the details to save your time and ours. When you send an e-mail message, it will go through the following chain of support:

❑ **Customer Support**

Your message is delivered to our customer support staff. They have files on most frequently asked questions and will answer anything general about the book or the web site immediately.

❑ **Editorial**

More in-depth queries are forwarded to the technical editor responsible for that book. They have experience with the programming language or particular product, and are able to answer detailed technical questions on the subject. Once an issue has been resolved, the editor can post the errata to the web site.

❑ **The Authors**

Finally, in the unlikely event that the editor cannot answer your problem, they will forward the request to the author. We do try to protect the author from any distractions to their writing (or programming); but we are quite happy to forward specific requests to them. All Wrox authors help with the support on their books. They will e-mail the customer and the editor with their response, and again all readers should benefit

The Wrox support process can only offer support for issues that are directly pertinent to the content of our published title. Support for questions that fall outside the scope of normal book support, is provided via our P2P community lists – ttp://p2p.wrox.com/listindex.asp.

p2p.wrox.com

For author and peer discussion, join the P2P mailing lists. Our unique system provides Programmer to Programmer™ contact on mailing lists, forums, and newsgroups, all in addition to our one-to-one e-mail support system. Be confident that the many Wrox authors and other industry experts who are present on our mailing lists are examining any queries posted. At http://p2p.wrox.com/, you will find a number of different lists that will help you, not only while you read this book, but also as you develop your own applications.

To subscribe to a mailing list follow these steps:

❑ Go to http://p2p.wrox.com/

❑ Choose the appropriate category from the left menu bar

❑ Click on the mailing list you wish to join

❑ Follow the instructions to subscribe and fill in your e-mail address and password

❑ Reply to the confirmation e-mail you receive

❑ Use the subscription manager to join more lists and set your mail preferences

Apache Tomcat Security

Handbook

Index

Index

A Guide to the Index

The index is arranged hierarchically, in alphabetical order, with symbols preceding the letter A. Classes derive from the System namespace unless another namespace is specified. Most second-level entries and many third-level entries also occur as first-level entries. This is to ensure that users will find the information they require however they choose to search for it.

A

access control, 88
AccessControlException, 81
admin application, Tomcat, 16, 18
  see also manager application.
  see also examples application.
  see also WebDAV application.
  deployment example, 18
  features, 18
  manager application, compared to, 18
  UserDatabase Realm
    adding roles, 109
    adding users, 111
  Valves, use of, 18
AJP (Apache JServ Protocol)
  definition, 173
  mod_jk module, 173
  SSH tunneling, 175
    deployment guidelines, 177
    mod_jk module configuration, 176
    tunnel establishment, 175
  Tomcat SSL configuration, 153
aliases, 55
Apache
  popularity of use, 5
  SSL deployment
    mod_ssl module, using, 168
  Tomcat application server, working with, 12
    advantages, 168
    multiple server architecture, 169
    single server architecture, 168
Apache-SSL, 168, 169

application security
  see also database security.
  see also file system security.
  see also SSO.
  application components, 6
  authentication misuse, 189
  authentication, mechanisms employed
    Basic, 164
    Client-certificate, 165
    Form based, 165
  cookies, use of, 189
  database security, 193
  invoker servlet
    problems with, 203
    workaround, 203
  J2EE, protection mechanism provision
    by, 164
  Java
    features provided by, 51
    package security, 199
    Security Manager deployment, 53
  JK connector
    problems with, 205
    workarounds, 205
  securing the application
    defining roles, 100
    login-config element, specifying
      authentication, 100
    role-name element, defining roles, 100
    security-constraint element, defining, 99
    steps, 98
    transport-guarantee element, defining
      transport layer requirements, 100
    url-pattern, defining, 99
  sessions, 191

application security (Cont'd)
symbolic links
problems with, 204
workarounds, 204
Tomcat WEB-INF folder
security problems, 206
workarounds, 206
vulnerabilities
broken access control, 6
broken account and session
management, 7
buffer overflows, 7
command injection flaws, 7
Cros-Site Scripting (XSS) flaws, 7
error handling problems, 7
insecure use of cryptography, 7
remote administration flaws, 7
unvalidated parameters, 6
web and application server
misconfiguration, 7
appName attribute
JAAS Realm configuration, 137
asymmetric encryption algorithms
definition, 145
private keys, use of, 145
public keys, use of, 145
SSL, use within, 149
authenticate() method
Custom Realms development, 138
authentication
application security, misuse in, 189
definition, 88
guidelines in choosing
custom login and error page, 95
ease of deployment, 94
security, 95
SSL, within, 149
types
Basic, 88, 89
Client, 88
Digest, 88
Form Based, 88, 90
HTTP Digest, 90
HTTPS Client, 92
authorization
Container-Managed Security, 95
programmatic security model, 96

B

Base64 encoding
Basic authentication, use within, 90
Basic authentication
see also Digest authentication.
see also client authentication.
see also Form based authentication.
application security, use in, 164
Base64 encoding, use of, 90
definition, 89

deployment example, 89
Digest authentication, compared to, 90, 95
disadvantage, 90
Form based authentication, compared
to, 90, 95
HTTPS, advantage of using, 90
Realms, use of, 88
SSL, use in, 94
CONFIDENTIAL protection type, 94
INTEGRAL protection type, 94
deployment example, 94
bind mode authentication
comparison mode authentication,
compared to, 128
OpenLDAP directory server, user
authentication, 127
broken access control vulnerability, 6
broken account and session
mismanagement vulnerability, 7
buffer overflows, 7, 11
BUGTRAQ
Tomcat, keeping track of vulnerabilities, 8

C

CA (Certificate Authority)
certificate chains, 148
CSR, 146
definition, 146
digital certificates, use with, 146
examples, 147
HTTPS Client authentication deployment,
use within, 93
keytool utility, trusting using, 159
web browsers, viewing within, 147
cacerts keystore
definition, 157
keytool utility, listing trusted CAs using, 157
cacls utility, 36
certificate chains, 148
root certificates, 148
certificates
see digital certificates.
chmod command
parameters listing, 38
Unix permissions, changing, 38
chown command
Unix permissions, changing ownership, 39
className attribute
Custom Realms development, 138
JAAS Realm configuration, 137
JDBC Realm configuration, 121
JNDI Realm configuration, 130
Memory Realms configuration, 102
UserDatabase Realm configuration, 108
client authentication
application security, use in, 165
handshake protocol, SSL, using, 151

Client authentication, HTTPS
see also Basic authentication.
see also Digest authentication.
see also Form based authentication.
deployment process
adding users matching certificate name, 93
configuring Tomcat for SSL client
authentication, 92
obtaining and installing digital
certificates, 93
specifying CLIENT-CERT authentication
constraint, 93
code, downloading samples, 209
command injection vulnerability, 7
command-line permissions, Windows, 35
cacls utility, 36
comparison mode authentication
bind mode authentication, compared
to, 128
OpenLDAP directory server, user
authentication, 128
CONFIDENTIAL protection type, 94, 100
connectionName attribute
JDBC Realm configuration, 121
JNDI Realm configuration, 130
connectionPassword attribute
JDBC Realm configuration, 121
JNDI Realm configuration, 130
connectionURL attribute
JDBC Realm configuration, 121
JNDI Realm configuration, 130
connectors, Tomcat
connectors list, 15
definition, 14
disabling connectors, 15
enabling connectors, 15
vulnerabilities, 15
Container-Managed Security
advantages, 97
definition, 95
disadvantages, 97
Tomcat Realms, derived from, 95
contextFactory attribute
JNDI Realm configuration, 130
cookies
application security, use in, 189
disadvantages, 189
minimizing usage, 189
remember me function, 190
validation guidelines, 190
CSP (Cryptographic Service Provider)
definition, 154
JSEE, use within, 154
CSR (Certificate Signing Request), 146
keytool utility, generation using, 158
Custom Realms, 138
implementation steps, 138
authenticate() method, 138
customer support, 210

D

data integrity, 88
data privacy, 88
database security
see also application security.
see also file system security.
developer control, 193
importance of, 193
prepared statements, use of, 196
securing connection parameters, 193
getConnection() method, 193
JNDI, advantage of using, 194, 195
JSP, vulnerabilities in using, 194, 195
stored procedures, 198
validation, 196
debug attribute
JAAS Realm configuration, 137
JDBC Realm configuration, 121
JNDI Realm configuration, 131
Memory Realms configuration, 102
UserDatabase Realm configuration, 108
digest attribute
Digest authentication, compared to, 105
encrypted passwords, setting, 105
JDBC Realm configuration, 121
JNDI Realm configuration, 131
Memory Realms configuration, 102
UserDatabase Realm configuration, 108
UserDatabase Realm, password
encryption, 112
Digest authentication
see also Basic authentication.
see also client authentication.
see also Form based authentication.
Basic authentication, compared to, 90, 95
definition, 90
deployment example, 90
digest attribute, compared to, 105
Form based authentication, compared
to, 90, 95
MD5 encryption algorithm, use of, 90
replay attacks, effects of, 95
digital certificates
certificate chains, 148
components, 146
definition, 145
deployment management, 177
HTTPS Client authentication deployment,
use within, 93
installation problems
Incorrect passwords, 164
Keystore Files Not Found, 163
Keystore tampering, 164
No Such Algorithm Exception, 163
keytool utility, import into keystores
using, 160
mod_ssl module, installation testing, 171
digital signatures, 149

DoS (Denial of Service) attacks, 183
driver attribute
JDBC Realm configuration, 121

E

encryption
definition, 144
encryption algorithms
asymmetric, 144
symmetric, 144
errata, feedback on, 210
error handling vulnerability, 7
Examples application, Tomcat, 19
see also admin application.
see also manager application.
see also WebDAV application.
vulnerabilities, 19
expandProperties property
security policy files, Java, 59

F

FAT (File Allocation Table) file system, 24
NTFS, compared to, 24
FAT32 file system, 24
NTFS, conversion to, 25
file permissions, NTFS, 26
file system security
see also application security.
see also database security.
groups, 27
owners, 28
permissions, 23
Unix permissions, 27
Windows permissions, 24
read only file systems, 49
superuser accounts, 28
user accounts, 27
firewalls
definition, 12
Tomcat, working with, 12
fierwall rule example, 13
Linux solutions, 13
Windows server solutions, 13
folder permissions, NTFS, 26
Form based authentication
see also Basic authentication.
see also client authentication.
see also Digest authentication.
application security, use in, 165
Base64 encoding, use of, 92
Basic authentication, 90
compared to, 90, 95
deployment example, 90
Digest authentication, compared to, 90, 95
HTTPS, advantage of using, 92
login page example, 91–92
SSL, use in, 94

G

get() method, sessions, 192
grant entry, 56
deployment example, 57
keystore entry, necessity for, 58
Principals, use of, 58
implementation example, 58
syntax, 56
usage guidelines, 57
groups, Unix, 27
adding, 30
deleting, 30
groups, Windows, 27
creation, 28
permissions
setting, 33
viewing, 31
verifying, 35

H

handshake protocol, SSL
definition, 151
functions, 151
HTML form vulnerabilities
action handlers, in, 183
form values, in, 183
HTTP Basic authentication
see Basic authentication.
HTTP Digest authentication
see Digest authentication.
HTTPS (HyperText Transfer Protocol Secure)
Basic authentication, advantage of
use in, 90
Client authentication deployment, use
within, 92
connector configuration
administrative interface, using, 162–63
Tomcat configuration file, using, 161
Form based authentication, advantage of
use in, 92
JSSE, handler within, 155
SSL, use with, 152
Tomcat SSL configuration, 153
HttpServletRequest class
methods list, 96
programmatic security model, implementation
of, 96
inherited permissions, 32
revoking, 33
setting, 32
verifying, 35

I

Injection attacks, 183
inscure use of cryptography vulnerability, 7
INTEGRAL protection type, 94, 100
Internet Explorer 5.0
    HTTPS Client authentication
        deployment, 93
Intrusion Detection Systems, 49
    Tripwire, 49
invoker servlet, Tomcat
    security exploits, 203
        operation mechanism, 203
        workarounds, 203
isNew() method, sessions, 192
isSecure() method, 188

J

J2EE (Java 2.0 Enterprise Edition)
    application security, protection mechanism
        for, 164
J2SE (Java 2.0 Standard Edition)
    regex utility, 184
JAAS Realm, 98, 134
    adding users/roles, 138
    configuration attributes
        appName, 137
        className, 137
        debug, 137
        roleClassNames, 137
        userClassNames, 137
        deployment example, 137
    configuring
        authentication mechanism setup, 135
        changing Java Security policy, 136
        configuring Realm Directive, 137
        configuring the provider, 135
        writing or obtaining providers, 135
    deleting users/roles, 138
    JAAS, authentication using, 134
    PAMs, use of, 134
Jakarta
    Jakarta-ORO library, 185
    Regexp package, 185
Java
    see also Security Manager, Java
    application security, features for, 51
    class loader
        definition, 51
    Java Virtual Machine
        definition, 51
        Security Manager, working with, 52
    keytool utility, 59
    security architecture, 62

Java package security, 199
    package-insertion attack, 199
    sealed JAR file, using, 200
        advantages, 202
        implementation example, 201
        manifest, 200
    Security Manager, 199
    security properties file, using, 200
        package-access attack, prevention of, 200
        package-insertion attack, prevention
            of, 200
java.io.FilePermission class, 73
    actions, 74
    deployment example, 74
    deployment targets, 74
java.lang.reflect.ReflectPermission
    class, 77
    deployment example, 77
    deployment target
        supressAccessChecks, 77
java.lang.RuntimePermission class
    deplotment targets
        accessClassInPackage, 72
        accessDeclaredMembers, 73
        createClassLoader, 69
        createSecurityManager, 70
        defineClassInPackage, 72
        exitVM, 70
        getClassLoader, 70
        getProtectionDomain, 72
        loadLibrary, 72
        modifyThread, 71
        modifyThreadGroup, 71
        queuePrintJob, 73
        readFileDescriptor, 72
        setContextClassLoader, 70
        setFactory, 71
        setIO, 71
        setSecurityManager, 70
        shutdownHooks, 71
        stopThread, 71
        writeFileDescriptor, 72
    deployment example, 73
java.net.NetPermission class, 76
    actions, 76
    deployment example, 77
    deployment targets
        RequestPasswordAuthentication, 76
        setDefaultAuthenticator, 76
        SpecifyStreamHandler, 76
java.net.SocketPermission class, 75
    actions, 75
    deployment examples, 75
    deployment targets, 75
java.security package
    java.security.Permission class, 61
    properties file, 200
    Security Manager, 199

java.security.AllPermission class, 80
actions, 80
deployment example, 81
deployment target, 80
java.security.SecurityPermission class, 78
actions, 80
deployment example, 80
deployment targets
addIdentityCertificate, 79
clearProviderProperties, 79
getPolicy, 78
getProperty, 78
getSignerPrivateKey, 79
insertProvider, 78
printIdentity, 79
putProviderProperty, 79
removeIdentityCertificate, 79
removeProvider, 78
removeProviderProperty, 79
setIdentityInfo, 79
setIdentityPublicKey, 79
setPolicy, 78
setProperty, 78
setSystemScope, 79
java.util.PropertyPermission class, 68
actions, 68
deployment example, 69
deployment target, 68
javac tool, 64
JDBC Realm, 98, 117
adding roles, 124
adding users, 123
digest password enabling, 123
advantages/disadvantages, 125
configuration attributes
className, 121
connectionName, 121
connectionPassword, 121
connectionURL, 121
debug, 121
digest, 121
driverName, 121
roleNameCol, 121
userCredCol, 122
userNameCol, 122
userRoleTable, 122
userTable, 122
configuring
database driver installation, 118
deployment example, 122
FLUSH PRIVILAGES directive, 119
PASSWORD() function, MySQL, 119
Populating Realm database, 120
Realm database creation, 118
User creation, 119
definition, 117
deleting roles, 125
deleting users, 124
Memory Realms, compared to, 125
MySQL, use of, 117
UserDatabase Realm, compared to, 125

JK connector
definition, 205
exploit susceptibility, 205
operation mechanism, 205
workarounds, 205
JNDI (Java Naming and Directory Interface)
architecture, 126
database security, advantage of use in, 194, 195
definition, 126
JNDI Realm, 98, 126
adding roles and users, 133
ldapadd command, 133
advantages/disadvantages, 133
configuration attributes
className, 130
connectionName, 130
connectionPassword, 130
connectionURL, 130
contextFactory, 130
debug, 131
digest, 131
roleBase, 131
roleName, 131
roleSearch, 131
roleSubtree, 132
userPassword, 132
userPattern, 132
userRoleName, 132
userSearch, 132
userSubtree, 132
configuring
deployment example, 132
JNDI driver installation, 127
LDAP schema creation, 127
populating the directory, 128
user creation, 129
user role assignment, 128
Memory Realms, compared to, 102
OpenLDAP directory server, use of, 126
removing roles or users, 133
ldapremove command, 133
UserDatabase Realms, compared to, 133
JSESSIONID, 191
JSSE (Java Secure Sockets Estension)
CSP, use of, 154
HTTPS, handler for, 155
SSL, use with, 152
Tomcat installation, 153

K

keystore
aliases, 55
cacerts keystore, 157
definition, 155
security policy files, use in, 55
Tomcat, issues of use with
keystore and alias passwords must be equal, 164
mulitple certificates in keystore, 164

keystore entry, 55
  declaration examples, 56
  grant entry, necessity of working with, 58
  guidelines, 56
  syntax, 56
keytool utility, 59
  CA trusting, 159
    importing root CA certificate into cacerts
      keystore, 160
    importing root CA certificate into
      keystore, 159
  cacerts keystore, listing trusted
    CAs in, 157
  CSR generation, 158
    certificate information validation, 158
    CSR content, 159
    generating certificate key, 158
    submitting CSR to trusted CA, 159
  definition, 155
  importing certificates into keystores, 160
  keystore creation, 155
    access password definition, 156
    alias referencing, 157
    private and public key generation, 156
    RSA encryption algorithm, use of, 157
    self-signed certificate creation, 155
    storage, 157

L

ldapadd command, 129, 133
ldapremove command, 133
login-config element
  application security, 100
ls command
  Unix permissions, viewing, 36

M

MAC (Message Authentication Code)
  handshake protocol, SSL, within, 151
mailing lists, subscribing to p2p.wrox.com, 211
manager application, Tomcat, 16
  see also admin application.
  see also examples application.
  see also WebDAV application.
  access restriction, 17
    Valves, using, 17
  admin application, compared to, 18
  application accessing, 17
  deployment, 16
  enabling the application, 17
  features, 16
manifest, JAR
  attributes table, 200
  definition, 200
  implementation example, 201
  Sealed attribute, 200

MD5 encryption algorithm
  Digest authentication, use in, 90
  Memory Realms, encrypted password
    generation, 106
  SHA digest algorithm, compared to, 106
Memory Realm, 98, 102
  adding users, 103
    defining security constraints, 103
    improved security measures, 105
    manager role, adding users to, 104
    multiple users, 104
    user element, 104
  advantages/disadvantages, 107
  configuration attributes
    className attribute, 102
    debug attribute, 102
    digest attribute, 102
    pathname attribute, 102
  configuring, 102
    MemoryRealm class, 102
  definition, 102
  deleting users, 107
  encrypted passwords, 105
    digest attribute, use of, 105
    MD5 encryption algorithm, generation
      using, 106
    SHA digest algorithm, generation
      using, 106
  JDBC Realm, compared to, 125
  JNDI Realms, compared to, 102
  Tomcat 4.0.x, default realm for, 102
MemoryRealm class
  Memory Realms configuration, 102
mod_jk module, Apache
  AJP, defined under, 172
  definition, 173
  installation
    distribution forms, 173
    implementation example, 174
    loading the module, 174
  SSH tunneling, use in, 176
  WidgetWorld example, use in, 174
mod_ssl module, Apache, 168, 169
  installation, 170
    certificate, testing using, 171
    compiling Apache, 171
    compiling mod_ssl, 170
    created files, 172
    obtaining source files, 170
    running install command, 172
    testing installation, 172
  OpenSSL, encryption based on, 170
Mozilla 1.0
  HTTPS Client authentication
    deployment, 93
MySQL
  see also database security.
  JDBC Realm, use in, 117

N

Netcraft, 5
NTFS (NT File System), 24
FATfile system, compared to, 24
FAT32 file system, conversion from, 25
file system security, importance within, 25
permissions
file permissions, 26
folder permissions, 26

O

OpenLDAP directory server
JNDI Realms, use in, 126
ldapadd command, 129
ldapremove command, 133
user authentication
Bind mode, 127
Comparison mode, 128
OpenSSL
mod_ssl module, encryption basis for, 170
ORO library, Jakarta
regular expressions, validation of, 185
OSI (Open Systems Interconnection) model
SSL, position of, 150
**OWASP (Open Web Application Security
Project)**
vulnerabilities compilation, 6
owners, Unix, 28
owners, Windows, 28

P

p2p.wrox.com mailing list, 211
package-access attack, 200
security properties file, prevention
using, 200
package-insertion attack, 199
security properties file, prevention
using, 200
PAM (Pluggable Authentication Modules)
JAAS Realms, use in, 134
pathname attribute
Memory Realms configuration, 102
Permissions, Java
custom permissions creation, 61
debugging permissions, 81
definition, 52
deployment diagram, 53
java.security.Permission class, 61
Tomcat, classes used by
java.io.FilePermission, 67, 73
java.lang.reflect.ReflectPermission, 68, 77
java.lang.RuntimePermission, 67, 69
java.net.NetPermission, 68, 76

java.net.SocketPermission, 67, 75
java.security.AllPermission, 68, 80
java.security.SecurityPermission, 68, 78
java.util.PropertyPermission, 67, 68
usage syntax, 61
permissions, NTFS
see permisssions, Windows.
permissions, Unix, 27
changing
chmod command, 38
changing ownership, 39
chown command, 39
SUID/SGID bits, 39
Tomcat
additional files, securing, 48
configuring as a service, 43
SysV-style mechanism, using, 43
disabling login, 40
file permissions, modifying, 47
suggested account settings, 40
tomcat-users.xml, problems with, 47
version, importance of, 40
Webapps directory, setting as read only, 48
viewing, 36
ls command, 36
Windows permissions, compared to, 37
permissions, Windows
command-line permissions, 35
denial precedence, 34
file permissions, 26
folder permissions, 26
group permissions, 33
inherited permissions, 32
Security Policies, 41
Tomcat
additional files, securing, 48
configuring as service, 44
disabling login, 41
file permissions, modifying, 45–47
suggesed account settings, 41
tomcat-users.xml, problems with, 47
version, importance of, 40
Webapps directory, setting as read only, 48
Unix permissions, compared to, 37
verifying, 35
viewing, 31
Windows 2000, additional permissions
in, 35
PKI (Public Key Infrastructure), 144
see also encryption.
policytool
Tomcat security policy files, editing
using, 63
port forwarding, SSH, 175
prepared statements
database security, use in, 196
definition, 196
implementation example, 197

Principals, Java
authenticated Principal, 58
definition, 52
deployment diagram, 53
grant entry, use within, 58
implementation example, 58
private keys
see also keystores.
asymmetric encryption algorithms,
use in, 145
deployment management, 177
programmatic security model, 96
HttpServletRequest class, implementation
by, 96
implementation example, 96
Protection domain, Java, 52
deployment diagram, 53
public keys
see also keystores.
asymmetric encryption algorithms, use in,
145
digital certificates, use with, 146
Public-Key encryption
see asymmetric encryption algorithms.

R

read only file systems
file system security, 49
Realms
applications security, role in, 98
Basic authentication, use in, 88
contents, 87
definition, 87
implementations
Custom Realm, 98
JAAS Realm, 98, 134
JDBC Realm, 98, 117
JNDI Realm, 98
Memory Realm, 98
UserDatabase Realm, 98, 107
selection criteria
adding/changing users and roles without
restarts, 139
custom management applications, 140
managability, 139
performance, 139
security, 139
record protocol, SSL, 151
regex utility
regular expressions, checking for, 184
Regexp package, Jakarta
regular expressions, validation of, 185
regular expressions
definition, 183
example, 184
Jakart-ORO library, validation using, 185
regex utility, checks using, 184
Regexp package, validation using, 185

'remember me' function, 190
remote administration vulnerability, 7
removeAttribute() method, sessions, 192
replay attacks
definition, 95
Digest authentication, effect on, 95
resourceName attribute
UserDatabase Realm configuration, 108
ResourceParams element
UserDatabase Realm configuration, 108
roleBase attribute
JNDI Realm configuration, 131
roleClassNames attribute
JAAS Realm configuration, 137
roleName attribute
JNDI Realm configuration, 131
role-name element
application security, 100
roleNameCol attribute
JDBC Realm configuration, 121
roleSearch attribute
JNDI Realm configuration, 131
roleSubtree attribute
JNDI Realm configuration, 132
root certificates, 148
RSA encryption algorithm, use of
keystore, creation, 157
mod_ssl module, installation testing, 171

S

Sealed attribute, JAR, 200
advantages, 202
usage implications, 202
Security Manager, Java
application security, use in, 199
deployment mechanism, 53
definition, 51
features, 52
functions, 62
implementation improvements, 52
installation checks, 82–84
procedure, 82
installation debugging, 81
AccessControlException, 81
SecurityException, 81
JVM, working with, 52
Permissions, 52
policy files, 52
context based security, use in, 54
Principals, 52
Protection domains, 52
setSecurityManager() method, 53, 54
Tomcat
access controls definition for, 62
Security Policies, Windows, 41
Tomcat account settings, modifying, 42

security policy files, Java, 52
components
grant entry, 56
keystore entry, 55
context based security, use in, 54
default deployment, 54
property expansion, 59
deployment example, Unix, 60
deployment example, Windows, 60
expandProperties property, 59
guidelines, 60
Tomcat security policy files, basis for, 63
security policy files, Tomcat, 64
Catalina code permissions, 65
debugging permissions, 81
Java security policy files, based on, 63
policytool, editing using, 63
system code permissions, 64
Web applications permissions, 66
security-constraint element
application security, 99
SecurityException, 81
server authentication
handshake protocol, SSL, using, 151
Servlet 2.3 specification, 87
disadvantage, 88
security models
Container-Managed Security, 95
programmatic security, 95
sessions
advantages, 192
disabling sessions, 191
enabling sessions, 191
JSESSIONID, using, 191
get() method, 192
implementation example, 191
isNew() method, 192
removeAttribute() method, 192
setAttribute() method, 191
setAttribute() method, 191
setSecurityManager() method, 53
context-based security, use in, 54
SGID bits, 39
SHA digest algorithm
JDBC Realm, enabling encrypted
passwords, 123
MD5 encryption algorithm, compared
to, 106
Memory Realms, encrypted password
generation, 106
UserDatabase Realm, password
encryption, 113
shared secret
handshake protocol, SSL, exchange
using, 151
symmetric encryption algorithms, 145

SSH (Secure Shell)
AJP, working with, 175
definition, 175
OpenSSH, 175
port forwarding, 175
tunneling, 175
deployment guidelines, 177
mod_jk module configuration, 176
tunnel establishment, 175
SSL (Secure Socket Layer)
AJP, working with
mod_jk module, using, 173
Apache, deployment with, 168
Apache-SSL, using, 168
mod_ssl module, using, 168
StrongHold, using, 168
application validation, 188
example, 188
asymmetric encryption algorithms, use of, 149
authentication, 149
Basic authentication, use with, 94
definition, 149
Form based authentication, use with, 94
handshake protocol, 151
HTTPS, use with, 152
JSSE, use with, 152
need for, 150
OSI model, position within, 150
record protocol, 151
resource management, 177
SSL accelerators, 168
TCP/IP, use of, 150
Tomcat configuration, 152
AJP, using, 153
HTTPS, using, 153
JSEE, installing, 153
Unix sockets, compared to, 149
WidgetWorld example, 165–68
WinSocks, compared to, 149
SSO (Single Sign On)
definition, 101
guidelines, 101
Tomcat configuration, 101
stored procedures
definition, 198
implementation example, 198
StrongHold
Apache, SSL deployment for, 168
SUID bits, 39
superuser accounts, 28
symbolic links, Tomcat
disadvantages, 204
lack of current support, 204
workarounds, 204
symmetric encryption algorithms
definition, 144
shared secret, 145
SysV-style mechanism
creation, 43
Tomcat, configuring as a service, 43

T

TCP/IP (Transfer Control Protocol/Internet Protocol)
SSL, use by, 150
timestamps
digital certificates, use with, 146
Tomcat
Apache, use with, 12
applications
admin, 16
examples, 16, 19
manager, 16
WebDAV, 16, 19
buffer overflows, effect of, 11
connectors
connectors list, 15
disabling connectors, 15
enabling connectors, 15
vulnerabilities, 15
firewalls, working with, 12
fierwall rule example, 13
Linux solutions, 13
Windows server solutions, 13
permissions, setting
see permissions, Unix.
see also permissions, Windows.
Realms, 87
service, use as
Linux/Unix, running on, 10
SysV-style mechanism, using, 43
Windows operating system, running on, 10
stand-alone web server, use as, 11
disadvantage, 12
unprivilaged user accounts, using, 11
user-level application, use as, 10
vulnerabilities, 9
BUGTRAQ, keeping track using, 8
webappsec, keeping track using, 9
tomcat-users.xml
problems, 47
transport-guarantee element
application security, 100
CONFIDENTIAL protection type, 100
INTEGRAL protection type, 100
Tripwire, 49
tunneling
see SSH (Secure Shell).

U

Unix/Linux
SSL, sockets compared to, 149
Tomcat, running as service, 10
unprivilaged user accounts
Tomcat, effect of using in, 11
unvalidated parameters vulnerability, 6
url-pattern element
application security, 99

user accounts, Unix, 27
adding new user, 30
deleting, 30
groups
determining users within, 29
modifying users within, 30
viewing, 29
user accounts, Windows, 27
creation, 28
permissions, viewing, 31
user element
Memory Realms, 104
password attribute, 104
roles attribute, 104
username attribute, 104
userClassNames attribute
JAAS Realm configuration, 137
userCredCol attribute
JDBC Realm configuration, 122
UserDatabase Realm, 98, 107
adding roles, 109
admin application, using, 109
role element attributes, 110
adding users
admin application, using, 111
user element attributes, 112
advantages/disadvantages
implementation examples, 116
configuration attributes
className, 108
debug, 108
digest, 108
resourceName, 108
configuring, 107
deployment example, 108
ResourceParams element, 108
deleting roles, 114
deleting users, 114
JDBC Realm, compared to, 125
JNDI Realms, compared to, 133
password encryption
digest attribute, using, 112
SHA digest algorithm, use of, 113
Tomcat 4.1.12, problems in, 112
UserDatabase API methods
implementation examples, 115
role management, 115
user managament, 115
userNameCol attribute
JDBC Realm configuration, 122
userPassword attribute
JNDI Realm configuration, 132
userPattern attribute
JNDI Realm configuration, 132
userRoleName attribute
JNDI Realm configuration, 132
userRoleTable attribute
JDBC Realm configuration, 122
userSearch attribute
JNDI Realm configuration, 132

userSubtree attribute
    JNDI Realm configuration, 132
userTable attribute
    JDBC Realm configuration, 122

V

validation, 183
    database security, good practice, 196
    form data values, using, 185
    regular expressions, using, 183
    SSL, using, 188
        example, 188
        isSecure() method, 188
    vailidity monitoring, 177
Valves
    admin application, use within, 18
    manager application, use within, 17
vulnerabilities
    broken access control, 6
    broken account and session
        management, 7
    buffer overflows, 7
    command injection flaws, 7
    Cross-Site Scripting (XSS) flaws, 7
    error handling problems, 7
    insecure use of cryptography, 7
    OWASP, compiled by, 6
    remote administration flaws, 7
    Tomcat connectors, within, 15
    unvalidated parameters, 6
    web and application server
        misconfiguration, 7

W

web/application server misconfiguration
    vulnerability, 7
webappsec
    Tomcat, keeping track of vulnerabilites, 9
WebDAV application, Tomcat, 16, 19
    see also admin application.
    see also examples application.
    see also manager application.
    compatible clients, 19
    read-write acess setting, 20
    role configuration example, 20
WEB-INF folder, Tomcat
    security problems, 206
    workarounds, 206
WidgetWorld example, 165–68
    client script, 165
    mod_jk module, working with, 174
    server script, 166
Windows 2000
    additional permissions, 35
Windows operating system
    file systems
        FAT, 24
        FAT32, 24
        NTFS, 24
    Tomcat, running as service, 10
Windows XP Professional
    permissions, viewing, 32
WinSocks
    SSL, compared to, 149

X

XSS (Cross-Site Scripting) atacks, 7

WROX PRESS INC.

Wrox writes books for you. Any suggestions, or ideas
about how you want information given in your
ideal book will be studied by our team.
Your comments are always valued at Wrox.

Free phone in USA 800-USE-WROX
Fax (312) 893 8001

UK Tel. (0121) 687 4100 Fax (0121) 687 4101

NB. If you post the bounce back card below in the UK, please send it to:
Wrox Press Ltd., Arden House, 1102 Warwick Road, Acocks Green, Birmingham. B27 9BH. UK.

Registration Code : 83090G8X2C2I5EC01

Apache Tomcat Security Handbook - Registration Card

Name

Address

City _____ State/Region

Country _____ Postcode/Zip

E-mail

Occupation

How did you hear about this book?

☐ Book review (name)
☐ Advertisement (name)
☐ Recommendation
☐ Catalog
☐ Other

Where did you buy this book?

☐ Bookstore (name) _____ City
☐ Computer Store (name)
☐ Mail Order
☐ Other

What influenced you in the
purchase of this book?

☐ Cover Design
☐ Contents
☐ Other (please specify)

How did you rate the overall
contents of this book?

☐ Excellent ☐ Good
☐ Average   ☐ Poor

What did you find most useful about this book?

What did you find least useful about this book?

Please add any additional comments.

What other subjects will you buy a computer
book on soon?

What is the best computer book you have used this year?

*Note: This information will only be used to keep you updated
about new Wrox Press titles and will not be used for any other
purpose or passed to any other third party.*

Check here if you DO NOT want to receive further support for this book.

8309

8309

wrox

PROGRAMMER TO PROGRAMMER™